Successful Social Activism and Unintended Market Emergence

Sayako Miura

Successful Social Activism and Unintended Market Emergence

The Fight Over Foot Health and Fashion in Japan

Springer

Sayako Miura
Faculty of Global Business
Showa Women's University
Setagaya City, Tokyo, Japan

ISBN 978-981-99-9290-4 ISBN 978-981-99-9291-1 (eBook)
https://doi.org/10.1007/978-981-99-9291-1

This Springer imprint is published by the registered company Springer Nature Singapore Pte Ltd.
The registered company address is: 152 Beach Road, #21-01/04 Gateway East, Singapore 189721, Singapore

Paper in this product is recyclable.

Preface

This book considers the relationship between social movements targeting companies and the emergence of new markets. Social movement organizations (SMOs) seek to change corporate behavior as their immediate goal, and thereby change society in the direction they want as a superordinate goal. Existing research has demonstrated that the activities of SMOs can change corporate behavior, and the change, in turn, leads to new market categories. The transformation in corporate behavior elicited by SMOs represents the direct effect of activism, while the emergence of new market categories because of such changes comprises the indirect effect of activism. This book addresses two key questions related to the findings of existing research on the direct and indirect effects of activism:

- *Direct effect of activism*: How can SMOs positioned on the periphery of an industry change corporate behavior?
- *Indirect effect of activism*: Are the markets that emerge owing to the activities of SMOs always intended, and thus aligned with the superordinate goals of the SMOs? When the market emergence is unintended by SMOs, specifically one that is inconsistent with the superordinate goals of SMOs, how does this emergence occur?

With regard to the question of the direct effect of activism, previous research has assumed that SMOs, positioned on the periphery of an industry as secondary stakeholders in companies, lack familiarity with the affairs of the industry. The question then arises: How do these SMOs influence corporate behavior? This book will examine this issue.

Regarding the question of the indirect effect of activism, existing research has considered cases where changes in corporate behavior lead to the emergence of markets that are intended, and thus consistent with the superordinate goals of SMOs. However, this book suggests that markets unintended by SMOs may also emerge. This book demonstrate this phenomenon and clarify how such markets emerge.

In considering these two questions, the book analyzes Japan's post-war footwear industry. In the 1960s, a small private organization, Japan Institute of Footwear (JIF), began efforts to emphasize the importance of foot health, and by the 1980s, it had succeeded in changing corporate behavior. JIF started training shoe fitters, experts in selecting shoes that fit customers' feet, and succeeded in having this practice adopted by shoe retailers. In clarifying how this transformation was achieved, this book will consider the first question regarding how SMOs located on the periphery of an industry can influence changes in the behavior of companies within that industry.

Within the footwear industry, the ripple effects of the activities of JIF led to the emergence of various new market categories: the comfort shoe market, the European comfort shoe market, and the fashion-oriented transparent insole market. The comfort shoe market was JIF's intended market that emerged as a result of the popularization of shoe fitters. The European comfort shoe market was even more dedicated to foot health than the comfort shoe market. Although not its intention, the market was consistent with the superordinate goal of JIF in terms of protecting foot health. The fashion-oriented transparent insole market was inconsistent with JIF's superordinate goal as it focused on "cute" insoles that made high-heeled trendy shoes comfortable, which raised questions regarding their impact on foot health. By clarifying how these markets emerged, the second question, regarding the unintended emergence of markets and the mechanisms behind them will be examined.

Existing research fails to answer these two questions adequately. However, the case of JIF's initiatives in promoting foot health and their consequences provide pertinent context for addressing these questions. By comparing historical accounts of the Japanese footwear industry with the findings of exisiting research on social movements that target companies, this book aims to clarify the implicit assumptions of existing research, contributing to the field of research on social movements targeting companies.

This book addresses questions regarding how SMOs, located on the periphery of an industry but envisioning to change it, can influence companies, and the corresponding ripple effects of their success. I sincerely hope that this book offers an opportunity for researchers and practitioners interested in social movements targeting companies and market emergence to broaden and deepen their analysis and discussions.

All the chapters of this book are interrelated, collectively exploring the relationship between social movements, companies, and markets. However, readers may also focus on specific sections of interest. For those interested in the first question of how SMOs located on the periphery of an industry can influence corporate behavior, Part II is particularly relevant. For those interested in the second issue, which focuses on unintended market emergence resulting from SMOs' activities and the mechanisms behind its emergence, Part III is recommended.

Those interested in understanding the survival strategies adopted by small and medium-sized enterprises should read Chaps. 2, 4, 5, and 7–10, which provide a historical description of the footwear industry. Conversely, Chaps. 1, 3, 6, and 11 can be skipped, as they mainly offer theoretical discussions on social movements targeting companies. The long-term single case study of the footwear industry presented in this book can be viewed as the case of survival strategies for small and medium-sized enterprises. Considering that many companies in the Japanese footwear industry, including manufacturers and retailers, are small in scale, this book elucidates the strategic actions they adopted for survival and the complex interactions among them.

Moreover, the case examined in this book should be valuable to individuals who are interested in the Japanese footwear industry and its history. Chapters 2, 4, 5, and 7–10 provide historical insights into the footwear industry. In 2019, Japan witnessed the emergence of the #KuToo movement (a term coined by combining *kutsū* (pain), *kutsu* (shoes), and #MeToo), which subsequently became very prominent. This movement contends that forcing women to wear high heels in the workplace is discriminatory. Simultaneously, it highlights the irrationality of forcing the use of shoes that cause physical strain (Ishikawa, 2019). The case study of the footwear industry in this book provides a partial contextual backdrop to this movement. Please note that this book does not directly address discrimination against women in Japan. However, the cases explored provide explanation into how Japanese people adopted Western-style footwear, including high heels, and coped with the related challenges.

Tokyo, Japan Sayako Miura

Acknowledgements

It was approximately 10 years ago that I became interested in the issue of foot health in the Japanese footwear industry and began my research journey. I had just completed my doctoral studies on technology strategies of large companies in the high-tech industries at Hitotsubashi University and was searching for a new research theme. At this point, I decided to investigate the footwear industry based on my experience with shoes. I have always loved shoes. However, I was getting shoe sores even though I thought I was choosing the right pairs for my feet at the store. Moreover, I was not the only one experiencing this problem, so I decided to embark on an investigation of the footwear industry. In the process, I learned of the existence of shoe fitters, a profession fostered by JIF, a small private organization. I was curious about how JIF was able to establish shoe fitters in the footwear industry. At the same time, although shoe fitters had become more prevalent, some people, including myself, suffered from shoe-related foot problems. Thus, in addition to examining the increase in the number of shoe fitters, I naturally became interested in the consequences of their proliferation. Alongside my research on the footwear industry, I became interested in social movements research. Social movement research focuses on how relatively socially marginalized people and organizations achieve their goals. Therefore, applying this research to analyze the process of a small private organization promoting shoe fitters in the footwear industry seemed appropriate. Fortunately at that time, organizational theorists were beginning to focus on social movements targeting companies and rapidly advancing their studies in this field.

Having started with little knowledge of the subject matter and the theoretical framework for analyzing it, I was able to compile my research into a book, thanks to the assistance of many people who supported me throughout the research process.

This book could not have been completed without those who cooperated in the survey. A list of those who agreed to be interviewed for the study is provided in Appendix 1. Everyone cooperated with my request to participate in the survey even though I was a complete stranger. What they shared with me from their perspectives was essential to this study, and all of them were very kind and inspiring.

In addition to the official interviews, various people engaged in the footwear industry showed me their work and shared their thoughts on shoes and the industry.

This assistance was essential for understanding shoes and the industry. I would like to thank Tomoko Ōya (footwear industry journalist), Saburō Endoh (former president of Valerian Shoes), Taiki Nishimura (owner of Shoe Fit Koubeya), the late Katsumi Shigeru, aka Moge (owner of Moge workshop), M. D. Toshihiko Uchida (Totsuka Kyoritsu Rehabilitation Hospital), Nobuko Hiroshima (owner of Mama to Kodomo no Ashi no Salon Nemunoki), Toru Nakamura (Grato), Chikashi Katashima (Asahi Shoes, Ltd.), Kentaro Nakayama (owner of Nakayama Shoe Shop Ltd.), Kazuko Ohi (President of Ohi Manufactureing), Miki Hayashi (Sogo & Seibu Co., Ltd.), Hiroshi Yoshino (President of Ortho Fits Co., Ltd.), Nahoko Nakamura (Chief Manager of Ortho Fits Co., Ltd.), Shinsuke Hamanaka (Moonstar Company), Kazuyuki Iwase (Iing Co., Ltd.), Emmylou Suzuki-Johnson (shoe and footwear researcher), Kazufumi Inagawa (Leather Industry Museum), Natsumi Okamoto (Gyōda City Local Museum), and Kazufumi Suzuki (Saitama Prefectural Museum of History and Folklore), in no particular order.

I am indebted to Keiko Yamaki. She was my colleague at Shujitsu University and encouraged me to publish this study in English. Without her encouragement, this book would not have been published.

I received insightful ideas and comments on this study at academic conferences, workshops, and study groups. I apologize for being unable to list them all due to space limitations. I am indebted to and would like to thank, in no particular order, Nobuyuki Inamizu, Momoko Kawakami, Jaehyang Han, Makoto Fujita, Minoru Shimamoto, Ken Sakai, Takahiro Endo, Masaya Onuma, Hiroshi Watanabe, Koichiro Kodama, Ken Okura, Aoyama Mitsutaka, Hajime Oda, Suzunosuke Aizawa, Rie Sakuraki, Niitsu Yasuaki, Yasuyuki Sakai, Shu Watanabe, Kei Fujiyama, Takanori Kato, Hidetsuna Sasaki, Philip Debroux, David Chiavacci, Sébastien Lechevalier, Markus Heckel, Harald Conrad, Karen Shire, and Peter Scott.

During the course of this research, I worked at Shujitsu University, Teikyo University, and Showa Women's University. I received valuable advice and support for my research from my colleagues. I would like to express special thanks, in no particular order, to Shinsaku Sugiyama, aka Sam, Kenji Taniguchi, Akenari Nomoto, Yasumasa Osaki, Shozo Saegusa, Toshikatsu Hayashi, Masatsugu Sanada, Xianghua Jiang, Kanae Teramoto, Arata Suzuki, Taiki Kagami, Yoshiki Enatsu, Akiko Imai, Akashi Hongo, and Akiko Komori. I also would like to thank Nobuko Tabata and Yuko Tsuchidate of the Institute of Modern Culture, Showa Women's University.

This research was initiated after I completed my Ph.D. at Hitosubashi University. However, my case study experiences at the graduate school undoubtedly served as the foundation that propelled this research. I am immensely indebted to Tsuyoshi Numagami, my graduate school supervisor. His incisive comments on my graduate studies and the values he practices as a researcher always inspired me. Without his help and advice in graduate school, I would not be a researcher. I would also like to thank Kentaro Nobeoka, my secondary supervisor. He always provided me with precise comments on my graduate study. I am also greatly indebted to Takeo Kikkawa, Chuma Hiroyuki, Seiichiro Yonekura, Ikuya Sato, Christina Ahmadjian, Yuko Yamashita, Yaichi Aoshima, Kazuhiko Tanaka, Makoto Nakano, Toshihiko

Kato, Masaru Karube, and Hiroshi Shimizu for their guidance and support through classes and workshops.

I am greatly indebted to Isuke Koto, my supervisor at the undergraduate school of Waseda University. I decided to pursue a career in teaching and researching at a university because of my encounter with him. To this day, he has guided and encouraged me as a senior teacher and researcher.

I am deeply grateful for the contributions of the team at Springer. I would like to extend my gratitude to Yutaka Hirachi, Misao Taguchi, Vinothini Elango, and Gayathri Kumar, who have graciously supported me in the publication of this book.

Finally, I would like to express my deep appreciation to my family. Without the understanding and support of my family, this research would have been impossible. My daughter Yuzuko was born around the same time as this research commenced. Her presence has always been a source of strength for me. Soon after she was born, my husband was transferred to work in another country, and Yuzuko and I lived apart from him for four and a half years. Those who always came by to take care of my daughter and encouraged me during that time were my mother, Hideko Kimura; my father, Yasunori Kimura; my mother-in-law, Kyoko Miura; and my father-in-law, Kiyoshi Miura. I want to express my deep gratitude to my husband, Masashi. He always listened to me and encouraged me, even though he was in a foreign country. Since returning to Japan to live with us, he has taken on half or more of the housework and childcare. Although my grandfather, Hamao Kimura, passed away before the book was published, he was supportive of my pursuit of a career as a researcher. I also believe that my original interest in shoes was influenced by him. He loved to polish shoes.

This research project was funded by *Grants-in-Aid for Scientific Research* (20K13596), Wesco Science Promotion Foundation, Shujitsu University Research Grant, Teikyo University Research Encouragement Grant, and Showa Women's University Research Grant.

Contents

About the Author

Sayako Miura a full-time lecturer at Showa Women's University, obtained her Ph.D. in Commerce from Hitotsubashi University. She has published many papers on market emergence and strategies of SMEs and NPOs based on in-depth case studies of the Japanese shoe industry. These include "Adjustments of social activist strategies and new market creation: The interplay of an activist group, companies and their primary stakeholders in the shoe industry (in Japanese with English abstract)," *Organizational Science*, *52*(3), 20–32, 2019; and "The developmental history of the insole market in Japan: Rising health consciousness and an unintended shift toward fashion (1984–2010)," *Japanese Research in Business History 38*, 43–61, 2021. She has also published "Component sharing across product categories leads to functional diversification: Evidence from the Japanese digital products market," *Asiatische Studien—Études Asiatiques*, *70*(1), 75–88, 2016.

List of Figures

List of Tables

Part I
Two Issues Related to Research on Social Movements Targeting Companies

Part I serves as preparation for the case analysis in Parts II and III. Chapter 1 briefly examines existing research on social movements targeting companies, presents the two unsolved issues, and explains the methodology for examining these issues. These two issues are explored through a case analysis of the Japanese post-war footwear industry. Chapter 2 provides the necessary background knowledge to understand the case, offering an overview of the awareness of foot health in post-war Japan, the characteristics of shoes as a product, the history of Japanese footwear, and an overview of the post-war footwear industry.

Chapter 1
Introduction

How can social movement oganizations (SMOs) positioned on the periphery of an industry change corporate behavior? Are the resulting changes in the market always intended, and thus aligned with the superordinate goals of the SMOs? These questions underlie this study. This chapter briefly examines existing research on social movements targeting companies, clarifying how it cannot address the two issues examined in this book owing to its implicit assumptions. Then, the chapter explains the methodology for examining these issues–a case analysis of the Japanese post-war footwear industry.

1.1 Theoretical Background: Direct and Indirect Effects of Social Movements

This book considers the relationship between social movements targeting companies and the emergence of new markets. SMOs attempt to change society by influencing corporate behavior as well as changing laws (de Bakker et al. 2017). In the context of corporate power expanding relative to the government and the increasing number of social movements that target companies, social movement studies expanded their focus from movements targeting the government to those targeting companies (Bartley and Child 2011; Fremeth et al. 2022; Jaffee 2012; King and Pearce 2010; Rao 2009; Soule 2009; Walker et al. 2008).

Existing research has addressed both the direct and indirect effects of social movements targeting companies. SMOs seek to change corporate behavior as their primary goal, and thereby change society in the direction they want as a superordinate goal (Snow and Soule 2010). The direct effect of activism is the change in corporate behavior brought about by SMOs, and the indirect effect of activism is the change in society because of the spillover effect from the direct effect of activism (Briscoe

S. Miura, *Successful Social Activism and Unintended Market Emergence*,
https://doi.org/10.1007/978-981-99-9291-1_1

and Gupta 2016). One of the changes that occurs in society as the indirect effect of activism is the emergence of new market categories (Briscoe and Gupta 2016).

The change in corporate behavior as a direct effect of activism leads to the emergence of new market categories as an indirect effect through the following process. SMOs attempt to change corporate behavior to achieve their superordinate goals. They attempt to either delegitimize existing corporate behavior they want to stop or legitimize new corporate behavior they want to promote (den Hond and de Bakker 2007; Sine and Lee 2009). Through these actions, SMOs attempt to create sociocultural changes in the market. These changes can be opportunities for entrepreneurs to start businesses, thereby leading to new markets. For example, in the US, activists positioned conventional industrial agriculture production as manipulated, exploitative, and artificial, and contrasted grass-fed production as authentic, sustainable, and natural (Weber et al. 2008). These frames resonated with some producers and consumers, and their mobilization resulted in the birth of a market category of grass-fed meat and dairy products.

This book explores the phenomenon of social movements targeting companies and the resulting emergence of new markets. It addresses two key issues that existing research on social movements targeting companies has overlooked owing to implicit assumptions. One relates to the direct effect of activism and the other relates to the indirect effect of activism.

The first issue relates to the direct effect of activism: How can SMOs positioned on the periphery of an industry change corporate behavior? As SMOs are secondary stakeholders of companies, it is difficult for their claims to be accepted (Stevens et al. 2005; Vasi and King 2012). Existing research has clarified that SMOs must not only appeal directly to companies but also reach out and mobilize primary stakeholders of companies, such as the media, consumers, and shareholders (Balsiger 2010; Dubuisson-Quellier 2013; King and Soule 2007; Weber et al. 2008). By mobilizing the primary stakeholders of companies, SMOs can exert influence on these companies. For instance, SMOs can change a company's behavior by encouraging consumers to boycott its products and media to cover the boycott to risk the company's reputation and sales (King 2016). However, as SMOs are secondary stakeholders in a company, they are located on the periphery of the industry and would not be familiar with the industry and the companies in it. This would make it difficult to formulate effective strategies for identifying the corporations and primary stakeholders that should be targeted and the frames that should be used to mobilize them. As such, this book explores how SMOs located on the periphery of industries can formulate effective strategies.

The second issue relates to the indirect effect of activism: Are the markets that emerge owing to the activities of SMOs always intended, and thus aligned with the superordinate goals of the SMOs? When the market emergence is unintended by SMOs, specifically one that is inconsistent with the superordinate goals of SMOs, how does this emergence occur? Existing research has considered cases where changes in corporate behavior lead to market emergence consistent with the superordinate goals of SMOs. For example, the emergence of the grass-fed meat and dairy products market was intended by activists who aimed to promote grass-fed production and consistent with their superordinate goals of realizing "sustainable agriculture, rural community development, health, and alternative consumption" (Weber et al. 2008, p. 533). Existing studies assume that companies and consumers react only according to the superordinate goals of SMOs. However, companies and consumers have their interests and intentions, and they do not necessarily react in accordance with the goals of SMOs. This point, specifically regarding consumer behavior, has been overlooked. If companies and consumers have diverse reactions to the activities of SMOs, a market that does not conform to the goals may emerge. Hiatt et al. (2009) have suggested that the initiatives of SMOs, having successfully achieved their initial goals, can have unintended consequences contrary to their superordinate goals; however, studies of social movements targeting companies have paid little attention to such a phenomenon. This book examines how and why these unintended consequences occur.

1.2 Methodology

1.2.1 Case Selection

This book examines two issues related to research on social movements targeting companies. (1) How can SMOs on the periphery of an industry change corporate behavior? This relates to the direct effect of activism. (2) Are the markets that emerge owing to the activities of SMOs always intended by the SMOs, and when the market emergence is unintended by SMOs, specifically one that is inconsistent with the superordinate goals of SMOs, how does this emergence occur? This relates to the indirect effects of activism. The selected case for analysis is the post-war Japanese footwear industry from the 1960s through the 2000s because the case is suitable for examining these two issues. In the footwear industry, (1) Japan Institute of Footwear (JIF),[1] an SMO that was initially unfamiliar with the industry, was successful in changing corporate behavior, and (2) owing to JIF's activities, various markets emerged including the one that was inconsistent with its superordinate goal.

In the post-war Japanese footwear industry, JIF, despite its lack of resources and knowledge regarding the industry, managed to change corporate behavior. This circumstance is suitable for addressing the first issue. Following World War II (WWII), JIF took issue with the Japanese footwear industry's emphasis on fashion while ignoring foot health and initiated activities to encourage companies in the footwear industry to prioritize foot health. Founded in 1965, JIF started as a fringe, resource-poor organization whose activities were initially ignored (Katō 2002).

[1] JIF was founded in 1965 as the Japan Institute of Women's Footwear (IWF). In 1969, it expanded its scope to include men's shoes and changed its name to JIF. Later, in 1997, it was renamed the Foot, Footwear and Health Association (FHA) and became a general incorporated association in 2009. For simplicity, this study primarily uses "JIF" to refer to the organization and uses "IWF" and "FHA" as needed.

However, in the mid-1980s, the group started training shoe fitters, who provided shoe fitting services at shoe stores, and succeeded in encouraging shoe retailers to adopt shoe fitters. Therefore, the first research question in this case study addresses how JIF succeeded in spreading shoe fitters among shoe retailers.

As a result of JIF's success, markets that JIF did and did not envision emerged: the comfort shoe market, the European comfort shoe market, and the fashion-oriented transparent insole market. The last one was inconsistent with JIF's superordinate goal of protecting foot health, providing an opportunity to consider the second issue. The comfort shoe market was one that JIF intended and envisioned, resulting from the popularization of shoe fitters. The other two markets were unintended consequences for JIF: the European comfort shoe market involved a stricter pursuit of foot health, whereas the fashion-oriented transparent insole market was less concerned with foot health, featuring products of questionable value from the perspective of protecting foot health. Therefore, the fashion-oriented transparent insole market serves as an example of a market that is inconsistent with JIF's superordinate goal. Thus, the second research question for this case addresses how JIF's activities and successes led to the emergence of these three markets, including the one that was inconsistent with JIF's superordinate goal.

The footwear industry offers an ideal context to examine the two issues related to research on social movements targeting companies. This is because the influence of political and technological factors on companies and markets can be naturally excluded. JIF clearly targeted companies to change their behavior, without targeting national and local governments to change laws. Although there was some desire to make the shoe fitter qualification a national requirement, there was practically no appeal to political bodies to achieve this goal.[2] Therefore, regarding the effects of social movements on companies, we can largely dismiss legal influences.

The footwear industry has not experienced significant technological change in manufacturing or materials over the past half-century in Japan. The production of Western-style shoes in Japan began during the Meiji period in the mid-nineteenth century. Thereafter, following WWII, efforts to improve productivity by adopting technology and machinery from the West continued until the 1960s (Hikakusangyō Enkakushi Hensan Iinkai 1959, 1989; Inagawa 2013; Satō 1971). However, by the 1970s, Japan had caught up (Katō 1977), and there have been no major changes in manufacturing technology since then. This situation is consistent with global trends, where production methods have seen no radical changes that significantly transformed the competitive environment of the industry.[3] Even today, some processes are performed by craftsmen, while others are mechanized. The primary materials—leather, rubber, and plastic—have remained largely unchanged globally. While future developments in automated machinery and materials may bring about significant

[2] Yashiro, a former chairman of the Shoe Fitter Committee of JIF, presented documents indicating that the FHA was considering making shoe fitters a National Trade Skill Test occupation (FHA 2002; Hiroo Yashiro, interview, May 17, 2017). However, this plan did not materialize, and there is no evidence in the remaining records that the FHA actively promoted this idea.

[3] Shoe manufacturing technology largely developed in the nineteenth and early twentieth centuries. For more details, see Church (1968, 1970) and Miranda (2004).

changes, during the period following WWII, there were no major technological innovations in manufacturing technology or materials that drastically impacted the competitive environment of the industry. This contrasts with industries such as the electronics industry, where advances in digital and semiconductor technology changed the competitive environment from the 1990s onwards, leading to a decline in Japanese electronics companies' global competitiveness in the 2000s (Aoshima et al. 2010).

Since the 2010s, the footwear industry has experienced significant technological changes in distribution owing to the shift toward online sales. However, it was not until after 2010 that online sales fully developed, which is well after the period this study covers. In 2008, Amazon Japan launched Javari.jp, a website specializing in shoes and bags with free returns including shipping charges, within the first 30 days of purchase. Javari was later integrated into Amazon.co.jp in 2014. In 2011, Jade launched Locondo.jp, a shoe-shopping site that offers free returns, including shipping cost, for up to 99 days. According to statistical data from *Shoes Book*, a footwear industry yearbook, in 2016, the Internet came to possess its own category for shoe sales share by retail format, which was valued at ¥210 billion (11.1% of the total market share) (Posty Corporation 2018).

1.2.2 Single Case Study

This study adopts a single-case study design because the footwear industry "case represents an *extreme* case or an *unusual* case, deviating from theoretical norms or even everyday occurrences" (Yin 2014, p. 52). The unusual occurrences in the footwear industry case are (1) JIF, an SMO that was not familiar with the industry, successfully changed corporate behavior, and (2) this change resulted in a market emergence that did not align with JIF's superordinate goal.

Therefore, this study aims to clarify why and how these unusual consequences occurred in the footwear industry. By doing so, this book contributes to research on social movements targeting companies. Case studies are suitable for elucidating causal mechanisms behind "how" and "why" questions (Yin 2014) and for identifying implicit assumptions and overlooked variables in existing research (George and Bennett 2005). This is because case studies are adept at accommodating long-term, complex causal mechanisms (George and Bennett 2005). It is important to note that although this study is a single case study, it is an embedded single case study with the post-war Japanese footwear industry as the unit of analysis, and SMOs, firms, and consumers in multiple market categories within the footwear industry as sub-units of analysis (Yin 2014).

In the process of unveiling causal mechanisms, this study aims to ensure validity. Internal validity assesses the validity of the causal relationship, that is, the extent to which the possibility of other variables having caused the outcome has been excluded. Single case studies can overcome the problem of internal validity through rich descriptions that exclude other potential explanations (George and Bennett 2005;

Numagami 1995, 2000). Efforts have been made to eliminate competing hypotheses throughout the case descriptions.[4] Construct validity evaluates whether operational measures are appropriate for the concepts. To ensure construct validity, triangulation using multiple sources of evidence is useful (Yin 2014). Available data and interview data are triangulated in this book.

1.2.3 Data

The Japanese footwear industry case presented in this book draws on various sources. Detailed data sources and the methods used are described in each relevant section. Here, I provide a brief overview of the main data sources used throughout the case descriptions.

1.2.3.1 Interviews

Interviews were conducted with 58 individuals, including JIF officials, shoe manufacturers, wholesalers, and retailers, and insole suppliers. Some participants were interviewed multiple times, resulting in a cumulative total of 64 interviews. The list and profiles of the interviewees are summarized in Appendix 1. These interviews were conducted over a ten-year period from 2013 to 2022.

A semi-structured interview format was used, where a questionnaire was sent to respondents in advance, with interviewees asked to reply at their leisure. The questionnaire was not standardized but tailored to each interviewee and their affiliated company. After conducting extensive research on the interviewees and their affiliated organizations through available secondary sources, specific questions were designed to clarify their actions and intentions at the time. Interviews typically lasted 1–2 h, with some interviews involving multiple respondents lasting more than 3 h. In addition, in some cases, hour-long tours of stores or factories were also conducted. During the interviews, notes were taken simultaneously and recordings were made with the interviewees' permission. After the interviews, the content was transcribed for preservation and reproduction.

Interviewees sometimes provided personal documents, although none were specifically requested. These documents ranged from a few to, in some cases, hundreds. All borrowed materials were photocopied, and a list consisting of dates and titles was created and used in the analysis.

[4] Two efforts, in particular, are presented here. First, Chap. 4 provides a detailed description of JIF's initial resources to demonstrate that its success does not stem from an abundance of ex ante resources, including industry knowledge, but from resources learned and accumulated ex post. Second, to illustrate that the growth of the fashion-oriented transparent insole market cannot be solely attributed to the expansion of the drugstore channel, sales of insole suppliers using the channel are compared in Chap. 10. The sales figures differ depending on whether the suppliers offered transparent insoles or not.

Interviews and private documents obtained from the interviewees were indispensable in clarifying the strategic actions, interactions, intentions, and perceptions of JIF and companies. As most of the subjects of analysis were small organizations and companies, secondary materials were insufficient. Therefore, interviews and private documents obtained from the interviewees were essential. Nonetheless, to avoid relying on a single source, triangulation was conducted wherein the contents of interviews with different people and secondary data were mutually confirmed to corroborate accounts and to improve construct validity (Yin 2014).

1.2.3.2 Fieldwork

Fieldwork was also conducted, including on-site observations and conversations in the form of short informal interviews. This fieldwork deepened the understanding of the footwear industry and identified new interviewees. As shown in Appendix 2, the sites included shoe exhibitions, shoe and foot health-related academic conferences, lectures on foot health, the Shoe Fitter (SF) Training Workshops of Foot, Footwear and Health Association (FHA, successor to JIF), and the FHA 50th party. Since most of the sites were places where many people gathered to study, I was able to observe them without drawing excessive attention. Notes were taken during the observations, and clean copies were made as field notes.

1.2.3.3 Newspaper and Magazine Articles

Although this paper draws on various available sources, articles in magazines and newspapers were useful for understanding the context, tracking the transition of historical facts, and checking for retrospective bias in interview data. The collection of these data allowed this study to tailor the questions to the interviewees and made the interviews more fruitful.

Among the papers and magazines, the most important was *Footwear Press*, a monthly trade publication. It is the only trade magazine of the footwear industry that covers the main period of this study—the 1980s through the 2000s. All the issues of *Footwear Press* from 1983 to 2010 were reviewed, and copies of necessary articles were made. A list of the articles with titles, dates, summaries, and keywords was created for later retrieval, amounting to 4,228 articles. As *Footwear Press* was not digitized and no library had every volume, I visited various libraries to check and collect the articles.

1.3 Structure of This Book

This book consists of four parts. Part I confirms that there are two issues related to research on social movements that target companies. Each of the two issues in existing research is reviewed more in depth, followed by case analysis in Parts II and III, respectively. Part II discusses the direct effect of activism: How can SMOs positioned on the periphery of an industry change corporate behavior? Part III examines the indirect effect of activism: Are the markets that emerge owing to the activities of SMOs always intended by SMOs, and when the market emergence is unintended by SMOs, specifically inconsistent with the superordinate goals of SMOs, how does this emergence occur? Although both issues are related to research on social movements targeting companies, the first issue covered in Part II examines the process until the SMO is successful in its strategy, whereas the second issue covered in Part III evaluates market changes occurring as a result of this success. Part IV presents a comprehensive overview of the book, as well as the discussion and conclusions. By reading the introduction in Part I, the case analyses in Parts II and III, and the summary in Part IV, the reader can gain a better understanding of the overall case of social movements in the Japanese footwear industry during the post-war period, from the process of JIF's success to its aftermath.

A brief overview of the contents of each chapter is provided below.

Part I, which includes this chapter, serves as preparation for the case analysis in Parts II and III. Chapter 1 briefly examines research on social movements targeting companies, presents the two issues, and explains the methodology for examining these issues. These two issues are explored through a case analysis of the Japanese post-war footwear industry. Chapter 2 provides the necessary background knowledge to understand the case, offering an overview of the awareness of foot health in post-war Japan, the characteristics of shoes as a product, the history of footwear in Japan, and an overview of the post-war footwear industry.

Part II examines the direct effect of activism: How can SMOs positioned on the periphery of an industry change corporate behavior? Chapter 3 clarifies that this issue remains unresolved by reviewing existing research on social movements targeting companies and presents an analytical framework for explaining this issue using JIF's activities in the footwear industry as an example. Chapter 4 describes JIF's original resources and its strategy based on these resources, as well as its evolution. JIF's founding and early resources were limited, and its original strategies based on those resources were ineffective. However, the new strategy of having shoe retailers acquire shoe fitter certification emerged by learning by doing. Chapter 5 explains the process by which JIF further revised its strategies and shoe fitters spread to shoe retailers and summarizes and discusses Part II. The analysis of the JIF case reveals that SMOs can develop effective strategies *ex post facto* by learning by doing.

Part III addresses the indirect effect of activism: Are the markets that emerge owing to the SMOs' activities always intended by the SMOs, and when the market emergence is unintended by SMOs, specifically one that is inconsistent with the superordinate goals of SMOs, how does this emergence occur? Chapter 6 explains that research on social movements targeting companies has given little thought to the possibility of markets unintended by the SMOs emerging. However, the case of JIF demonstrates the emergence of unintended markets, including the one inconsistent with the superordinate goals of JIF. An analytical framework for considering why and how such markets emerge is presented. Chapter 7 explains how the awareness of foot health increased because of JIF's initiatives and the proliferation of shoe fitters. As a result, the comfort shoe market emerged, which was intended by JIF. Chapter 8 reveals that the European comfort shoe market emerged in response to the interest in foot health stimulated by JIF. It was a market that JIF did not intend but was in line with JIF's superordinate goal of protecting foot health. In contrast, Chaps. 9 and 10 describe the process that led to the emergence of the fashion-oriented transparent insole market that did not align with JIF's superordinate goals because of JIF's initiatives. Chapter 9 confirms the emergence of a market for insoles that provide walking support. Chapter 10 describes the process by which the walking-support insole market became fashionable, and the fashion-oriented transparent insoles flourished. The chapter also summarizes and discusses Part III. The analysis of the JIF case reveals that the initiatives of SMOs stimulate various consumer needs and company responses, potentially leading to the emergence of markets that either align or do not align with the superordinate goals of SMOs.

In Part IV, Chap. 11 summarizes the discussions presented in this volume. It reviews the discussions aimed at resolving the issues associated with research on social movements targeting companies developed in Part I through Part III and clarifies the contributions made. It then discusses three implications of the book: unintended market emergence resulting from successful social movements, difficulties in mobilizing consumers, and expanding the scope of research on social movements targeting companies.

Chapter 2
Characteristics of Shoes and the Footwear Industry

This chapter provides basic information about shoes and the footwear industry in Japan to help understand the case analyses presented in Parts II and III. The information is organized into four sections. The first section discusses awareness of foot health in Japan. Until the mid-1980s, before JIF started to train shoe fitters, Japanese people did not pay attention to foot health. The second section examines the features of shoes. While both shoes and clothing are apparel, they exhibit different characteristics. The margin of error of shoe sizes is smaller. The third section includes a general outline of the history of footwear in Japan. Both traditional Japanese footwear and footwear adopted from the West became positioned as fashion items. The fourth section provides a general outline of the post-WWII footwear industry in Japan. The footwear industry has been a fragmented industry with no clear dominant firms (Porter 1980; Seki 1975). This information should clarify the descriptions in subsequent chapters regarding the Japanese footwear industry since the 1960s.

2.1 Awareness of Foot Health in Japan

Some experts have pointed out that in the 1970s and 1980s, Japanese people focused only on the fashion of shoes and were unable to choose shoes that fit, which was detrimental to correct walking and health. For example, Eijirō Sugano, a doctor of agriculture and leather researcher, and Tadao Ishizuka, a medical doctor, both pointed out that many people prioritized the fashionable features of shoes while remaining

This chapter consists of restructured and revised version of Miura, S. (2020). Naze eranda kutsu de ashi o itamerunoka: Shijō deno kutsu erabi no muzukashisa o saguru [Why do we have trouble with the shoes we wear? The difficulty of finding shoes that fit in Japan]. *Gakuen*, (958), 16–36. https://swu.repo.nii.ac.jp/records/7011.

S. Miura, *Successful Social Activism and Unintended Market Emergence*,
https://doi.org/10.1007/978-981-99-9291-1_2

indifferent to their health benefits (Ishizuka 1983; Sugano 1975). Michiko Inukai, a journalist, wrote in *Asahi Shimbun* on July 11, 1967:

> The essence of Italian shoes is tireless study on leather and research on the human feet that need to fit into it. In other words, it is their dedication to comfort. After all, shoes exist for human feet. Shoes are not for decoration—much less something people should wear while enduring foot pain for outward displays of fashion. After three hours of wearing and walking in Japanese shoes, you cannot help but become conscious of them. When it comes to Japanese shoe-related companies in general, why not devote some of the attention that is used so much for appearance to the study of the human foot? What they are doing is putting the cart before the horse and running ahead while forgetting the basics of the starting point.[1]

Consumer surveys conducted in the 1980s also showed that foot health was largely overlooked. A 1988 survey by the Nada-Kobe Consumer Cooperative found that half of the respondents (the total number of respondents is unknown) said that they still wore shoes that hurt their feet (Ōtsuka and Abe 1990). A 1985 study by the Consumer Science Research Institute of Hyogo Prefecture ("Fujin-gutsu ni kan suru jittai chōsa hōkoku" [fact-finding report on women's shoes]) found similar results (Ōtsuka and Abe 1990). Examining these surveys, Ōtsuka and Abe (1990) concluded that consumers "tended to prioritize design and color over comfort" (p. 19).[2]

However, it is more accurate to say that consumers were largely unaware of the impact of shoes on foot and overall health than to say that they had decided to prioritize fashion over health. Consumers took it for granted that new shoes were, by nature, painful at first (Kuze 1999), and they did not realize that those painful shoes would harm their feet and overall health in the long run. People understood that ill-fitting shoes could create shoe sores and blisters in the short term, but they did not understand that those short-term problems could lead to hallux valgus (or bunions) and other serious foot deformities over time. Retailers and manufacturers also did not have much knowledge or understanding of foot health (Katō 1977; Sugano 1975). Michiko Kubota, a salesclerk in the women's shoe department of Seibu Ikebukuro, Seibu Department Stores, said that sellers also thought it was normal for new shoes to be painful and for shoe sores to occur.[3] Takeo Kikuchi, president of Dinus Shoe Corporation, a small shoe manufacture, noted the same (Takesawa 2005). This lack of awareness of foot health persisted owing to the absence of specialized university laboratories in engineering, medicine, or home economics dedicated to shoe research. Additionally, shoe manufacturers focused primarily on manufacturing methods, with limited investment in research on the health function of shoes (Katō 1977; Sugano 1975; Yamazaki 1987).

---

[1] Translated from Japanese by the author and secondary citation from Sugano (1975, pp.13–14).

[2] Translated from Japanese by the author.

[3] Michiko Kubota, sales consultant at Shoes Frontier (interview, May 15, 2017).

2.2 Shoe Product Features

The previous section explained that, until the 1980s when JIF achieved success, Japanese people's awareness of foot health was low, and some experts claimed that people should have focused on the health function of shoes rather than their fashion function. What are the health functions and fashion functions of shoes? How are they related to each other? This section will briefly explain the health and fashion functions of shoes while paying attention to the product characteristics of shoes.

2.2.1 Health Function of Shoes

Foot health, walking, and general health mutually affect each other, as shown in Fig. 2.1. The relationships between foot health and walking, walking and general health, and how all of these are associated with shoes will be explained sequentially.

Foot health and walking balance interact with each other. With healthy feet, one can walk with good balance because no problems need to be compensated for. When the individual's foot is experiencing a problem, such as Hallux valgus (or bunions) and digitus minimus varus (or bunionettes), which are often observed at the same time as flat feet and splay feet (Takayama 2014),[4] it becomes impossible to maintain good balance when walking because of the need to compensate for pain. If one can walk with good balance, the muscles and bones in the feet will be used properly, and the walker's feet will remain healthy. Unbalanced walking puts an excessive burden on parts of the foot, which may cause the problems noted above.

Well-balanced walking is good for overall health, and conversely, good health is conducive to well-balanced walking. Well-balanced walking is good for overall health, as it promotes good circulation. In contrast, unbalanced walking restricts circulation and puts undue stress on the knees and hips. If one is in good health, maintaining a good balance while walking should not be difficult. In contrast, individuals with bodily ailments will have to compensate for this as they walk, leading to an unbalanced gait.

Shoes have a bearing on walking, which in turn affects foot health and general health. Well-fitting shoes promote a well-balanced gait, whereas poorly fitting shoes hinder one's gait. Shoes that are too loose require the wearer to put extra pressure on their feet, especially the toes, to keep the shoes from slipping off. Shoes that are too tight prevent the toes from functioning properly, as there is no room for the toes

[4] Similar to the relationship between the chicken and the egg, it is not known whether hallux valgus develops before or after splayfeet/flatfeet (Uchida 2003). Hallux valgus is a common condition among women, but it is also observed in men and children (Meshida 2017; Shibata 2007; Takegawa 2007; Tanaka 2010). It is more common in women because women have weaker joint structures and muscles that support the joints. It has also been pointed out that hallux valgus in men may not become evident because of the belief that men do not develop it or because they are embarrassed to admit it (Shionoya 2012).

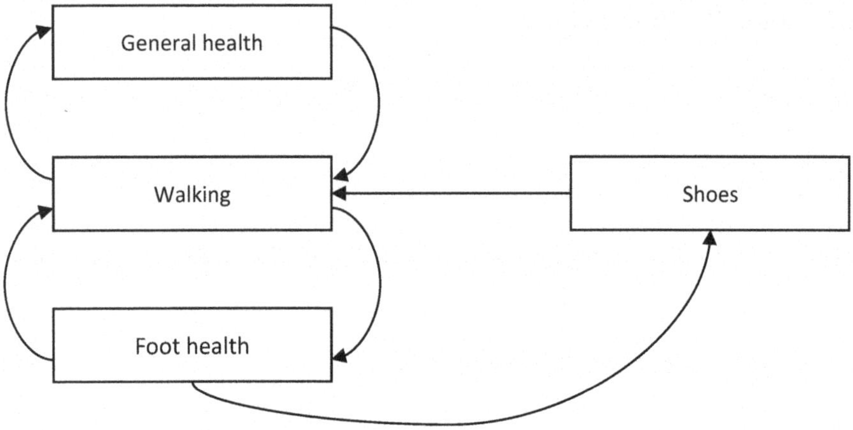

Fig. 2.1 Relationship between walking, health, and shoes. *Source* Miura (2020, p. 20, Fig. 1), translated from Japanese and modified by the author

to move. In both cases, walking balance is sacrificed, and as noted earlier, walking balance affects foot health as well as general health.

Healthy feet are more tolerant of shoe fit. This is because, with stronger muscles, one can walk without losing balance, even when the fit is not perfect. This may be easier to understand if thought of in the opposite manner. Individuals with problematic feet are more limited in the choice of shoes they can select. They must consider avoiding pain and loss of balance when selecting a pair of shoes.

Given that well-fitting shoes are important for foot and general health, what defines a good fit between a foot and a shoe? Shoes that simply replicate the exact size of the foot do not properly accommodate the foot or support walking (JIF 1984h, 1995). To support the foot's dynamic changes while walking, shoes have parts that should fit just right, parts that should be small, and parts that should be big relative to the foot. The names of each part of the foot referenced in the following explanation are listed in Figs. 2.2 and 2.3. When one's heel encounters the ground, the shape of the heel does not change much, but as the individual takes a step, the three arches of the foot collapse (Fig. 2.3). In other words, the foot's length and width expand. Finally, when extending the toes by kicking, the length and width of the toes expand. Therefore, the heel part of the shoe should fit tightly around the heel to provide support to the heel. The instep (waist section) should be narrower than the waist section to support the arches and prevent the feet from sliding forward. The toe part should be roomy for the toes to spread and push off the ground.

It is significantly challenging to find shoes that meet the criteria described above. First, achieving a proper shoe fitting requires millimeter-to-millimeter conformity to prevent a foot from slipping within the shoe (Oohori and Yamazaki 1990; Yamazaki 1983, 1992). In this regard, shoes differ greatly from clothing. While various sizes of clothing are acceptable as long as they do not slip off the body, the margin of error of shoe sizes is smaller to adequately support the activity of walking (Kondō 1995).

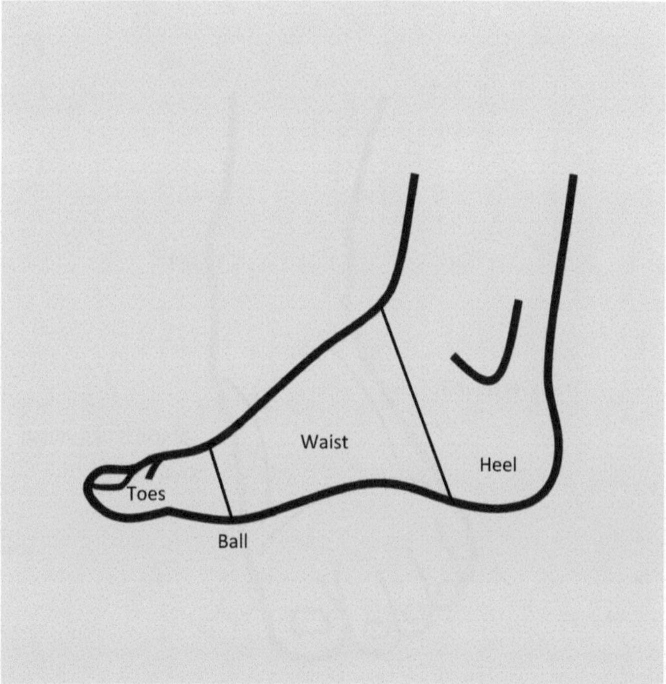

Fig. 2.2 Names of parts of the foot. *Source* iStock.com/3xy. Modified by the author

Second, although there are standards for shoes, these serve only as general guidelines. In Japan, the Japan Industrial Standards (JIS) S5037 determines the standards for shoe sizes.[5] JIS S5037 stipulates foot length and ball girth (foot circumference) (Fig. 2.2). For example, indications such as E or EE denote the ball girth of the foot. Foot length is specified in 5 mm and ball girth in 6 mm increments. These foot lengths and ball girths established by JIS S5037 are foot sizes, not shoe sizes, referred to as "nude size." For example, a 23 cm E shoe will fit a person with a foot length of 23 cm and a ball girth of E, but the shoe itself is not 23 cm and E in size. Therefore, each shoe manufacturer determines the shoe size that should fit that specific foot nude size, leading to differences in sizing estimates by shoe manufacturer (Kuremoto 2011). As a result, shoes with the same size notation, such as a 23 cm E shoe, may come in various sizes. Furthermore, even shoes with the same design may have individual differences when natural leather is used to manufacture them. Leather is made from

[5] From 1977 to 1979, under the contract from the Ministry of International Trade and Industry, Zennihon Hakimono Dantai Kyōgikai, a trade association in the footwear industry, conducted foot shape measurements of 10,000 people. This project aimed to establish a JIS sizing system for shoes. JIS S5037 was established on August 1, 1983, and revised on August 20, 1998 (Japan Standards Association n. d.).

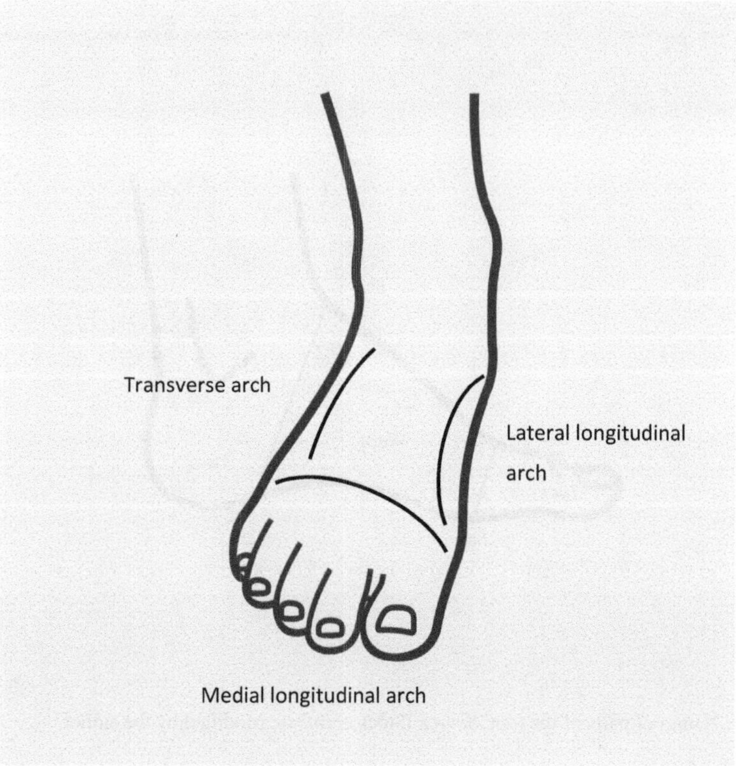

Fig. 2.3 Foot arches. *Source* iStock.com/3xy. Modified by the author

animal hides and is not homogeneous like synthetic leather (Ishida and Yoshinaga 2009; Kuremoto 2011; Nakajima 2012).[6] Thus, shoe size remains elusive.

Third, as shoe size is elusive, foot size is also elusive. Even if the three sizes specified by JIS S5037 are identical, other parts of the foot may still differ in size because of variations in foot shape from one person to another (Nikkei Business Publications and Kuze 1999). Furthermore, the degree of change in foot shape during walking also varies (Nakajima 2011a).

To summarize, finding well-fitting shoes is important for foot and general health, but it is a difficult task. Although proper shoe fitting requires millimeter-to-millimeter conformity, both foot sizes and shoe sizes remain elusive. Therefore, people cannot select shoes depending only on JIS S5037. Finding shoes that fit well requires trying on real shoes (Kajiyama 2018; Kuremoto 2011; Shionoya 2012).

[6] Shoemakers ascertain these conditions, cut the leather, sew it together, place it on the shoe last, and complete the lasting process (Kuremoto 2011). "Lasting" refers to the task of pulling the leather upper around the circumference of the shoe last, ensuring it conforms closely to the last, and attaching the shoe to its sole with pins or adhesive.

2.2.2 Fashion Function of Shoes

Shoe selection becomes even more difficult when considering both fashion and size (Miura, 2020). The fashionableness of shoes relates to the style that their appearance conveys. Finding shoes that both fit comfortably and appeal to you owing to their design can be quite challenging.

Shoe styles that are considered popular and fashionable tend to change with the times. However, in general, since the end of WWII, shoes with narrow toes have been considered more fashionable than those with wider toes. For women, pumps with pointed toes are a typical example of this trend (Fig. 2.4). Even for men, leather shoes with a tapered toe section, as shown in Fig. 2.5, are generally considered more fashionable than those with a round, wide toe.

Shoes with a tapered toe design tend to be inconsistent with the health functionality of shoes. As mentioned in the previous section, the toe part is a space for the toes to spread out, providing energy to the walker's gait by kicking off the ground. Therefore, the toe parts should be roomy for a shoe to support walking. Fashionable women's or men's shoes that have a tapered toe design cannot offer sufficient room for toes. Furthermore, in the case of pumps, as there is nothing to hold the instep of the foot, the foot tends to slip forward, putting stress on the toes. High-heeled pumps also place the feet in an unnatural position, much like being placed on a slanted board, with feet tending to slip forward, causing much strain on the balls of the feet and toes.

Fig. 2.4 Pointed toe pumps. *Source* iStock.com/GeorgeDolgikh

Fig. 2.5 Cap toe shoes. *Source* iStock.com/GeorgeVieiraSilva

In this way, all things being equal, fashionable shoes—that is, shoes with a tapered toe and, in some cases, high heels—tend to be inconsistent with health functionality.[7]

If people only pay attention to the fashion function of shoes, lack knowledge regarding the health function and proper fit of shoes, and take it for granted that it is normal for shoes to hurt, it will be difficult for them to select shoes that do not hurt their feet. This is the issue that some people viewed as problematic as pointed out in the previous section.

2.3 History of Footwear in Japan

How did shoes come to be positioned as fashion items in Japan? This section briefly explains the history of footwear in Japan. Both traditional and Western footwear were not initially fashion items but became so over time.

2.3.1 Traditional Japanese Footwear

Western footwear spread to ordinary people in Japan after WWII. Before that period, people commonly wore *waraji* (straw sandals), *zōri* (thonged sandals), and *geta* (wooden clogs) (Kishimoto and Ichida 2000; Notsu 1969).[8] As shown in Figs. 2.6, 2.7, 2.8 and 2.9, each of these shoes features a platform where the foot is placed and a cord-like strap that protrudes from the platform, passing between the big toe and the second toe and over the top of the foot. This strap secures the foot to the platform (Miyamoto 1933). *Waraji* are a type of footwear woven from rice straw. They have a long strap that protrudes from the front and passes through loops on the sides and at the heel; the strap is then wrapped around the ankle and tied (Fig. 2.6). *Zōri* have a simpler strap than *waraji* and can be made with materials other than rice straw, such as hemp (Akita 2002) (Fig. 2.7). Therefore, *zōri* are essentially flip-flops made from plant materials. *Geta* also utilize a strap, but their platform is made of wood, with one to three teeth or heels serving to raise it above the ground (Figs. 2.8 and 2.9).

Similar to other cultural items, these types of footwear were developed in Japan with Chinese and Korean influences (Akita 2002). *Waraji* and *zōri* appeared around the second half of the seventh century, during the Asuka period, and became widespread among the masses around the 10th century, in the middle of the Heian period (Akita 2002). *Geta* appeared between the fourth and fifth centuries, during the Kofun period, but they became popular among the masses after the diffusion of

[7] However, not all shoes designed with ample room in the toe are necessarily healthy. Even if shoes are designed with enough room for the toes, if the heel and waist parts of the shoes are too large, the foot may slide forward when walking, which is not healthy (Nishimura 2016; Tanaka 2010). Conversely, even if shoes are tapered and fashionable, if the sizes of the heel and waist parts are appropriate, the foot will not slide forward, reducing the burden on the ball of the foot and toes.

[8] For more details on Japanese traditional footwear, see Suzuki-Johnson and Nakagawa (2021).

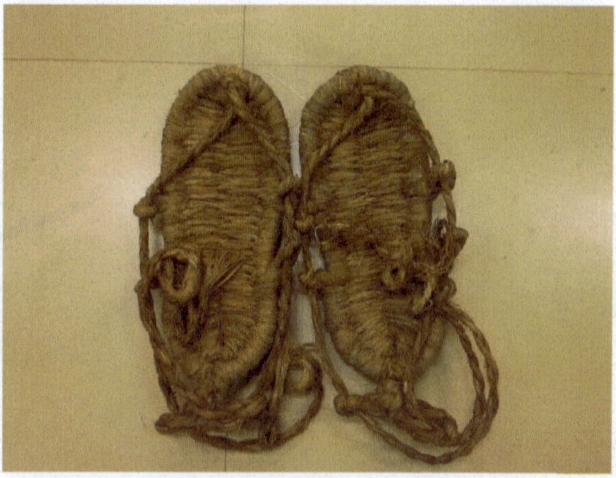

Fig. 2.6 *Waraji* (straw sandals). *Source* Photo by courtesy of Saitama Prefectural Museum of History and Folklore

Fig. 2.7 *Zōri* (thonged sandals). *Source* Photo by courtesy of Gyōda City Local Museum

waraji and *zōri*. Influential individuals began wearing *geta* around the 10th century in the Heian period. From the Kamakura period in the 12th century onwards, affluent commoners also began to wear them. Ordinary people did not start wearing *geta* until the seventeenth century, at the beginning of the Edo period, and *geta* continued to diversify in the middle of the Edo period (mid-18th century) (Imanishi 1962; Notsu 1969).

Fig. 2.8 *Geta* (wooden clogs). *Source* Photo by courtesy of Gyōda City Local Museum

Fig. 2.9 *Geta* and their repairer. *Source* Photo by courtesy of Minoru Inagawa (Director of Leather Industry Museum). *Note* A photograph of Japanese customs taken for an overseas audience, probably from the end of the Edo period to the early Meiji period

Table 2.1 Average pairs of footwear per person (1966)

		Male	Female
Geta	Paulownia	2.1	3.6
	Pine	0.9	0.4
	Japanese cedar	0.5	0.3
Zōri		1.4	3.2
Leather shoes		1.8	1.3
Rain boots, long boots		1.7	1.5
Total		8.4	10.3

Source Calculated by the authors based on Notsu (1969), Table 1 (p. 44) and Table 3 (pp. 46–47)
Notes Participants included 501 men and 500 women aged 20 years or older from the San'in region. Participants were divided into groups by age, i.e., 20s, 30s, 40s, and 50s. Each group had 100 participants, except for men in their 50s, which had 101 participants

The difference in the popularization of *waraji* and *zōri* compared with *geta* stemmed from their different uses. *Waraji* and *zōri* were well-suited for agricultural work and thus quickly gained popularity among the masses. In contrast, *geta* were not as practical for daily use, owing to the small ground contact surface. They were used only in exceptional cases, such as during rainy weather or for water-related tasks such as laundry and drawing water (Akita 2002; Ichida 2000).[9] As the purchasing power of town-dwelling commoners increased during the Edo period and their *kimono* (clothing) became a fashion item, the design and ornamentation of *geta* diversified (Akita 2002: Ichida 2000). In short, *geta* became popularized as an accessory to coordinate with *kimono*. In the Meiji period, which began in the mid-19th century, the design and ornamentation of *zōri* also began to diversify as an accessory to complement *kimono* as Japan was influenced by an influx of Western culture (Imanishi 1962).

From that time until before WWII, *zōri* and *geta* continued to be mainstream footwear. Even in 1966, a survey conducted in the San'in region revealed that adults possessed as many or more pairs of traditional footwear than they did Western-style leather shoes (Table 2.1). At the time, it was typical to wear Western shoes with Western clothing, but some older people continued to wear their favorite *geta* and *zōri* along with *kimono* on a daily basis (Notsu 1968, 1969).

Today, hardly anyone in Japan wears *zōri* or *geta* on a daily basis. However, *zōri* and *geta* live on as fashion items used for special occasions. *Kimono* are still worn as festive clothing for the New Year, weddings, and other special occasions, and *geta* and *zōri* are indispensable footwear choices when wearing *kimono* (Fig. 2.10).

[9] In addition, straw and common rush, materials used for *waraji* and *zōri*, were relatively easy to obtain (Akita 2002).

Fig. 2.10 *Kimono* and *Zōri* for *Shichi-Go-San* celebration. *Source* Photo by courtesy of the author. *Note Shichi-Go-San*, literally meaning seven, five, and three, is a festival celebrating the growth of children who have reached the age of three, five, and seven

2.3.2 Western-Style Shoes in Japan

Western shoes were introduced in Japan due to military demand, and they were later popularized as a fashion item after WWII. This section briefly reviews the process of this transition. Japanese people began wearing Western-style leather shoes during the mid-19th century, marking the transition from the Edo period to the Meiji period. Domestic production of these shoes began in 1870, three years after the end of the Edo period's isolation and the start of the Meiji period (Inagawa 2013). The Japanese footwear industry was transplanted from the West, initially focusing on manufacturing combat boots (Hikakusangyō Enkakushi Hensan Iinkai 1959, 1989; Koshō 1966; Satō 1971). Therefore, the industry was initially a segment of the defense industry. With the successive conflicts of the Sino-Japanese War, Russo-Japanese War, and World War I during the late 19th and early 20th centuries, the capacity of the footwear industry increased (Koshō 1966; Miura 2017) as major shoe manufacturers imported production machinery to mechanize their operations. Because much of the demand came from the military, wholesale and retail capacity did not develop significantly outside of micro in-house manufacturing retailers (Seki 1975).

Japan's defeat in WWII spelled the end of the footwear industry's orientation within the defense industry. Shoes were subsequently repositioned within their second industrial context: the clothing industry. The big, mechanized players that had carved out dominant positions in the shoe sector before the war transitioned their operations from satisfying military needs to meeting private demand. Small and medium-sized manufacturers increased their production of women's shoes (Satō 1971). By the 1970s, one of the dynamics characterizing the footwear industry, where market power diverged both horizontally and vertically, was the multi-dimensional competition over creating brands that consumers would align with (Seki 1975). In the field of men's shoes, the premiere manufacturers from the prewar era had established brand names. For example, Nippon Seika (currently Regal Corporation), which supplied shoes to the Army, had the Regal brand, while Otsuka Seika, which supplied shoes to the Navy, had the brand Otsuka (Nippon Seika Shashihensan Iinkai 1990; Otsuka Seika 1976). In addition, rubber shoe manufacturers, such as Japan Rubber (currently Asahi Shoes) and Tsukihoshi Gomu (currently Moonstar), known for manufacturing athletic shoes and rubber boots, entered the leather shoe market and grew in strength (Gomuhouchi Shinbunsha 1979; Seki 1975; Tsukihoshi Gomu 1967). In women's shoes, wholesalers had a dominant brand presence, and they had their shoes produced by small and medium-sized manufacturers. The four largest women's shoe wholesalers were Shinei Sangyo, Tokutsu, Suganuma, and Ogitsu (Yano Research Institute 1981). However, since shoes were considered fashion items designed as secondary accessories to pair with clothing (Iwamoto 2014; Seki 1975), those product brands could not perfectly control the market. At the same time, store brands of major shoe retail chains held sway over the contemporary marketing landscape. In the 1970s, Washington Kutsuten and Americaya Kutsuten emerged as leading retail chains (Gomuhouchi Shinbunsha 1978).

2.4 Post-War Footwear Industry in Statistics

This section outlines the details of the post-war footwear industry. Seki (1975) pointed out that market power diverged both horizontally and vertically in the footwear industry in the 1970s. These trends have remained largely unchanged, and it would be difficult to argue that any industry-dominating manufacturer has emerged. Thus, the footwear industry remains fragmented (Porter 1980). What has changed since the 1970s is the increase in imported goods. As manufacturers were unable to establish powerful product brands, the imports of overseas products increased, and the industry was hollowed out as Japan relied heavily on imported footwear.[10] Since shoe manufacturers were small, they lacked the extra capacity to differentiate their brands. Under these circumstances, there was no way that manufacturers could conduct research on foot health.

[10] In addition to the increase in foreign brands, the relocation of production bases overseas by major footwear companies has also been pointed out as a reason for the increase in imports (Miyakawa 1994). This shift is because of the strong yen and economic development, which have made production in Japan relatively more expensive. This transition has resulted in job losses among small and medium-sized domestic manufacturers that had been subcontracting for major footwear companies. It can be interpreted as a defeat due to imports, stemming from the failure of small and medium-sized manufacturers to establish their own brands (Inagawa and Yamamoto 2011).

2.4.1 Maturity of the Domestic Shoe Market

Figure 2.11 illustrates changes in the domestic retail market size based on data from Posty Corporation, changes in domestic market size based on data from the Yano Research Institute, and changes in domestic footwear demand based on official statistics. The figures from the Yano Research Institute and Posty Corporation are based on retail sales, whereas the official statistics are based on shipments from manufacturing establishments. Therefore, domestic demand from official statistics appears smaller than the others. The reason for the discrepancies between the figures from the Yano Research Institute and Posty Corporation is that each company makes its own estimates. However, all three figures indicate that the Japanese footwear market expanded in the 1960s and 1970s and matured in the 1980s and 1990s.

Figures 2.12 and 2.13 subdivide the domestic demand for footwear according to the difference in instep material: leather and others (plastic, rubber, and cloth). Plastic footwear is made of artificial or synthetic leather. In general, leather footwear is more expensive than plastic or rubber footwear. Figure 2.12 shows that leather footwear accounted for 40%–50% of domestic demand, peaking at 50% in 1990, and it has been shrinking since then. As the price of leather footwear is higher than that of plastic, rubber, and cloth footwear, leather footwear had a smaller share by quantity. In terms of quantity, leather footwear had shrunk from a peak of 20% in 1990 to less than 10% in 2011, as shown in Fig. 2.13.

2.4.2 Reliance on Imported Footwear

Imported footwear supports the domestic market. As of 2011, the import ratio for footwear as a portion of domestic demand was 70%, based on value: 47% for leather footwear and 85% for plastic and rubber footwear (Table 2.2).[11] Based on quantity, as of 2011, the import ratio for footwear was 90%: 60% for leather footwear and 93% for plastic and rubber footwear (Table 2.3). The higher percentage for quantity than value indicates that imports are considered low-priced goods.

As shown in Fig. 2.14, footwear imports have increased in response to exchange rate fluctuations. Appreciation of the yen lowers import prices and increases the level of imports. The footwear industry has consistently witnessed increased imports during periods of yen appreciation. The first significant surge in the yen's value after WWII occurred in 1971 during the Nixon shock. The yen rose in value from ¥360 to the dollar to ¥308 to the dollar and continued to appreciate thereafter. Figure 2.14 illustrates that imports of plastic and rubber footwear started to rise in the 1970s. However, when the yen depreciated owing to the Carter shock in 1978, imports of plastic and rubber footwear leveled off until the mid-1980s. The yen rose abruptly again because of the Plaza Accord of 1985, when the exchange rate shifted from

[11] Domestic demand is calculated by adding the import amount to the domestic production amount and then subtracting the export amount.

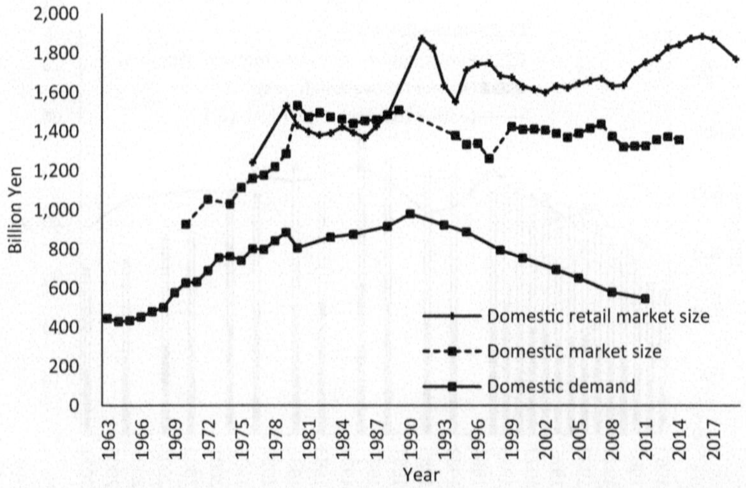

Fig. 2.11 Japanese domestic footwear market size. *Sources* Prepared by the author. For the domestic retail market size, Gomuhouchi Shinbunsha (later Posty Corporation) (1978, p. 1, 1979, p. 1, 1980, p. 1, 1981, p. 1, 1982, p.1,1983, p.1, 1984, p.1) and Posty Corporation (1985, p. 5, 1986, p. 5, 1987, p. 14, 1988, p. 6, 1989, p. 8, 1990, p. 9, 1991, p. 8, 1992, p. 10, 1993, p. 20, 1994, p. 16, 1995, p. 18, 2005, p. 18, 2012, p. 15, 2013. p. 17, 2014, p. 20, 2015, p. 29, 2016, p.9, 2017, p. 9, 2018, p. 8, 2020, p. 3, 2021, p. 3) were referred to. For the domestic market size, Yano Research Institute (1981, p. 57, 1983, p. 6, 1985, p. 5, 1989a, p. 5, 1990, p. 8, 1998, p. 11, 2003, p. 7, 2009, p. 13, 2014, p. 35, 2016, p. 29) was referred to. For the domestic demand, Ministry of Economy, Trade and Industry (METI) (n.d.a) and Ministry of Finance (n.d.) were referred to. *Notes* 1. The domestic retail market size is adjusted to real values with 2010 as the base year (2010 = 1) using the Consumer Price Index (Ministry of Internal Affairs and Communications n.d). 2. The domestic market size is adjusted to real values in the same manner as the domestic retail market size. Yano Research Institute changed its survey categories in 1989 and 1999, and so the data are not perfectly continuous. Values for the years 1988, 1997, and 2002 are outlooks. 3. The domestic demand is calculated by adding the import amount to the domestic production amount and subtracting the export amount. It is adjusted to real values with 2010 as the base year (2010 = 1) using the GDP deflator for domestic production (Cabinet Office n.d.), and Import and Export Price Indexes for import and export amounts (Bank of Japan n.d.b). The domestic demand values are shown up to 2011 because of a change in the estimation method from 2012 onward

¥235 to the dollar to ¥150 to the dollar within the space of one year. This sharp appreciation led to increased imports of plastic and rubber footwear. Meanwhile, imports of leather footwear, which had previously been minimal, surged from 1986. In addition to the appreciation of the yen caused by the Plaza Accord, leather shoe imports were liberalized from 1986. Until then, volume restrictions were imposed under the import quota (IQ) system. However, as of April 1986, it transitioned to a tariff quota (TQ) system, allowing the import of leather footwear at either no tariff or a lower tariff rate (primary tariff rate) within a certain quantity, and a higher tariff rate (secondary tariff rate) for quantities exceeding the limit. Thus, any quantity of leather footwear could be imported if the tariff was paid. Subsequently, quotas were

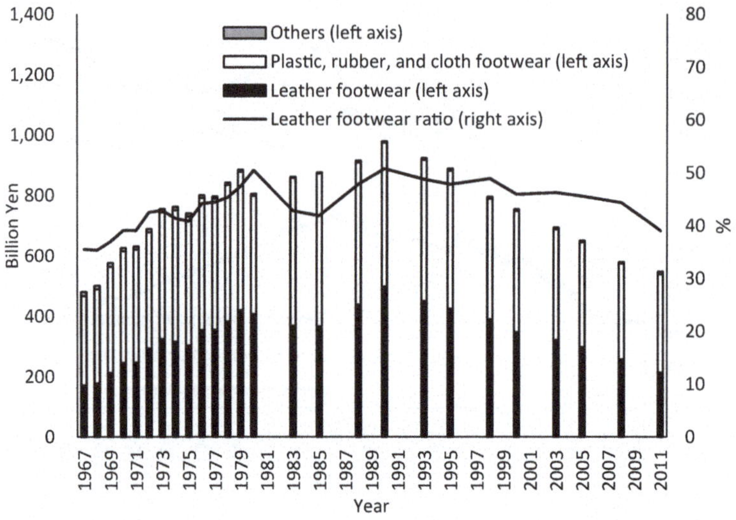

Fig. 2.12 Footwear market size by shoe material (value). *Source* Prepared by the author based on the same sources as the ones mentioned for domestic demand in Fig. 2.11. *Note* Adjusted to real values as shown in Fig. 2.11, with the base year set as 2010 = 1

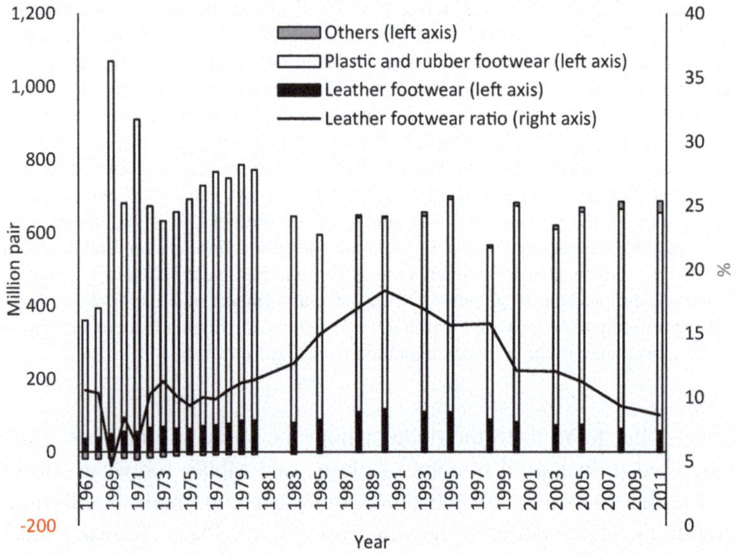

Fig. 2.13 Footwear market size by shoe material (quantity). *Source* Prepared by the author based on the same sources as the ones mentioned for domestic demand in Fig. 2.11. *Note* No statistical information is available for the quantity of cloth shoes. In 1969 and 1971, the increase in the quantity of plastic footwear exceeded the change in value, and the reason for this phenomenon is unknown. The negative figures for other footwear continue until 1983, as there is no equivalent category volume data in the Census of Manufactures, which estimates domestic production, and the quantity of exports exceeds that of imports in the Trade Statistics of Japan

Table 2.2 Percentage of imports in domestic demand by shoe material (value)

	1970	1975	1980	1985	1990	1995	2000	2005	2011
Leather footwear	1.3	1.6	1.7	1.9	12.5	25.1	31.0	41.3	46.5
Plastic, rubber, and cloth footwear	0.8	4.9	9.7	12.0	28.5	55.9	70.5	78.9	84.9
Total	1.0	3.5	5.3	7.5	19.9	40.9	52.3	61.8	69.9

Source Prepared by the author. The sources were the same as the domestic demand sources in Fig. 2.11

Table 2.3 Percentage of imports in domestic demand by shoe material (quantity)

	1970	1975	1980	1985	1990	1995	2000	2005	2011
Leather footwear	0.7	1.1	1.8	2.2	15.4	27.6	34.5	48.8	60.3
Plastic and rubber footwear	0.4	5.2	10.0	17.0	27.7	59.6	71.6	87.1	92.7
Total	0.5	4.9	9.1	15.0	26.0	55.1	67.5	83.0	90.2

Source Prepared by the author. The sources were the same as the domestic demand sources in Fig. 2.11

expanded and tariff rates reduced.[12] As a result, from the mid-1980s onwards, there was a rapid increase in leather footwear imports, propelled by the yen's appreciation and deregulation. Although the rapid rise in imports of both types of footwear slowed down in the mid-1990s, along with the slowing down of yen appreciation, the ratio of imports as a portion of domestic demand reached 70% by 2011.[13] It is important to note that the value of footwear exports is not discussed here because it is negligible.

As for import regions (Figs. 2.15 and 2.16), leather footwear had been imported from Europe and Asia, while plastic and rubber footwear had been imported from Asia. Leather shoes from Europe are high-end footwear, whereas leather footwear and plastic and rubber footwear from Asia are low-end products (Ministry of Economy, Trade and Industry 2022).

While in theory a stronger yen lowering import prices increases the number of imports, in practice a strong yen does not necessarily lead to an immediate increase in imports. If domestic items have advantages in non-price factors, import levels do not increase to the same extent that the yen rises (Itami 1998). Tariff barriers are one factor. This is one reason the rate of imports for leather footwear, while increasing, had been lower than that for plastic and rubber footwear. Another factor is the development of demand for higher-quality products through product differentiation by domestic manufactures (Itami 1998). If domestic manufactures can successfully differentiate their products, they can fend off the influx of low-priced imports

[12] See Appendix 3 for historical trends in quotas and tariff rates.

[13] Since 2011, imports have been increasing regardless of the trend of yen depreciation. Manufacturers had been struggling with increased imports for some time, but the 2008 global financial crisis and the 2011 Great East Japan Earthquake devastated shoe manufacturers and influenced the expansion of imports.

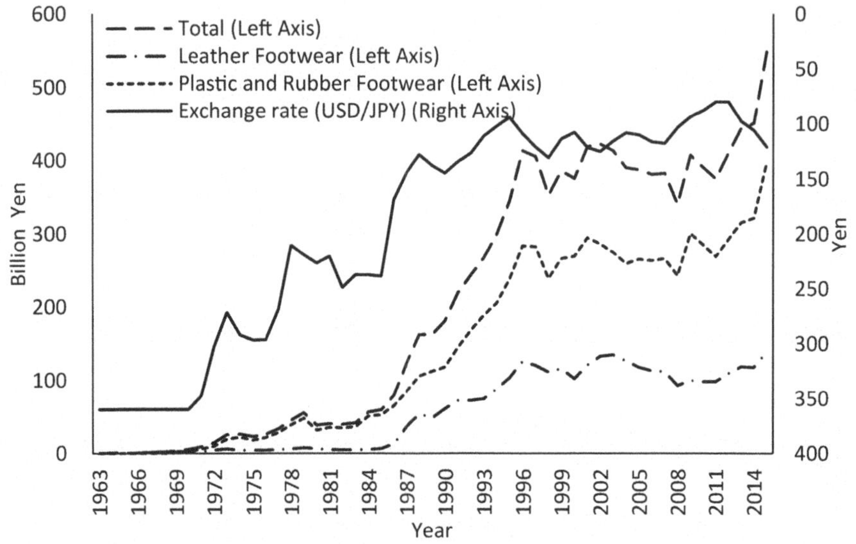

Fig. 2.14 Footwear import value by shoe material. *Source* Prepared by the author based on the same sources as the ones mentioned in Fig. 2.11 for imports and Bank of Japan (n.d.a.) for exchange rate. *Note* Imports were adjusted to real values as in Fig. 2.11, with 2010 = 1

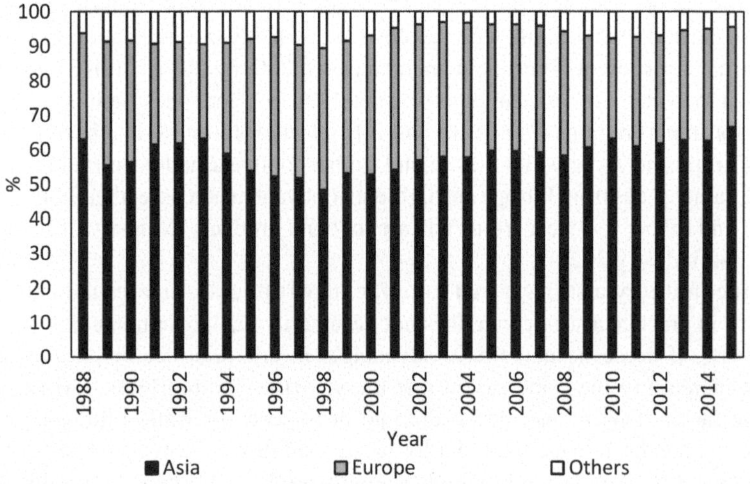

Fig. 2.15 Percentage of leather footwear by import region (value). *Source* Prepared by the author. The source is the same as the ones for import amount in Fig. 2.11

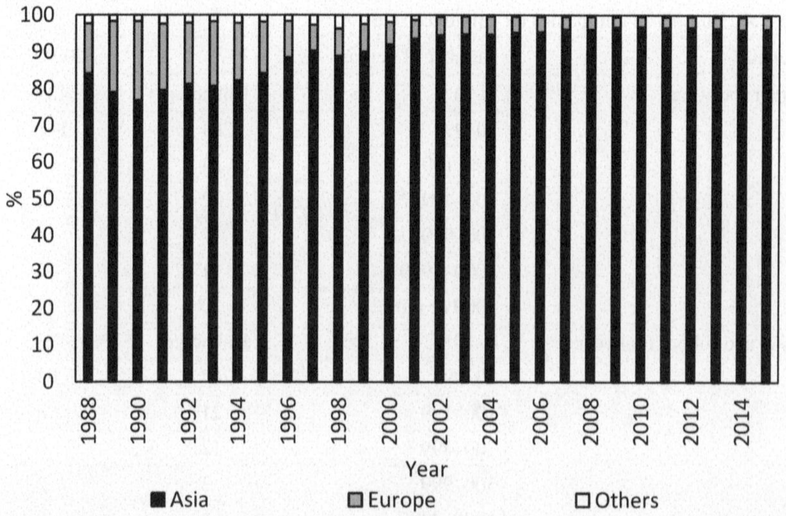

Fig. 2.16 Percentage of rubber and synthetic footwear by import region (value). *Source* Prepared by the author. The source is the same as the ones for import amount in Fig. 2.11

and prevent imports of high-priced products. The automotive manufactures, whose export pace was affected by the appreciation of the yen in the 1980s, turned their attention to the domestic market and redeveloped it by introducing high-value-added products (Itami 1998). The proportion of imports as a part of domestic demand in 2015 was 5%, based on value, for the automotive industry,[14] as the industry was not invaded by imports to the same degree as the footwear industry. In the case of footwear, however, domestic shoe manufactures had not developed strong product differentiation.

2.4.3 Small Manufacturers

Shoe manufacturers have been unable to establish strong product brands and dominate the industry to prevent the invasion of imported footwear because of their small size. Compared to the Japanese automotive industry, which dominates the domestic market and has established its brand worldwide, there have been far fewer large companies in the footwear industry. Simple comparisons cannot be made because the product characteristics are different. However, there have been almost no large companies in the footwear industry. As shown in Table 2.4, there were many small manufacturers that sustained the industry in both the footwear and automobiles industries as of 1975 and 2005. The major difference between the shoe and automotive

[14] Calculated based on statistical data from the Japan Automobile Manufacturers Association (Japan Automobile Manufacturers Association n.d.).

Table 2.4 Number of companies by employee size

Product	Number of persons	1975	2005
Leather footwear	4–10	Unknown	425
	20–99	204	141
	100–199	24	15
	200–499	12	2
	500–999	7	0
	1000–4999	1	0
	5000 or more	0	0
Plastic and rubber footwear	4–10	Unknown	476
	20–99	267	63
	100–199	21	8
	200–499	17	0
	500–999	3	2
	1000–4999	4	0
	5000 or more	1	0
Automobile	4–10	Unknown	4,856
	20–99	1,550	2,171
	100–999	271	446
	200–499	171	293
	500–999	69	101
	1000–4999	53	72
	5000 or more	17	23

Source Prepared by the author based on METI (n.d.a)
Note The number of companies with less than four employees is unknown

industries, however, is the number of large manufactures. In the footwear industry, there were only a few companies with more than 500 employees for leather footwear and plastic and rubber footwear. In contrast, there have been more than 100 companies with more than 500 employees in the automotive industry.

The fact that the footwear industry had fewer companies of any size in 2005 than in 1975 can be attributed to the expansion of imports. The number of domestic producers has decreased due to bankruptcies or the transfer of production bases overseas (Miyakawa 1994).

Because businesses were small, footwear manufactures did not have the capacity to make differentiated high-end shoes or research on foot health. The low level of awareness of foot health among Japanese people has been discussed in Sect. 2.1, and one of the reasons for this can be attributed to a lack of research due to the small size of shoe manufacturers.

Part II
Direct Effect of Activism: How an SMO Succeeded in Changing Corporate Behavior

Part II delves into the direct effect of activism, specifically examining the transformation in corporate behavior brought about by SMOs. It addresses the question: How can SMOs positioned on the periphery of an industry change corporate behavior? In this case study, which focuses on the postwar Japanese footwear industry, the research inquiry revolves around how JIF, a small voluntary organization operating on the industry's periphery, managed to induce changes in corporate behavior. The analysis of the JIF case reveals that SMOs can develop effective strategies *ex post facto* through learning by doing.

Chapter 3
Social Movement Targeting Companies

As of June 1, 2023, there were 3,595 shoe fitters working in the footwear industry (FHA 2023). Shoe fitters are experts in shoe fitting, a process involving taking measurements of the foot, selecting shoes that fit properly, and confirming the fit. JIF established its own Shoe Fitter (SF) Training Workshop and began appealing to shoe retailers about the need for shoe fitters to conduct fittings at their stores (Miura 2019a). JIF succeeded in persuading shoe retailers to adopt shoe fitters, and shoe fitters have subsequently become widespread throughout the footwear industry.

How did JIF succeed in convincing shoe retailers to adopt shoe fitters and popularize their use throughout the industry, despite lacking resources and knowledge regarding the industry, and being ignored by the industry, even when it claimed to improve the health functions of shoes (Katō 2002)?

This chapter reviews existing research on the strategies employed by SMOs that target companies and points out that existing research has not sufficiently addressed the issue: How can SMOs positioned on the periphery of an industry change corporate behavior? It then proposes a dynamic framework to analyze this issue by adopting an emergence strategy perspective based on strategic theory (Itami and Roehl 1991; Mintzberg 1978; Mintzberg and Waters 1985).

This chapter consists of restructured and revised version of Miura, S. (2019a). Shakai katsudōdantai no senryaku shūsei to shijō sōzō: kutsusangyō ni okeru shakaikatsudōdantai, kigyō, shōhisha, media no sōgosayō [Adjustments of social activist strategies and new market creation: The interplay of an activity group, companies and their primary stakeholders in the shoe industry]. *Organizational Science*, *52*(3), 20–32. https://doi.org/10.11207/soshikikagaku.52.3_20.

S. Miura, *Successful Social Activism and Unintended Market Emergence*,
https://doi.org/10.1007/978-981-99-9291-1_3

3.1 Existing Research

One of the main issues in research on social movements that target companies has been how SMOs change corporate behavior as secondary corporate stakeholders (Eesley and Lenox 2006; King 2008; King and Soule 2007). From the perspective of resource dependence theory (Pfeffer and Salancik 1978), companies do not depend on SMOs for resources necessary for operation or survival. Therefore, compared with primary stakeholders essential to the company's survival, such as shareholders, business partners, and customers, it is difficult for SMOs to make companies accept their demands (Stevens et al. 2005; Vasi and King 2012).

When considering this issue, it is helpful to classify SMOs' strategies into disruptive and persuasive strategies (Briscoe and Gupta 2016). Some SMOs targeting companies aim for deinstitutionalization by stopping current corporate behavior and industry practices, whereas others aim for (re)institutionalization, attempting to disseminate new corporate behavior and turn it into an industry practice (den Hond and de Bakker 2007). The differences between the ambitions of these groups are caused by their different ideologies (den Hond and de Bakker 2007). According to den Hond and de Bakker (2007), "The concept of ideology comprises an interconnected set of beliefs and attitudes relating to problematic aspects of social and political topics that are shared and used by members of a group and that inform and justify choice and behavior" (p. 903). The beliefs and attitudes of SMOs fall somewhere between two stances: companies are the problem, or companies are both a part of the problem and a part of the solution. SMOs that believe companies are the problem aim to stop their conventional behavior. They tend to employ disruptive strategies that damage them (Yaziji & Doh, 2013). Disruptive strategies are "focused on creating material or reputational costs for organizations" (Briscoe and Gupta 2016, p. 5). SMOs that believe cooperating with companies is essential to solving problems aim to convince companies to adopt new behaviors. They tend to employ persuasive strategies (Briscoe and Gupta 2016; den Hond and de Bakker 2007). Persuasive strategies are "geared toward convincing decision-makers about the merits of activist claims" (Briscoe and Gupta 2016, p. 5).

Extensive research has been conducted regarding disruptive strategies adopted with the aim of deinstitutionalization (Briscoe and Gupta 2016). Companies do not depend on SMOs for resources, but these groups do not depend on companies for resources either. Therefore, SMOs can employ disruptive tactics that cause damage or the possibility of damage to a company (Briscoe and Gupta 2016). Based on the theory of resource dependence, it is more effective for losses to a company to be caused by primary stakeholders than by SMOs (Frooman 1999). For example, a consumer boycott and the associated media attention may damage a company's sales and reputation; thus, the company is forced to comply with the demands of SMOs (King 2008, 2016; Schurman 2004). Therefore, SMOs need to mobilize primary stakeholders (King and Soule 2007), which they do by presenting the problem in a way that resonates with and arouses action from them. This presentation is referred to as framing, which is the act of creating an interpretive framework that gives meaning to a certain event and guides action, and then presenting it to other actors (Benford and Snow 2000).

In recent years, research on persuasion strategies has also been conducted. Extant research has identified the effectiveness of pressuring companies through primary stakeholders of a company, similar to disruptive strategies (Frooman 1999). New behaviors are often not understood or even noticed by companies because of their novelty (Aldrich and Fiol 1994). Therefore, to transform company behavior, SMOs need to frame the merits of the new behavior and convey it to the target companies (Sine and Lee 2009). They also use framing to mobilize primary stakeholders such as the media and consumers (Balsiger 2010; Dubuisson-Quellier 2013; Weber et al. 2008). They try to reveal consumers' latent demand for the goods and services of companies that have adopted these new behaviors. This change in demand encourages companies to adopt new behaviors. Media attention attracts the attention of consumers and other companies, inducing transformations in the behavior of target companies. Thus, SMOs accomplish a change in corporate behavior.

3.2 Perspectives Overlooked in Previous Studies

Previous studies on disruptive and persuasive strategies have clarified the effectiveness of tactics used to force change at companies through the mobilization of their primary stakeholders (Balsiger 2010; Dubuisson-Quellier 2013; King 2008; Schurman 2004; Weber et al. 2008). These studies presuppose that SMOs know the companies to target, the stakeholders to leverage, and the frames that will be effective for each. Based on these assumptions, studies have shown the effectiveness of stakeholder-mediated strategies. However, these assumptions conflict with others about SMOs.

Studies on social movements targeting companies have discussed how SMOs influence corporate behavior based on the premise of a lack of mutual resource dependence between the SMO and the company. If there is no interdependence, an SMO is likely to be positioned on the periphery of the industry and be unfamiliar with its circumstances. Therefore, it is difficult for SMOs to determine the companies to target, influential stakeholders to mobilize, and frames that will be effective for companies and their stakeholders. Without understanding these factors, SMOs cannot determine effective strategies. How can SMOs on the periphery of an industry change corporate behavior? This problem is more critical in the case of persuasive strategies for the following reasons.

First, it is difficult to define and convey the details of the new behavior that the SMO aims to make a company adopt in advance because the behavior is new. There is greater uncertainty when attempting to make a company start doing something than when attempting to make a company stop doing something. Second, SMOs may struggle to choose potential companies to adopt the new behavior if they are not familiar with the circumstances of the industry. The companies that are behaving in a way that SMOs aim to stop are apparent; however, the companies that SMOs want to adopt new behaviors are latent. Third, because of the multitude of options, it is difficult for SMOs to determine the appropriate frame for a company. It could be framed based on the economic benefits of the new action, the social benefits, or the costs of not changing the action.[1] A combination of these factors is also possible. The threat employed in a disruptive strategy that a company's sales and reputation will be damaged if the company continues its behavior is simpler. Fourth, SMOs with limited knowledge of the industry may struggle to identify influential stakeholders to change the behavior of the company. Fifth, it is difficult to determine the frame to mobilize promising stakeholders prior to actions. The fourth and fifth difficulties are also present in disruptive strategies. However, generally, it is more challenging to determine the strategies that will be effective when utilizing persuasive strategies.

These five factors are mutually dependent. If the target companies are not decided, for instance, the content of the new behavior and the frame may not be defined. The method of mobilizing important stakeholders may influence the selection of target companies, the details of demanded behavior, and the frame choice. The interdependence among the factors makes the determination of effective persuasive strategies more difficult.

Most previous studies have assumed that SMOs have no interdependence with the companies and have overlooked how that assumption also suggests that SMOs are not familiar with industry circumstances. Therefore, previous research has seldom discussed how SMOs establish an effective persuasive strategy.

3.3 Perspectives of This Research

How can SMOs on the periphery of an industry establish effective persuasive strategies to change the behavior of companies? This study suggests the dynamic strategic change model of SMOs (Fig. 3.1). Once SMOs take strategic action toward companies and their stakeholders, the companies and primary stakeholders either react or do not react, which educates the SMOs about the industry. Based on their learning, they modify their persuasive strategy. The dynamic perspective of strategy, where an organization learns from environmental feedback in response to its strategic action and then modifies the original, intended strategy, has been developed as an emergent strategy in strategic management theory (Itami and Roehl 1991; Mintzberg 1978;

[1] An example of framing the new behavior in terms of economic benefits is the US recycling industry, which prospered when the framing shifted from viewing recycling as a voluntary non-profit action to a for-profit action (Lounsbury et al., 2003). An example of framing the new behavior in terms of social benefits is the rise of wind power in the US; wind power was emphasized as an environmentally friendly energy production method (Sine & Lee, 2009). An example of framing the new behavior in terms of the costs of not adopting the behavior can also be seen in the case of wind power. It was highlighted that continuing to produce energy using oil, coal, and gas would destroy the environment (Sine & Lee, 2009).

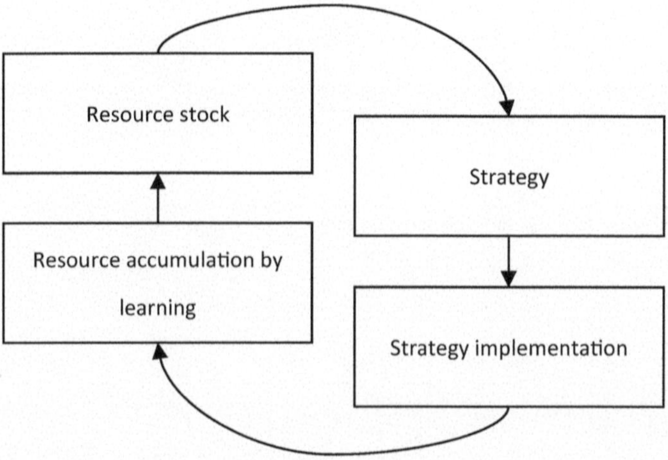

Fig. 3.1 Model of dynamic strategy change. *Source* Prepared by the author referring to Itami and Roehl (1991, p. 129)

Mintzberg and Waters 1985; Sakai 2018). The current study introduces this perspective in social movement studies discussing SMO strategy and answers the question: How do SMOs establish an appropriate persuasive strategy?

Strategies are formed based on the SMOs' resources (Freeman 1979), including physical resources such as funding and supplies, as well as information resources such as member knowledge, experience, and expectations. As SMOs are positioned at the fringes of existing industries, they lack detailed knowledge about the industry. The initial strategies built on that limited knowledge could be ineffective in changing corporate behavior. However, once SMOs implement strategies against the industry, they receive either reactions or no reactions from the industry. Through this experience, they learn about the industry, providing them with new resources, such as knowledge (Itami and Roehl 1991). Through this learning by doing, SMOs modify their persuasive strategy: whom to target, what behaviors to demand, and how to frame their problem. Thus, effective strategies emerge ex post (Mintzberg 1978; Mintzberg and Waters 1985).

Using the dynamic strategy change model, the next two chapters analyze JIF's case. JIF was a resource-poor organization located at the fringes of the industry, and it did not initially intend the strategy of having shoe fitters adopted by shoe retailers. How did JIF decipher the strategy and succeed in popularizing shoe fitters in the footwear industry? Chapter 4 analyzes JIF's original strategy and the process by which JIF's original strategy was modified to foster shoe fitters, and Chap. 5 examines how further revision and refinement of the strategy led to the proliferation of shoe fitters in shoe-related companies.

Chapter 4
JIF's Initial Strategy

The current and the following chapters analyze the process of modifying the strategies of JIF and successfully changing corporate behavior. JIF is a voluntary organization established to address the Japanese footwear market problem of emphasizing the fashion function of shoes and neglecting their health function. Despite being on the fringes of the footwear industry and resource-poor, JIF succeeded in persuading shoe retailers to adopt shoe fitters.

Nevertheless, JIF's initial strategy had nothing to do with shoe fitters (Miura 2018), as shown in Table 4.1. Its initial strategy was to develop standard shoe lasts, have shoe manufacturers adopt these standards, and ensure that manufacturers made shoes that would fit Japanese feet. The superordinate goal was to improve the health function of shoes and safeguard the foot health of the Japanese. As shoes should essentially fulfill health functions by supporting walking, the problem was framed as one where shoe manufacturers should make shoes that fit Japanese feet as a matter of course. However, JIF later modified its strategy. The emerging strategy entailed persuading shoe retailers to have shoe fitters at their stores to help customers in choosing well-fitting shoes. JIF highlighted the significant economic benefits of having shoe fitters in a shoe store because of the high customer demand for well-fitting shoes.

Behind the strategy change was JIF's learning process. This chapter describes how JIF modified its strategy from the initial standard shoe last dissemination strategy to a shoe fitter dissemination strategy. The next chapter further examines the process by which JIF modified its shoe fitter dissemination strategy and made it successful.

This chapter consists of restructured and revised version of Miura, S. (2018, August 3–4). *Partnering strategy between NPOs and business organizations: The case of the shoe industry in Japan* [Paper presentation]. Challenges of Sustainable Development and Social Impacts on Cooperatives and Social Enterprises, Bangkok, Thailand; and Miura, S. (2019b). Shikakunintei jigyō no setsuritsu process: Shoe fitter shikaku o jirei to shite [Establishing private qualification programs: How the shoe fitter qualification program was established]. *Shujitsu Management Studies*, (4), 33–68. https://shujitsu.repo.nii.ac.jp/records/453.

S. Miura, *Successful Social Activism and Unintended Market Emergence*,
https://doi.org/10.1007/978-981-99-9291-1_4

Table 4.1 JIF's initial and modified strategies

Aspect	Initial strategy in the 1960s and 1970s	Modified strategy in the 1980s
Superordinate goal	Improving the health function of shoes and safeguarding the foot health of the Japanese people	Improving the health function of shoes and safeguarding the foot health of the Japanese people
Target company	Shoe manufacturers	Shoe retailers
Requirement for target companies	Shoe manufacturers making shoes that fit the Japanese foot using standard shoe lasts	Shoe retailers completing shoe fitter accreditation and selecting shoes that fit the customer well
Frame	Shoe manufacturers have a responsibility to make shoes that fit Japanese feet and thereby support foot health. Nevertheless, they pursue only the fashion aspects of shoes	Customer demand for proper shoe selection by a shoe fitter is significant, and having a shoe fitter is an advantage for the store

4.1 Establishment of IWF (JIF) and Its Initial Strategy

Kazuo Katō, an editor of one of the trade magazines in the footwear industry, established the Japan Institute of Women's Footwear (IWF, later JIF) in 1965 (Katō 2002) to address the prevailing situation in the Japanese footwear industry. At the time, shoe manufacturers, distributors, and consumers only paid attention to how fashionable the shoes were, often neglecting the health function of footwear, as discussed in Chap. 2. Katō's concerns were expressed in an essay he wrote two years after IWF was founded (Katō 1967). In this essay, he highlighted that the primary function of footwear should be to support walking by proper fitting. He observed that research on the topic was lacking in Japan (Katō 1967). Thus, his goal was to develop standard shoe lasts that could contribute to the Japanese people's foot health.

> It should be evident that the first condition of all articles of clothing is that they fit the human body. Still, it is not easy to meet this first condition with shoes, which have the roles of covering, protecting, assisting, and supporting the feet that support the weight of the body. However, considering the current situation in Japan, research on functional aspects is almost nonexistent, and we must use the expression "just before dawn." ... [Our group will start], in line with the following basic action plan, to accumulate measurements and experiments, find standard values [of foot shape], and draft reasonable standard table. A suggested future action plan includes (1) properly transferring foot shape measured values to shoe lasts, (2) making shoes easy to work with, and (3) classifying foot shape and shoe lasts (Katō 1967, p. 148).[1]

Although this essay was authored by Katō, it closely aligned with the strategy of IWF, an organization he founded.[2] The primary strategic target was shoe manufacturers, and IWF demanded that these manufacturers make shoes tailored to fit

[1] Translated from Japanese by the author. The square brackets were added by the author.

[2] Toshimi Fukui, board member of IWF and JIF at the time, stated, "Katō was the lead actor and went around trying to convince people like heads of an industry group or some other enthusiast [to join us]." (President of Fukui Shoelast Mfg. Co. Ltd., interview, April 28, 2016, translated from Japanese by the author).

Japanese feet using the standard shoe lasts that would be developed by IWF. The framing emphasized that shoes should contribute to health, and shoe manufacturers should make such shoes as a matter of course. Nevertheless, it was a problem that, despite this, shoe manufacturers were not focusing on the production of well-fitting shoes.

In 1969, IWF was reorganized into JIF to incorporate a broader range of shoe-related companies beyond women's shoes (Katō 2002). JIF inherited the strategy mentioned above at the time of this reorganization. The name "JIF" is therefore used throughout the book to avoid confusion, unless it becomes necessary to differentiate between IWF and JIF.

4.2 JIF's Initial Activities

While JIF (IWF) aimed to improve the health function of shoes and protect Japanese people's foot health, their specific action policy, which involved the development of standard shoe lasts, did not immediately move to the implementation stage. It was not until 1970, five years after its establishment, that the organization began measuring foot shape, an activity directly related to the development of standard shoe lasts.

IWF's initial activities during its first five years comprised self-publishing books and conducting seminars related to foot health and the health function of shoes. The first book was about the foot (Japan Institute of Women's Footwear 1967), the second was about shoes (Japan Institute of Women's Footwear 1968), and the third combined the contents of the first two books, which were reorganized (Japan Institute of Women's Footwear 1969). The contents of the third book included shoe material, customer handling, shoe maintenance, shoe types and designs, and a glossary. Its contents were ideal for newcomers entering shoe-related companies, providing them with foundational knowledge by documenting tacit industry knowledge.[3] Subsequently, its revised editions, *Yoi Kutsu no Kiso Chishiki* [Basic Knowledge of Good Shoes], were published repeatedly, as shown in Table 4.2 (Japan Institute of Women's Footwear 1969; Katō & Yamamoto 1976, 1980, 1983, 1987). These books significantly benefitted JIF's funding.[4] In addition, lectures on shoe ergonomics and shoe pattern-making workshops were organized (Table 4.3). Although these books and lectures were not directly related to the development of standard shoe lasts, they indirectly contributed to the improvement of the health function of shoes. According to the available records, IWF also conducted seminars on fashion (Table 4.4), although Katō—the founder and the executive director of JIF—criticized the footwear industry's exclusive focus on the fashion function of

[3] Jun'ichi Morino, Planning & Purchasing Dept., Ginza Yoshinoya Co. Ltd. and board member of FHA (interview, August 8, 2014).

[4] A total of 11,000 copies have been sold, from the first revised edition in 1976 to the 11th edition in 1995. It was unprecedented in the industry for a ¥2,000 (US$21) book to sell so many copies (Hiromu Yamamoto, interview by phone, December 8, 2015). The price is calculated based on the dollar-yen rate in 1995.

shoes.[5] The publication of books and organization of seminars continued even after the commencement of the foot shape measurement project in the 1970s which will be discussed in the next section; thus, Tables 4.2, 4.3 and 4.4 list them up to the 1980s.

4.3 Foot Shape Measurement Project

When IWF was reorganized into JIF in 1969 to incorporate shoe-related companies beyond women's shoes, JIF finally took the first step toward developing shoe lasts through a foot shape measurement project. On the occasion of the reorganization, the members discussed what they should do to improve the health function of shoes. In those discussions, the following points were listed as issues related to shoe sizing in the industry:

1. Shoe size labeling is inaccurate and inconsistent; thus, it is unfriendly to consumers.
2. Japanese people's physique has changed due to the Westernization of their lifestyles, causing contradictions in the existing JIS standard for shoe sizes (established in 1965).
3. Shoe last standardization has not progressed; therefore, production is poor.
4. Foot shape measurement methods up to now have been extremely varied and unestablished, and no large-scale survey has been conducted in the first place. (JIF 1970, pp. 1–4)[6]

Based on this understanding of the issues, JIF established the Size Committee in January 1970, who decided to conduct Japanese foot shape measurements to address the above issues (JIF 1970). One year and three months after the launch of the Size Committee, it completed the "First Stage Foot Shape Measurement Guidelines," which contained (1) objects of measurement, (2) measuring instruments, (3) measurement items and points, (4) how to measure, and (5) how to fill in record forms (JIF 1971; Takesawa 2005). JIF implemented a nationwide foot measurement survey during the period 1972–1973 with the help of 14 member companies (JIF 1975). The Size Committee aggregated and analyzed the results and compiled a report in 1975 (JIF 1975).

Measuring the foot shape of 2,000 people nationwide from 1972 to 1973 was groundbreaking, and JIF's standing in the industry improved after having implemented this project. While foot shape measurements had been conducted before, they had measured at most several hundred people (e.g., Kondō et al. 1950; Takeichi 1969; Uchimura 1972). From 1977 to 1979, Zennihon Hakimono Dantai Kyōgikai, the footwear industry trade association, was contracted by the Ministry of International Trade and Industry to conduct foot shape measurements for 10,000 people. This project aimed to create a JIS standard sizing system for shoes. JIF's original

[5] The fashion seminar was held with the aim of generating income by charging participation fees. Further details are discussed in Sect. 4.5, explaining JIF's initial resources.

[6] Translated from Japanese by the author.

Table 4.2 IWF and JIF's book published from the 1960s to the 1980s

No	Title	Year	Editor/ author	Publisher	Remark
1	Shoe report sensho no.1 [Shoe report selection no.1]	1967	IWF	IWF	Preface states Katō as the editor, Nakao as the supervisor, and Kagami as the person who provided materials
2	Shoe report sensho no.2 [Shoe report selection no.2]	1968	IWF	IWF	Preface states that the book was written by Kagami and edited by Katō
3	Shoe report sensho no.3 [Shoe report selection no.3]	1969	IWF	IWF	Afterword states that the book was edited by Yamamoto
4	Katagami technique [Technique of shoe pattern cutting]*	1971	Kido	JIF	
5	Shoe report tokushū [Shoe report selection]	1972	JIF	JIF	Recording of a seminar by Y. Nakao
6	Kutsu yōgo 6 kakoku taiyakushū [Footwear industry technical vocabulary]	1975	OECD	JIF	Translated by Katō and Yamamoto
7	Yoi kutsu no kiso chishiki (Revised ed.) [Basic knowledge of good shoes (Revised ed.)]	1976	Katō and Yamamoto (Eds.)	JIF	
8	Yoi kutsu no kiso chishiki (Revised 2nd ed.) [Basic knowledge of good shoes (Revised 2nd ed.)] *	1978	Katō and Yamamoto (Eds.)	JIF	
9	Shin-katagami technique [Technique of shoe pattern cutting, updated]	1979	Kido, T	JIF	
10	Yoi kutsu no kiso chishiki (Revised 3rd ed.) [Basic knowledge of good shoes (Revised 3rd ed.)]	1980	Katō and Yamamoto (Eds.)	JIF	
11	Yoi kutsu no kiso chishiki (Revised 4th ed.) [Basic knowledge of good shoes (Revised 4th ed.)]*	1981	Katō and Yamamoto (Eds.)	JIF	

(continued)

Table 4.2 (continued)

No	Title	Year	Editor/ author	Publisher	Remark
12	Kantō chiku kutsu kanren kigyō sōran [Kantō region footwear companies directory]*	1981	Unknown	JIF	
13	Sasō Keigo no kutsu sekkyaku know-how [Shoe salesperson's know-how by Keigo Sasō]	1982	Sasō, K	JIF	
14	Yoi kutsu no kiso chishiki (Revised 5th ed.) [Basic knowledge of good shoes (Revised 5th ed.)]	1983	Katō and Yamamoto (Eds.)	JIF	
15	84-nen ban kutsu sangyōo sōran*	1983	Unknown	JIF	
16	Itai kutsu wa mō hakanai [Say goodbye to wearing painful shoes]	1984h	JIF (Ed.)	Kodansha	
17	Yoi kutsu no kiso chishiki (Revised 6th ed.) [Basic knowledge of good shoes (Revised 6th ed.)]*	1985	Katō and Yamamoto (Eds.)	JIF	
18	Shoe fitter ga kaita kutsu no hon [Shoe book by a shoe fitter]	1986	Katō and Yamamoto	Sansuisha	
19	Yoi kutsu no kiso chishiki (Revised 7th ed.) [Basic knowledge of good shoes (Revised 7th ed.)]	1987	Katō and Yamamoto (Eds.)	JIF	
20	Kenkō ni ii kutsu erabi [Picking healthy shoes]	1988	JIF (Ed.)	Chikuma Shuhansha	Also stated as written by Katō and Yamamoto
21	Yoi kutsu no kiso chishiki (Revised 8th ed.) [Basic knowledge of good shoes (Revised 8th ed.)]*	1989	Katō and Yamamoto (Eds.)	JIF	

Source Miura (2019b, Table 4.5, p. 44), translated from Japanese and modified by the author
Note Asterisks indicate books whose existence is indicated in other documents but whose actual existence has not been confirmed; therefore, the books are not included in the reference list

Table 4.3 IWF and JIF's seminar on the health function of shoes

Organization	Seminar title	Date
IWF	Shoe ergonomics seminar	
	First	Unknown
	Second	1969, July 23–26
JIF	Shoe pattern-making workshop	
	12th	1979, August 27–29
	13th	1980, July 9–11
	15th	1981, August
	No. unknown	1984, November

Source Miura (2019b, Tables 4.4 and 4.3, p. 42), translated from Japanese and modified by the author
Note For the first–11th Shoe Pattern-Making Workshops, the dates are unknown

Table 4.4 IWF and JIF's seminar on the fashion function of shoes

Organization	Seminar title	Date
IWF	IWF seminar	1968, date unknown
JIF	Fashion forecasting seminar (men's and women's)	
	1980 SS	1979, October 30
	1980 AW	1980, February 20, April 21
	First 1981 SS	1980, July 17–18
	Second 1981 AW	Date unknown
	Third 1982 SS	1981, July
	Fourth 1982 AW	1981, November 30–December 1
	Fifth 1983 SS	Date unknown
	Sixth 1983 AW	1983, February 24
	Seventh 1984 SS	1983, July
	Eighth 1984 AW	1983, December 3
	Ninth 1985 SS	Date unknown
	10th 1985 AW	1985, January 28–29
	11th 1986 SS	Date unknown
	12th 1986 AW	1985, December 12–13

Source Miura (2019b, Table. 4.2, p. 41), translated from Japanese and modified by the author
Note SS indicates spring and summer and AW indicates autumn and winter

large-scale measurement results were recognized, and its guidelines were provided for the project (Katō 2003). Furthermore, JIF's president, Keigo Sasō, became a member of the project's steering committee (Zennihon Hakimono Dantai Kyōgikai 1978).[7] As such, the organization's standing in the industry had advanced greatly.

However, it was difficult to argue that JIF's Foot Shape Measurement Project was successful considering its initial goals. The foot shape data of 2,000 people did not lead to shoe lasts. As it was a pioneering initiative, they were prepared to sell the results; however, without any inquiries, there were no sales.[8] As foot shape values do not immediately lead to shoe lasts,[9] Fukui, a board member of JIF at the time, viewed that shoe-related companies did not know what to do with the numerical values they were given.[10] That is, JIF was unable to analyze, process, and provide their data in a way that companies could use when making shoe lasts. JIF itself embarked on the development of standard shoe lasts, but this initiative also ran into difficulties, as presented in the next section.

4.4 Standard Shoe Lasts Project

The Standard Shoe Lasts Committee was established in March 1981 after the dissolution of the Size Committee. Its purpose was to create shoe lasts that had the best fittings for Japanese people (JIF 1981a, n.d.c.). They began to develop shoe lasts based on the measurement data they had gathered. However, the development of a standard shoe last was not successful. Two years later, in October 1983, men's shoe lasts were listed in the JIF bulletin for approximately ¥50,000 (US$211) for members only (JIF 1983d),[11] but their presentation was postponed multiple times, and as of November 26, 1985, the shoe lasts had still not been officially announced (JIF 1983b, e, 1984b, f, 1985a, f). As documentation is limited, it is unclear whether a last was ever launched for either men's or women's shoes.[12] However, in JIF materials from the following years, the project was not mentioned.[13] Therefore, even if the lasts

[7] Zennihon Hakimono Dantai Kyōgikai (the footwear industry trade association), is a group that was formed in 1977 with the participation of 11 footwear-related industry groups. Its primary purpose was to standardize shoe last dimensions (Gomuhouchi Shinbunsha 1979; Ōtsuka 1991).

[8] Toshimi Fukui, President of Fukui Shoelast Mfg. Co. Ltd. (interview, April 28, 2016).

[9] Data from several foot points does not immediately lead to shoe lasts. "Shoe lasts need to have the volume to ensure sufficient space for the foot, and a shape that retains that of the foot without damaging its walking motion" (Nakajima 2011b, p. 6, translated from Japanese by the author). Therefore, feet and shoe lasts do not have the same dimensions (Ōtsuka 1991).

[10] Toshimi Fukui, president of Fukui Shoelast Mfg. Co. Ltd. (interview, April 28, 2016).

[11] The price is calculated based on the dollar-yen rate in 1983.

[12] Fukui, who is listed as the lead director of the Standard Shoe Lasts Committee (JIF 1983d), stated that his memories of this project are vague (Toshimi Fukui, President of Fukui Shoelast Mfg. Co. Ltd., interview, April 28, 2016).

[13] For example, the project was not mentioned in the FHA 50th Anniversary Celebration speeches and materials distributed (February 10, 2016), and the book published to commemorate the 50th anniversary did not mention it at all (FHA 2015).

were announced, they may not have received much of a response or been widely used.

The Standard Lasts Committee's activities stalled and the number of meetings gradually decreased. The committee met seven times in 1981, eight times over 1982–1983, and three times between 1984 to March 1985; thereafter, the frequency of their meetings is unclear (JIF 1981b, 1983d, 1985a, f). There are several possible reasons for this. First, an inherent problem of shoe lasts is that standard sizes cannot fit every individual foot. Shōichi Katō, who was involved in JIF activities as a member of the Fitting Workshop at the time (which will be discussed in Sect. 4.7), said, "Normal shoes and standard shoes are no different from ordinary shoes in terms of whether they fit [individual feet]. This is why it [developing standard shoe lasts] was at a standstill."[14] Fukui was a member of the Standard Shoe Lasts Committee, but his memories of their activities are vague. In an interview, he stated that he believed that they tried to make one, but it did not get any further than that.[15] Second, it is possible that there was little investment in resources for the activities of the Standard Shoe Lasts Project, causing its decline. Members' motivation may have waned when results from the difficult task were not forthcoming, or more resources may have been allocated to the Fitting Workshop that was launched at the same time. Ultimately, the committee's activities stagnated. Therefore, JIF came to believe that "trying on shoes [that is, fitting] in stores is important."[16]

4.5 JIF's Initial Resources Behind Its Activities

From its founding in 1965 through the Foot Shape Measurement Project of 1972–1973 to the Standard Shoe Lasts Project that began in 1981, JIF remained on the periphery of the industry. JIF had little dependence on the companies in the footwear industry, and these companies were also not dependent on JIF for resources. Nevertheless, several people and companies interested in the health function of shoes and foot health supported JIF's activities. With their support, JIF managed to self-publish books and conduct seminars about improving the health function of shoes and realized the Foot Shape Measurement Project, although it took some time to materialize, and attempted to develop a standard shoe last.

[14] Shōichi Katō, Bon Pied (interview, February 10, 2014). Translated from Japanese by the author. The square brackets were added by the author.

[15] Toshimi Fukui, President of Fukui Shoelast Mfg. Co. Ltd. (interview, April 28, 2016).

[16] Shōichi Katō, Bon Pied (interview, February 10, 2014). Translated from Japanese by the author. The square brackets were added by the author.

4.5.1 Peripherality

In the footwear industry, where both the demand and supply sides value the fashion function, JIF's emphasis on the importance of the health function of shoes was out of step with the industry's taken-for-grantedness (Suchman 1995). JIF was on the periphery of the industry. This is evident in the fact that it did not have many members, and many of the members were not interested in improving the health function of their shoes. Katō gathered approximately 100 companies from the footwear industry as members when IWF was founded (Katō 2002), but membership dwindled over the years. Around 1980, ten years after the reorganization, membership had fallen to 50 companies.[17] At the founding of IWF, Katō explained the importance of shoe health function to major women's leather shoe wholesale companies and persuaded them to join him. Their entry led many smaller subcontractors of the wholesale companies to join JIF, as the subcontractors wanted to maintain a good relationship with the wholesalers.[18] However, as the subcontractors were not exactly interested in the health functions of shoes, they gradually withdrew from the organization.

The fact that JIF was financially unable to rely on companies in the footwear industry also illustrates the peripheral nature of JIF. Although membership fee income was a source of funding for JIF, JIF was always in the red because the number of members was small to begin with and kept dwindling. Toshimi Fukui, a board member at the time, acknowledged that IWF and JIF tended not to have sufficient funding, so JIF (IWF) borrowed money from some board members.[19] At that time, the membership fee for JIF was ¥72,000 (US$289) per year (JIF 1982a), and the fees from the 50 member companies generated ¥3.6 million (US$14,454).[20] However, this amount did not cover the office rent in Tokyo and the salaries of two full-time members, Katō and Hiromu Yamamoto. Yamamoto was a junior journalist at the footwear industry trade magazine company where Katō worked and once joked that "I was dragged by Katō [into IWF] and had a hard time."[21] Consequently, JIF had to earn funds through various activities other than membership fees. To earn funds, JIF published various books and held several seminars related to foot health and the health function of shoes (Tables 4.2 and 4.3). It also held fashion seminars (Table 4.4), which were contrary to JIF's superordinate goal to improve the health function of shoes. Hence, the insufficient funding from footwear industry companies indicated that JIF occupied a peripheral position within the industry.

---

[17] JIF had 49 member companies in 1979 (JIF 1979), it had 40 in 1982 (JIF 1982c), and it had 43 in 1983 (JIF 1983h).

[18] Toshimi Fukui, President of Fukui Shoelast Mfg. Co. Ltd. (interview, April 28, 2016). Major women's leather footwear wholesale companies were leading companies and controlled small contractors in the women's leather footwear market (Seki 1975).

[19] Toshimi Fukui, President of Fukui Shoelast Mfg. Co. Ltd. (interview, April 28, 2016).

[20] The prices are calculated based on the dollar-yen rate in 1982.

[21] Hiromu Yamamoto (interview by phone, December 8, 2015). Translated from Japanese by the author. The square brackets were added by the author. Tokiko Hasegawa, who joined the office in the 1980s, said she had heard that Katō and Yamamoto had not always received their salaries every month in the 1960s and 1970s (interview, February 10, 2016).

4.5.2 Support from Enthusiastic Members

The organization lacked funds and supporters but had several members who agreed with Katō's ambition and supported JIF's activities.[22] With their support, JIF managed to conduct activities related to the health function of shoes.

Self-publishing and seminars were the main activities initially (Tables 4.2, 4.3 and 4.4) because Katō and Yamamoto were skilled in such activities as they were journalists.[23] One of the books that Katō and Yamamoto edited and which sold well was *Yoi Kutsu no Kiso Chishiki* [Basic Knowledge of Good Shoes]. The book was a formalized compilation of knowledge necessary for shoe sales (Japan Institute of Women's Footwear 1969). One of the contributors to the book's content was Fusao Kagami, a shoemaking expert who systematized and formalized shoemaking. He provided shoe-related information for JIF's first self-published book, *Shoe Report Sensho No.1: Kutsu no Tame no Ashi* [Shoe report selection no.1: Foot for shoes] (Japan Institute of Women's Footwear 1967) and collaborated extensively on the second book, *Shoe Report Sensho no.2: Yoikutsu no Jōken Nyūmonhen* [Shoe Report Selection No.2: Requirements for Good Shoes] (Japan Institute of Women's Footwear 1968). Based on these books, Katō and Yamamoto compiled the third book, *Yoi Kutsu no Kiso Chishiki* (Japan Institute of Women's Footwear 1969), which sold quite well. Kagami noted his resonance with Katō in the foreword to *Shoe Report Sensho no.2: Yoikutsu no Jōken Nyūmonhen.*

> Shoes have an extremely organic function, and their manufacture requires a broad range of knowledge, techniques, and skills spanning the three phases from feet to shoe lasts to shoes. Therefore, it had been difficult to document this in writing. Here, in compiling the "*Yoikutsu no Jōken Nyūmonhen*," it was a great pleasure for the author to have a good editor [Katō] (Japan Institute of Women's Footwear 1968, p. 3).[24]

Another contributer to *Yoi Kutsu no Kiso Chishiki* (Japan Institute of Women's Footwear 1969) was Yoshiyasu Nakao. He was a foot expert and provided knowledge about the structure and workings of the feet in *Shoe Report Sensho no.1* (Japan Institute of Women's Footwear 1967). He graduated from the Graduate School of Medicine at the University of Tokyo and was an expert in somatometry for product designers based on ergonomic considerations rather than medical or anthropological perspectives (Nakao 1965; Nishimura 1992). Nakao became involved in IWF due to his interest in shoes and a suggestion from a mutual acquaintance of Katō.[25] Beyond

---

[22] Fukui stated, "Under Katō-san, likeminded hardworking companions gathered" (Toshimi Fukui, President of Fukui Shoelast Mfg. Co. Ltd., speech at the FHA 50th Anniversary Celebration, February 10, 2016, translated from Japanese by the author).

[23] Hiromu Yamamoto (interview by phone, December 8, 2015).

[24] Translated from Japanese by the author. The square brackets were added by the author.

[25] He supported Chie Koike, a teacher at Bunka Fashion College, who aimed to make Japan's first dressmaking mannequin (Koike and Nakao 1966; Nishimura 1992). Koike was acquainted with Katō as a footwear industry journalist, and she introduced him to Nakao since Katō wanted to learn about feet (Katō 2003). Nakao began to collaborate with JIF's activities after receiving the nudge from Koike as well as his interest in shoes (Katō 2003).

book editing with Katō and Yamamoto, he also took on the role of a lecturer at "Shoe Ergonomics Seminars" in the second half of the 1960s (Table 4.3). Furthermore, he played a significant role in establishing the measurement method for the Foot Shape Measurement Project from 1972 to 1973. The established method was evaluated and used in national-level foot shape measurements from 1977 to 1979 (Katō 2003).

Other books related to the health function of shoes include *Katagami Technique* [Technique of shoe pattern-making] and *Shin Katagami Technique* [Technique of Shoe Pattern-Making, Updated], authored by Tsuneo Kido, a shoe designer and founder of K Studio (Kido 1979).[26] Kido wanted to "break away from the conventional pattern paper-making method [of shoes] centered on intuition and aimed for scientific and rational pursuit" (Kido 1979, p. 3)[27] and sympathized with Katō, whose stated goal was to research how to improve the health function of shoes. Kido also took on the role of a lecturer at the "Shoe Pattern-Making Workshop" in the 1970s (Table 4.3).

Keigo Sasō, the managing director of the long-established shoe retailer Heiwado Kutsuten in Tokyo and JIF president, wrote *Sasō Kego no Kutsu Sekkyaku Know-How* [Shoe Salesperson's Know-How by Keigo Sasō] (1982). He was also sympathetic to Katō's thoughts on the health function of shoes, and as a member who supported IWF since its establishment, he wrote the book for shoe retailers to "provide good shoes to consumers through sensitive and meticulous sales techniques" (Sasō 1982, p. 154).[28]

4.6 By-Product of the Foot Shape Measurement Project and JIF's Strategy Change

Along with foot shape data from 2,000 people, the Foot Shape Measurement Project created unexpected by-products. The committee found that most Japanese people's feet were damaged. In addition to tinea pedis, calluses, blisters, foot corns, and shoe sores, which were common at the time, problems such as hallux valgus (bunions), hammertoes, splay foot, and ingrown toenails were found in 95% of women and 65% of men. JIF believed that the trouble was due to poorly fitted shoes. According to JIF, "This was an unforeseen large percentage … It sent a chill down the spine" (Katō 2002, p. 124).[29] JIF members were aware that ill-fitting shoes were harmful for feet before the Foot Shape Measurement Project (e.g., Japan Institute of Women's Footwear 1967; Katō 1977), but the high percentages were shocking.

[26] The book is about the methods of designing shoe patterns. Just as cloth is cut to match patterns when making clothes, shoe materials are cut to match patterns when making shoes. As shoes are three-dimensional and composed of curved surfaces, it requires skill to develop them into flat paper patterns.

[27] Translated from Japanese by the author. The square brackets were added by the author.

[28] Translated from Japanese by the author.

[29] Translated from Japanese by the author.

While discussing how to address this surprising discovery, JIF learned of the "shoe fitter" job that was available in some Western countries. This individual assists in selecting shoes based on their expertise in feet and shoes. JIF decided to introduce shoe fitters in Japan.

JIF's changing viewpoint was behind this new policy. They had found that trying to improve shoes themselves by developing standard shoe lasts was not successful and thought it would be better to have wholesalers, retailers, and consumers understand what good shoes are: that is, educate and enlighten them. Fukui, a board member of JIF at the time, described this as follows.

> We did a lot of activities. However, the first goal we envisioned to make shoes better appeared increasingly distant and started to come apart—it just got too broad. We ended up doing too many things, and I remember thinking "Okay, then what do we do?"
>
> The strongest ones in the shoe industry, or the ones with the most influence, are retailers. Retailers and wholesalers have a strong voice. As they buy things from different manufacturers, they are powerful, relative to manufacturers, is what I mean. After thinking about all kinds of things, we thought it might be a better idea to approach from that end, to inform and educate them about how good shoes are. Rather than talking upstream about improving materials, shape, color, and so on, we thought things would move more quickly if we educated or opened their eyes to these things.
>
> Therefore, we came upon the issue of shoe fitters. This entailed approaching the problem from the opposite direction. The opinion was voiced that we should start downstream instead of upstream, and so I think that's how it took on that form. ... There's a saying that good shoes don't always sell. When we were told that the shoes that sell are good shoes, we were speechless. We were making all kinds of efforts to do research, and then they come at us with, "No, that's not how it is." So, then it occurred to us to go at it from the opposite direction. I think we had the idea that things would progress faster if consumers understood what shoe fitters are, and if shoe fitters did a few different things, then consumers would end up wanting to wear good shoes.[30]

JIF decided to initiate the Fitting Workshop to establish a training program for shoe fitters. The program became a central project for JIF beginning in the mid-1980s.

4.7 Fitting Workshop Project

To establish the shoe fitter training program, JIF started the Fitting Workshop in August 1979 (JIF, n.d.c; Katō 2002, 2003; Miura 2014),[31] with approximately 20 participants from member companies as shown in Table 4.5. Activities were broadly divided into the so-called "Nakao Seminar" for learning about the function and structure of the foot, with Nakao as the lecturer, and self-guided workshop sessions where members would deepen their understanding of shoes and fittings (Katō 2002). Once again, it was Nakao who assumed responsibility for conducting the lectures on

[30] Toshimi Fukui, President of Fukui Shoelast Mfg. Co. Ltd. (interview, April 28, 2016). Translated from Japanese by the author.

[31] Yōichi Funakawa's notebooks made between 1985 and 1986 (personal communication, May 19, 2014).

the foot. Shoe fitting requires knowledge in several areas: shoes, feet, and appropriate fit. JIF members had knowledge about shoes and some degree of knowledge about fitting as shoe-related companies, but they did not possess expertise in feet (Takesawa 2005).[32] Therefore, JIF continued to seek Nakao's guidance. Between 1979 and 1984, before the shoe fitter training program became available for the public in 1983, participants learned about feet, shoes, and fitting. One or two Nakao Seminars were held per year, conducted over one to three days to study foot anatomy and biology, with lectures running about eight hours per day (Takesawa 2005). Between these seminars, the participants engaged in the self-study of shoe fitting by making shoes, checking their fit, and engaging in discussions (Miura 2019b).

At first, Nakao declined Katō's requests to support the Fitting Workshop because of his busy schedule. However, Katō persisted because he believed that "without training shoe fitters, there is no hope of improving Japan's shoe culture" (Katō 2003, p. 135).[33] Nakao had two conditions before accepting the teaching role. The first was, "Learning is generally something that you understand less the more you do it. Shoes are on a wildly different level of difficulty than you are probably thinking, so do not turn back halfway through" (Katō 1990, p. 1).[34] The second condition was, "The study of shoes and educational institutions for shoes does not yet exist in Japan. When JIF begins an educational enterprise in some form in the future, I want participating members to act as instructors to guide the next generation" (Katō 1990, p. 1).[35] This statement indicates that he wanted the expertise he provided not to be monopolized by the companies participating in the course but to be of use to the entire footwear industry.

The members who gathered for the Fitting Workshop came from JIF member companies, but they did not necessarily aim to establish a shoe fitter training program. Instead, they aimed to acquire systematic expertise in function and structure of feet and legs from Nakao, which did not exist in the footwear industry at that time. Some companies urgently needed knowledge about feet because it was crucial for their business, while others wanted to acquire this knowledge, even if they did not necessarily need it right away. However, their shared objective was to learn about feet and legs. For example, Takeo Kikuchi, President of Dinus Shoe Corporation, a medium-sized women's shoe manufacturer, was working on making shoes that fit the feet of women, including those of his daughter, who had hallux valgus (bunions). He recognized the limitations of self-study and felt the need to learn about feet systematically. Kikuchi stated:

> I knew that I had to study the basics of foot function and structure, but in any case, I wanted solid academic backing and felt keenly that I wanted to create wooden models based on that backing. If I could create shoes that satisfied the needs of women whose shoes made

---

32 Jun'ichi Morino, Planning & Purchasing Dept., Ginza Yoshinoya Co. Ltd., and board member of FHA (interview, August 8, 2014); Shigemoto Satō, Sales Promotion Division, Asics Japan Corp and Vice President of FHA (interview, September 14, 2014).

33 Translated from Japanese by the author.

34 Translated from Japanese by the author.

35 Translated from Japanese by the author.

Table 4.5 Fitting Workshop members

No	Company name[a]	Type of business	Member name			Notes
			As of July 10, 1980	As of March 3, 1982	As of 1991	
1	Asics	Sports shoe manufacturer	Kiyosawa, Jun'ichi	Satō, Shigemoto	Satō, Shigemoto	
2	Dinus Shoe Corporation	Women's and men's shoe wholesaler and manufacturer	Kikuchi, Takeo	Kikuchi, Takeo	Kikuchi, Takeo	President
3	Ginza Yoshinoya Shōji	Women's shoe wholesaler	Morino, Jun'ichi	Morino, Jun'ichi	Morino, Jun'ichi	
4	Ginza Yoshinoya Shōji	Women's shoe wholesaler	Yashiro, Hiroo	Yashiro, Hiroo	Yashiro, Hiroo	
5	Hotei Gomu	Rubber shoe manufacturer	Fujiwara, Hiroshi	Fujiwara, Hiroshi	Fujiwara, Hiroshi[b]	
6	JIF	SMO	Katō, Kazuo	Katō, Kazuo	Katō, Kazuo	Director of Administrative Office
7	Ozaki	Shoe sub-material manufacturer	Matoba, Ken	Matoba, Ken	Matoba, Ken	
8	Ozaki	Shoe sub-material manufacturer	Ozaki, Teruhisa	Ozaki, Teruhisa	Ozaki, Teruhisa	President and JIF vice president
9	Secaicho	Rubber shoe manufacturer	Sakai, Kanji	Masuyama, Yoshifumi	Tamai, Yoshinobu	
10	Studio S.K. (Bon Pied)	Women's shoe design and custom-made shoe manufacturer	Katō, Shōichi	Katō, Shōichi	Katō, Shōichi	President
11	K Studio	Shoe design studio	Kido, Tsuneo	Kido, Tsuneo		President and JIF board member
12	Midori Anzen	Safety shoe manufacturer	Fukushima, Akinobu	Kojima, Toshio		
13	Rinzai	Shoe sub-material manufacturer	Fujita, Minoru	Fujita, Minoru		
14	Rōne Shoes	Unknown	Tanaka, Yoneji			
15	Seibu Department Stores	Department store	Yanagihara, Tomoe			

(continued)

Table 4.5 (continued)

No	Company name[a]	Type of business	Member name			Notes
			As of July 10, 1980	As of March 3, 1982	As of 1991	
16	Yoshinoya Kutsuten	Women's shoe retailer	Suzuki, Tomio			
17	Unknown		Uchida, Hyakuma			
18	Unknown		Yamaguchi, Michio			
19	Ken Planter	Shoe manufacture			Bando, Yukiko	
20	Morito	Shoe sub-material manufacturer			Funakawa, Yōichi[c]	

Source Prepared by the author based on Miura (2014, Table 7, p. 18) and memos from Shōichi Katō (personal communication, January 23, 2015) for 1980 and 1982, and JIF Fitting Kenshūkai (1991) for 1991

Notes [a] Company names are from the year in question. Unless specified otherwise, the term "shoe" refers to a leather shoe

[b] Fujiwara worked for Marisoru in 1991

[c] Funakawa started to participate in 1985 when he worked at Secaicho Gomu (Yōichi Funakawa's notebooks made between 1985 and 1986, personal communication, May 19, 2014)

> them cry, I could contribute to society in some small way. Sales would also go up, and the company would surely be able to grow (Takesawa 2005, p.89).[36]

Jun'ichi Morino from Ginza Yoshinoya Shōji, a well-known traditional shoe wholesaler and retailer, also attended the Fitting Workshop to learn about feet. In 1978, Ginza Yoshinoya Shōji launched the Hakiyoi Kutsu Kenkyūkai (good comfort shoe research society) to efficiently scale up their business while maintaining the "wearing comfort" achieved through their individual production and sales practices (Ginza Yoshinoya 90-nenshi Hensanshitsu 1997; Yashiro 1997). To that end, they needed information about feet. Morino stated:

> There are all kinds of customer foot shapes: for example, people with the same size 23[cm] could be an E, an EE, or an EEE. They could have wide feet or narrow feet and so on. We were trying to work on classifying these foot shape types. Therefore, we talked about fundamental knowledge, about sharing that knowledge among everyone. … So that's why I went to the seminar as a representative, to bring back that information and report on it.[37]

Shigemoto Satō mentioned that his company, Asics, sent him to the program because Asics, a large manufacturer of sports shoes, was "a company that was pretty eager

[36] Translated from Japanese by the author.

[37] Jun'ichi Morino, Planning & Purchasing Dept., Ginza Yoshinoya Co. Ltd. and board member of FHA (interview, August 8, 2014). Translated from Japanese by the author. The square brackets were added by the author.

to study and sought information from outside the company."[38] Hiroshi Fujiwara said that he participated in the Fitting Workshop because "the company [rubber shoe manufacturer Hotei Gomu] sent me to take Professor Nakao's course."[39]

Teruhisa Ozaki, president of the shoe sub-material manufacturer Ozaki, played an important role in uniting the members of the Fitting Workshop to establish a shoe fitter training program, the Shoe Fitter (SF) Training Workshop.[40] As a board member of JIF, he felt a sense of responsibility toward making the training program operational.[41] Morino states that the foundation of the SF Training Workshop was thanks to Nakao's knowledge and Ozaki's leadership.

> When we were on our way home [from the Fitting Workshop], and we got to the place where we usually part and say goodbye, that woods in Ueno where the statue of Saigo-san is, there was a kind of barbecue terrace outside on that hill. So, then Ozaki said, "Are you all just going home?" So, we said "No, we have time, it's fine." Since the people from Kansai were planning to stay overnight and we didn't have separate plans, we decided, "Alright, let's have some food." That was the first time we shared a meal and had a drink together. I think it was summer, probably. ... We sat in seats outside, since it was a terrace, and had beer and ate grilled meat or something like grilled mutton. That was when it felt like we finally started to open up to each other. I talk about this a lot with Satō, but if it hadn't been for Ozaki-san, we might never have opened. ... Katō-san and Professor Nakao may be the root source of shoe fitters, but another who pulled together our Fitting Workshop to establish shoe fitter training program was Ozaki-san, and I think his influence was huge there.[42]

Ozaki brought together members who were not necessarily enthusiastic about becoming instructors for the SF Training Workshop. Fujiwara explained:

> Everyone was not willing at first. "Can we really teach [at the SF Training Workshop]?" [I thought] it was just tiring. I talked with Ozaki-san because I didn't want to go. But he replied "What are you saying?" and gave us a pep talk, so we kept moving forward. ... He said we [the member of the Fitting Workshop] should put what we've learned out into the world. The office [JIF] had no money, so if it did the course, it would become a business. Ozaki-san was also a manager [of his own business]. He wasn't doing [the Fitting Workshop] as a charitable work. It seems he kept a close eye on both sides [i.e., social contribution and business].[43]

---

[38] Shigemoto Satō, Sales Promotion Division, Asics Japan Corp and Vice President of FHA (interview, September 14, 2014). Translated from Japanese by the author.

[39] Hiroshi Fujiwara, J.B. Co., Ltd. (interview, January 4, 2015). Translated from Japanese by the author. The square brackets were added by the author. In 1985, Yōichi Funakawa was also directed to study feet by his company, called Secaicho Gum. He was required to do so after becoming in charge of shoe lasts development (Yōichi, Funakawa, interview, May 19, 2014).

[40] Toshimi Fukui, President of Fukui Shoelast Mfg. Co. Ltd. (speech at the FHA 50th Anniversary Celebration, February 10, 2016); Yashiro Hiroo (interview, May 17, 2017). Note that Ozaki's path to membership is unclear, but since an advertisement from his company, Ozaki, appears in IWF (1969), he may had been a member from the early stages.

[41] Hiroshi Fujiwara, J.B. Co., Ltd. (interview, January 4, 2015).

[42] Jun'ichi Morino, Planning & Purchasing Dept., Ginza Yoshinoya Co. Ltd. and board member of FHA (interview, August 8, 2014). Translated from Japanese by the author. The square brackets were added by the author.

[43] Hiroshi Fujiwara, J.B. Co., Ltd. (interview, January 4, 2015). Translated from Japanese by the author. The square brackets were added by the author.

The members of the Fitting Workshop strengthened their unity through their activities.[44] Thus, the Fitting Workshop was not dissolved after the shoe fitter training program began in 1983, and it continued to engage in fitting-related research activities until 1993 (JIF Fitting Kenshūkai 1994). Nakao's lectures continued, but the workshop also conducted original research, including the establishment of a plaster molding method, an examination of packing work to adjust the inside of the shoe, and an exploration of changes in the foot caused by heel elevation (JIF Fitting Kenshūkai 1991, 1992, 1994).[45] The members continued to serve as instructors for the training program, participated in renewing the program's curriculum, and organized and conducted the advanced shoe fitter training program that began in 1988. In addition, they prepared and conducted the master's course introduced in 1991 (JIF Fitting Kenshūkai 1992). They also managed supplementary courses that were developed based on requests from qualified shoe fitters.[46]

Therefore, the SF Training Workshop program was developed by the JIF office and Fitting Workshop members with support from Nakao and Ozaki. The first workshop began in August 1983. Nakao was the primary instructor in charge of ergonomics, while Fitting Workshop members were in charge of subjects related to fitting (JIF, 1983g, 1984g, 1985i, j).

4.8 Summary

This chapter highlights that JIF lacked effective resources and an optimal strategy in the beginning and that JIF revised its strategy through learning by doing. JIF was located on the periphery of the industry and was resource-poor. However, with the help of some supporters, it managed to conduct some activities related to the health function of shoes. While there were partial successes, the strategy of developing a standard shoe last and persuading shoe manufacturers to adopt it and make shoes with a high health function was not successful. However, learning from those experiences, JIF modified its strategy; the strategy to improve the health function of shoes by training shoe fitters to select shoes at shoe retailers that fit individual feet emerged.

IWF (JIF) was founded with the aim of having the Japanese footwear industry improve the health function of shoes that support walking. It intended to develop shoe lasts that fit Japanese people's feet and have manufacturers make shoes based on these lasts. However, JIF could not fully realize its activities during the 1960s and the early 1970s because of resource constraints. To secure funds, they published books and held seminars using the expertise of two full-time staff members—former

[44] Shōichi Katō, Bon Pied (interview, February 10, 2014); Jun'ichi Morino, Planning & Purchasing Dept., Ginza Yoshinoya Co. Ltd. and board member of FHA (interview, August 8, 2014); Shigemoto Satō, Sales Promotion Division, Asics Japan Corp and Vice President of FHA (interview, September 14, 2014).

[45] Ken Matoba (interview, May 19, 2014).

[46] Yōichi Funakawa. (interview, May 19, 2014).

journalists of a footwear industry trade magazine—who excelled at such activities. A few members resonated with JIF founder Katō and cooperated on publishing books and running seminars related to the health function of shoes.

Upon its reorganization into JIF, the organization finally obtained foot shape measurements of 2,000 Japanese people, five years after it was founded. This project was a pioneering initiative due to the support received from a foot specialist, Nakao. Thus, JIF was involved in the foot shape measurement project conducted by the entire footwear industry.

However, they were unable to develop standard shoe lasts, which was their original goal. They put the foot shape measurement data up for sale, but no companies bought it, and even JIF's Size Committee was unable to use it to develop shoe lasts. Therefore, the strategy of improving the health function of Japanese shoes by developing shoe lasts based on the measurement data and requiring shoe manufacturers to develop shoes that fit Japanese feet failed.

Nevertheless, a by-product of the Foot Shape Measurement Project was that JIF discovered the prevalence of foot problems. JIF believed that the cause was not wearing the right shoes and learned that some Western countries had shoe fitting specialists called shoe fitters.

Based on the realization that it was difficult to convince shoe manufacturers to produce shoes with a high health function and by learning about the prevalence of foot problems, JIF changed its strategy. Their earlier requirement for shoe manufacturers to produce shoes that fit Japanese people well changed to having shoe retailers offer shoe fitting services. Along with this revised strategy, the Fitting Workshop was established and the personal connections that had been established propelled its activities, which led to the initiation of the SF Training Workshop program in 1983.

Chapter 5
Adjustment of JIF's Strategy and Diffusion of Shoe Fitters

This chapter analyzes how the use of shoe fitters became widespread among shoe retailers because of JIF's activities. The analysis in this chapter reveals that JIF further learned from its activities and modified its strategy, which led to the diffusion of shoe fitters to shoe retailers.

The previous chapter revealed that JIF had arrived at the strategy of improving the health function of shoes by training shoe fitters to select shoes at shoe stores that fit individual feet, and the strategy emerged through learning by doing. However, this strategy did not yield immediate results, and more strategy revisions were made through learning by doing. The difference between the original SF Training Workshop and the revised one is summarized in Table 5.1. JIF learned that latent consumer demand for shoe fittings was strong; therefore, it clearly narrowed its target from shoe-related companies in general to shoe retailers. JIF also revised the frame by appealing to the economic advantages of attracting more customers through shoe fittings because the need for shoe fitter-based shoe selection was high, although originally the frame conveyed that learning shoe fitting is necessary to be a shoe professional. The requirements for shoe retailers to acquire shoe fitter certification were also changed from two 3–4-day courses to a 3-day course followed by an examination, reducing the burden on companies (Luders 2006).

This chapter consists of restructured and revised version of Miura, S. (2018, August 3–4). *Partnering strategy between NPOs and business organizations: The case of the shoe industry in Japan* [Paper presentation]. Challenges of Sustainable Development and Social Impacts on Cooperatives and Social Enterprises, Bangkok, Thailand; Miura, S. (2019a). Shakai katsudōdantai no senryaku shūsei to shijō sōzō: kutsusangyō ni okeru shakaikatsudōdantai, kigyō, shōhisha, media no sōgosayō [Adjustments of social activist strategies and new market creation: The interplay of an activity group, companies and their primary stakeholders in the shoe industry]. *Organizational Science*, *52*(3), 20–32. https://doi.org/10.11207/soshikikagaku.52.3_20.

S. Miura, *Successful Social Activism and Unintended Market Emergence*,
https://doi.org/10.1007/978-981-99-9291-1_5

Table 5.1 JIF's strategy revisions

Aspect	Original workshop	Revised workshop
Superordinate goal	Improving the health function of shoes and safeguarding the foot health of the Japanese people	Improving the health function of shoes and safeguarding the foot health of the Japanese people
Target company	All shoe-related companies	Shoe retailers
Requirement for target companies	All shoe-related companies completing shoe fitter accreditation To be accredited, attendance in two sets of 3–4 consecutive days' training workshop	Shoe retailers completing shoe fitter accreditation and selecting shoes that fit the customer well To be accredited, attendance of a 3 consecutive days' training workshop, passing a written test, and clearing 50 foot measurement tests
Frame	Learning shoe fitting is necessary to be a shoe professional	Customer demand for proper shoe selection by a shoe fitter is high, and having a shoe fitter is an advantage for the store

This chapter describes the process of JIF's strategy modification and the resulting diffusion of shoe fitters. This chapter also summarizes the description of JIF's strategy changes developed in Part II, clarifies the contribution of the study, and discusses the implications for research on the direct effect of activism targeting companies.

5.1 Diffusion of Shoe Fitters to Shoe Retailers

JIF-trained shoe fitters had penetrated the footwear industry. Figure 5.1 shows the number of participants in the SF Training Workshop and the number of qualified shoe fitters. A qualified shoe fitter is one who was once certified by JIF and continued to renew their registration for certification. Both the number of SF Training Workshop participants and qualified SFs increased from the beginning of the program until the collapse of the Japanese bubble economy in 1991. Although the number of SF Training Workshop participants decreased and the number of qualified shoe fitters stagnated because of the subsequent recession after the collapse, the program survived. Beginning in 1996, both numbers began to increase. Awareness of shoe fitter among consumers has also increased. A survey conducted in 1997 indicated that 50% of men and 70% of women were aware of shoe fitters (JIF 1997). Thus, JIF has succeeded in promoting shoe fitter in the footwear industry.

The companies that accepted shoe fitters were primarily shoe retailers. Table 5.2 shows the business categories of JIF member company, a company that SF Training Workshop participants belong to, and a company that qualified shoe fitters belong to.[1]

[1] Specialist shops refer to the retail business categories that are not department stores, supermarkets, general merchandise stores, cooperatives, or convenience stores. That is, specialist shops are a

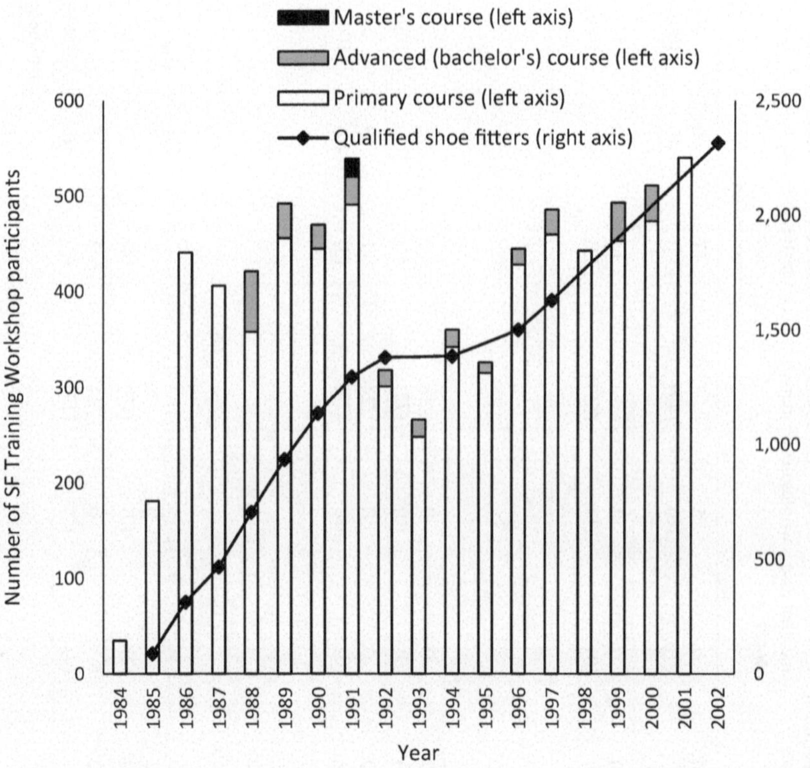

Fig. 5.1 Number of participants in SF Training Workshops and number of qualified shoe fitters. *Source* Miura (2018, p. 68), modified by the author

---

residual category (Tamura 2008). This study classified shoe specialty stores into small and medium shoe retailers, large high-end shoe retailers, and large mass shoe retailers by combining available data (Miura 2019a). The specific procedure is as follows. First, large and small-to-medium retailers were differentiated by the sales figures. If a company had entered the top 50 sales rankings of shoe specialty stores in the industry yearbook *Kutsu Nenkan* [Shoe Yearbook] and its successor *Shoes Book* at least once in the two years before and after the year in question, it was considered a large company (Gomuhouchi Shinbunsha 1981, 1982, 1983, 1984; Posty Corporation 1985, 1987, 1988, 1990, 1991, 1992, 1993, 1994, 1995, 1996). The top 50 companies were usually nationwide chain stores and the best regional stores. Best regional stores are companies that operate multiple stores in a local area and boast the top sales in that area. Note, however, that as JIF member companies of 1979 (Table 5.2, Sect. 1), the top 15 companies at the time were used due to limited available materials. Second, large companies were further categorized into high-end and mass market. In the company's profile data in the industry yearbook *Kutsu, Hakimono Sangyō Nenkan* [Shoes and Footwear Industry Yearbook], companies were classified according to whether their main products had a selling price of ¥10,000 yen or more or whether they had at least one branch in a department store (Yano Research Institute 1983, 1985, 1989a, b). Articles from the industry magazine *Footwear Press* were also used as supplements for price and store information ("Fukyō shirazu" 1992; Sugawara 1991, 1992).

Table 5.2 Classification of JIF members, SF Training Workshop participants, and qualified shoe fitters by business category

	Shoe retailers				Department stores	General merchandise stores	Shoe wholesalers	Shoe manufacturers	Shoe materials, repairs, and design	Others and unknown	Total
	Small and medium-sized	Large high-end	Large mass-market	Large unknown							
1. JIF member company, 1979	1 (1)	2 (2)	0 (0)	0 (0)	0 (0)	0 (0)	5 (10)	24 (49)	17 (35)	0 (0)	49 (100)
2. JIF member company, 1983	2 (5)	1 (2)	0 (0)	0 (0)	0 (0)	0 (0)	2 (5)	23 (55)	14 (33)	0 (0)	42 (100)
3. SF Training Workshop participants, 1983											
No. of companies	2 (8)	1 (4)	0 (0)	0 (0)	0 (0)	0 (0)	0 (0)	18 (72)	1 (4)	3 (12)	25 (100)
No. of people	2 (6)	1 (3)	0 (0)	0 (0)	0 (0)	0 (0)	0 (0)	24 (77)	1 (3)	3 (10)	31 (100)
4. SF Training Workshop participants, revised 1st (1984) and 2nd (1985)											
No. of companies	18 (38)	9 (19)	2 (4)	1 (2)	2 (4)	1 (2)	0 (0)	8 (17)	2 (4)	4 (9)	47 (100)
No. of people	22 (33)	15 (23)	2 (3)	2 (3)	2 (3)	6 (9)	0 (0)	11 (17)	2 (3)	4 (6)	66 (100)

(continued)

Table 5.2 (continued)

	Shoe retailers				Department stores	General merchandise stores	Shoe wholesalers	Shoe manufacturers	Shoe materials, repairs, and design	Others and unknown	Total
	Small and medium-sized	Large high-end	Large mass-market	Large unknown							
5. Qualified shoe fitter, 1992											
No. of companies	238 (58)	10 (2)	4 (1)	7 (2)	31 (8)	3 (1)	37 (9)	49 (12)	6 (1)	27 (7)	412 (100)
No. of people	325 (24)	278 (21)	27 (2)	48 (4)	335 (25)	22 (2)	88 (6)	192 (14)	10 (1)	30 (2)	1355 (100)
Average no. of people	1.4	27.8	6.8	6.9	10.8	7.3	2.4	3.9	1.7	1.1	3.3

Sources Section 1, prepared by the author based on (JIF 1979) and Gomuhouchi Shinbunsha (1980, p. 46). Sections 2–5, Miura (2019a, Table 1, p. 25), translated from Japanese and modified by the author

Note Percentage in parentheses

Section 5 of Table 5.2 indicates that shoe retailers, specifically small and medium-sized shoe retailers, had the most shoe fitters as of 1992 and were supporters of the shoe fitter system. In the case of small shoe stores, such as mom-and-pop shoe stores, the owners often served as shoe fitters. Although the number of large, high-end shoe retailers and department stores with shoe fitters was relatively small, their large workforce resulted in a similar number of shoe fitters compared to small and medium-sized shoe retailers. In contrast, few companies among the large mass-market shoe retailers or general merchandise stores, which handled mass-market shoes through self-service, had shoe fitters.

Although shoe retailers were supporters of the shoe fitter system, JIF was not originally an organization heavily involved with shoe retailers but rather had significant involvement with shoe manufacturers, including materials, repairs, and design. In 1979, when IWF was reorganized into JIF, 41 out of 49 member companies (84%) were in manufacturing, materials, repairs, and design, with only three in retail (Table 5.2, Sect. 1). By 1983, six months before the start of the SF Training Workshop, 37 out of 42 member companies (88%) were in manufacturing, materials, repairs, and design, with only three in retail (Table 5.2, Sect. 2). Therefore, in the original SF Training Workshop in 1983, the majority of participating companies were in the shoe manufacturing business, accounting for 76% of the 25 companies and 80% of the 31 participants (Table 5.2, Sect. 3).

However, in the revised workshops in 1984 and 1985, more shoe retailers began to participate. Shoe retailers accounted for 64% of the 47 participating companies and 62% of the 66 participants (Table 5.2, Sect. 4). Among participant companies, the highest number came from small and medium-sized shoe retailers, followed by large high-end shoe retailers. Participation from large, mass-market shoe retailers remained limited. This trend of participating companies continued in subsequent years, as reflected in the distribution of qualified shoe fitters by business category in 1992 (Table 5.2, Sect. 5).

The adoption of shoe fitters became widespread among shoe retailers, specifically among small and medium-sized shoe retailers, even though JIF was not originally closely associated with shoe retailers. The next sections describe the strategic actions taken by JIF that led to these changes in the mobilized companies.

5.2 Original SF Training Workshop

The members of the Fitting Workshop established the shoe fitter training program, and JIF launched the SF Training Workshop in 1983 (JIF 1983a, c). The main content of the program included shoe ergonomics and leg structure, provided by Nakao, and shoe fitting, taught by the Fitting Workshop members serving as instructors (JIF 1983g). The remaining content covered shoe parts and the production and design of shoes. These topics were divided into two sets, each comprising a 3-day workshop.

The leaflet that advertised the workshop was distributed to approximately 150 salient shoe companies, including JIF member companies, shoe retailers, general merchandise stores, department stores, footwear industry groups, shoe manufacturers, and shoe material manufacturers (JIF 1983i). The first seminar was held from August 29 to August 31, and while JIF had initially planned for 30 participants, a total of 31 participants from 25 companies ultimately attended (JIF 1983d).

In a questionnaire administered after the completion of the workshop, many participants indicated their interest in attending a second workshop (JIF 1983d). Given the positive response and JIF's original plan to conduct two courses, each lasting between 3 and 4 days (JIF 1982b), JIF prepared for the second workshop and announced that those who completed both workshops would be certified as primary shoe fitters (JIF 1983d).

The second 3-day workshop was held from February 13 to February 15, 1984, and it was only open to members who had completed the first 3-day workshop. However, only 12 participants returned for the second workshop (Katō 2002)[2] because many companies could not close or had employees absent from work for three or more days.[3]

Based on the original two workshops, JIF learned that there were shoe companies that were interested in its shoe fitter training program. However, it became evident that attending both workshops placed a heavy burden on these companies.[4]

5.3 Book Publication

In April 1984, JIF published a book titled *Itai Kutsu wa Mō Hakanai* [Say Goodbye to Wearing Painful Shoes] through Kodansha (JIF 1984h), one of the major publishing companies in Japan. This publication was based on JIF's long history of seeking better functionality of shoes and the preparation of the SF Training Workshop by the Fitting Workshop. The book highlighted two key points: the harm caused by ill-fitting shoes and tips for proper shoe fitting. JIF had initially planned to publish a book summarizing the Fitting Workshop's activities in early 1983, but it was just an idea at that time (JIF 1983a). However, in May 1983, they received an offer from Kodansha to write a book on shoes (JIF 1983c). Kodansha had planned a series of books on apparel accessories, with the first covering makeup, the second focusing on lingerie, and the third on shoes. The preface of the book noted that in European shoe stores, "customers choose the design, but it is the fitter's role to choose the shoes that fit" (JIF 1984h, p. 7),[5] and a photo from the first SF Training Workshop was included (p. 6).

[2] Number of companies unknown.

[3] Hiromu Yamamoto (interview by phone, December 8, 2015).

[4] Hiromu Yamamoto (interview by phone, December 8, 2015).

[5] Translated from Japanese by the author.

Table 5.3 Media appearance of the book, *Itai Kutsu wa Mō Hakanai* (JIF 1984h), and JIF

Media		Before the book publication	After the book publication							
			Apr	May	Jun	Jul	Aug	Sep	Oct	Total
Number of articles about the book										
	Trade press/magazine	–	8	4	2	2	1	0	0	17
	General paper/magazine	–	0	0	3	10	0	0	0	13
Number of articles/television programs that JIF appears in										
	Trade press/magazine	Unknown	0	0	0	0	0	1	0	1
	General paper/magazine	1(1973)	1	1	1	1	1	4	3	12
	Regional television	Unknown	0	0	0	0	0	0	4	4
Total		–	9	5	6	13	2	5	7	47

Source Miura (2018, Table 1, p. 75), modified by the author

The book received a response from consumers, newspapers, and magazines that were greater than JIF had ever experienced before (Table 5.3).[6] The overwhelming response made JIF realize that many consumers faced shoe-related problems and that the demand for shoe fitting services was high (JIF 1984d). On the day of publication, April 17, 1984, JIF received a phone call from a consumer, and from that date through July 31, 1984, they received 98 calls and nine letters, totaling 107 inquiries. Afterward, inquiries continued to come in every day (JIF 1984e). Out of these 107 inquiries, 70% of consumers stated their desire to find a store with a shoe fitter because they had never owned well-fitting shoes and/or had experienced various foot problems, such as irregular sizes, foot corns, calluses, or hallux valgus (bunions). An additional 21% of the queries were about which shoe brands might provide a better fit. Although they did not explicitly mention a shoe fitter, their reasons for seeking stores or brands were intrinsically the same: they had never worn shoes that fit them well and/or had experienced problems with their feet.

The book, and therefore JIF, also attracted attention from the media. Table 5.3 lists the media appearances related to the book and JIF. Articles on the book appeared not

[6] Post-publication media appearance is based on internal JIF documents. Pre-publication media appearance was confirmed by four national newspapers, *Asahi Shimbun, Nikkei Shimbun, Mainichi Shimbun, and Yomiuri Shimbun,* and a magazine database, Magazine Plus, which covered major Japanese magazines. All articles mentioning "shoe" were reviewed and no article was related to JIF.

only in trade press and magazines, but also in general papers and magazines. The articles covered not only the book itself, but also JIF as an organization. In addition, in October, a four-consecutive-day television program about footwear, with full cooperation from JIF, aired on regional television in Kansai through Asahi Broadcasting (JIF 1984e).

As far as the remaining materials are concerned, there is no indication that the book was aimed to stimulate consumer demand and boost the SF Training Workshop prior to its publication.[7] Rather, it seems that JIF compiled the findings from the Fitting Workshop activities for consumers following its longstanding strategy of generating funds by self-publishing a book about their activity content.[8] Therefore, the volume of the response was an unexpected lesson for JIF. Based on these experiences, JIF strengthened its belief that there was a significant need for shoe fitters and that demand had started to emerge (JIF 1984e).

5.4 Revision of SF Training Workshop

Based on the consumer and media response to the book, JIF realized that the potential demand for shoe fitters' fitting services could have economic benefits for shoe retailers. Based on the response of shoe companies toward the training program, they also learned that while companies were interested in shoe fitters, it was too demanding for them to attend two 3–4-day workshops. Thus, JIF modified the targets, requirements for participation, and the frame for the SF Training Workshop (Table 5.1).

The target participants of the SF Training Workshop were modified from "all shoe-related companies" (JIF 1983g) to "shoe retailers" (JIF 1984g, 1985i, j). JIF changed the target because it had learned that there was a high demand for shoe fitting at shoe stores based on reactions to the book from consumers and the media. When JIF commenced the Fitting Workshop, it already had a vision to educate shoe retailers to change the footwear industry, as described in Chap. 4. However, the original SF Training Workshop did not clearly focus on shoe retailers, as the title of the workshop, "The First Fitter Training Workshop for Top and Middle Management," indicates (JIF 1983g).[9] JIF rather targeted all shoe-related companies. In the revised SF Training Workshop, however, JIF clearly targeted shoe retailers, as the workshop title, "SF Training Workshop for a Shoe Retailer's Sales" (JIF 1984g, 1985i, j), shows.[10] The

---

[7] There was no reference to shoe fitters in the accompanying notes when the book was distributed to members (JIF 1984c). The same is true for other materials issued by JIF in relation to the book (JIF 1983a, c, d, f, 1984a, n.d.a).

[8] One of the business plans for 1983 was listed as "prepare an overall summary of feet for publication" (JIF 1983a). Later, in May 1983, Kodansha approached JIF to contribute to a series of books on apparel accessories (JIF 1983c). It remains unclear whether JIF initially proposed the book idea to Kodansha. This marked the first time JIF's book was published by a major publishing house.

[9] Translated from Japanese by the author.

[10] Translated from Japanese by the author.

program was still open to all shoe-related companies. However, the change in the workshop's title suggested that JIF's primary target companies had become shoe retailers ("Shoe fitter" 1988).

JIF also modified its requirements for the companies. JIF had learned that it was a heavy burden for the companies to attend both workshops. Therefore, the program was shortened from two sets of 3-day workshops to one. Although JIF believed that a 3-day workshop was too short to certify someone as a shoe fitter, it had no choice but to shorten the program length.[11] To compensate for the reduced number of workshop days, JIF incorporated additional certification criteria. After attending the workshop, participants were required to pass a written exam, submit foot shape measurement sheets of 50 people, and pass the accuracy assessment of those sheets before being certified. JIF later stated that it changed the requirements to prioritize "sending stores as many people as possible who have an awareness about fitting," even though it believed that the 3-day workshop was insufficient ("Shoe fitter" 1988, p. 38).[12]

JIF changed the frame of the program, which is the reason why shoe-related companies needed to learn about shoe fitting. JIF made this change after learning that the potential demand for shoe fitters' fitting services could have economic benefits for shoe retailers, and this point would be useful in mobilizing shoe retailers. For the original workshops, JIF claimed that learning shoe fitting was necessary to become a shoe professional and to improve the health function of shoes. Specifically, they asserted in the workshop flyer, "There are very few people who can be called true shoe professionals with extensive knowledge of feet and shoes. … It is vital to call for excellent fitters in all sectors related to shoes to improve shoe functionality" (JIF 1983g).[13] However, for the revised workshops, JIF stated that the need for shoe fitters was so great that companies would witness an economic benefit from having them. Specifically, JIF wrote in the workshop flyer as follows.

> There was a bigger reader response to the book than we expected, and we are still receiving calls from consumers who are having trouble choosing shoes, asking 'Let us know stores with fitters' and 'I'd like to find shoes that fit my feet.'... even now, we receive these voices every day. Consumer groups from all over the country, as well as media organizations coming to cover the story, have asked us to hurry up with the training since they'll cooperate fully in making shoe fitters well known. (JIF 1984g, 1985i, j)[14]

A flyer inviting people to join JIF was issued around the same time, stating that "fitting is the most important issue in the future and the biggest selling point for shoes" because of consumer needs and a significant amount of mass media attention (JIF 1984d).[15] These flyers were sent to major companies in the industry, and invitations to the SF Training Workshop were also published in industry trade magazines.[16]

[11] Hiromu Yamamoto (interview by phone, December 8, 2015).

[12] Translated from Japanese by the author.

[13] Translated from Japanese by the author.

[14] Translated from Japanese by the author.

[15] Translated from Japanese by the author.

[16] Toshiyuki Ozawa, Marketing Director of Ozawa Ichiba Ltd. (e-mail, June 1, 2017).

These changes in strategy brought success. In the first and second revised workshops, there were more participants than the number of available seats; 35 participants from 22 companies participated in the first revised workshop in December 1984, and 31 participants from 25 companies attended the second revised workshop in February 1985 (JIF n.d.b.). Shoe retailer presence expanded as JIF intended. In the original workshop in August 1983, shoe retailers constituted 12% of the 25 companies (Table 5.2, Sect. 3), whereas they constituted 59% of the 22 companies in the first revised workshop and 68% of the 25 companies in the second workshop (Table 5.2, Sect. 4). These results imply that JIF's target and frame changes were bearing fruit.

Changing the requirements for becoming a certified shoe fitter was also a success. JIF designed the workshop to cost ¥60,000 (US$356) for three days in the revised workshop.[17] The single workshop allowed stores to close for a shorter period and reduced their financial burden. "Toukutsu Shoe Fitter Course" by the Toukutsu Association, which imitated JIF's course and began in 1986, was set at two days for ¥10,000 (US$59) (Toukutsu Kyōkai 1986).[18] As the Toukutsu Association was the largest alliance of small and medium-sized shoe retailers in Tokyo with 902 member stores in 1986 (Toukutsu Kyōkai 2021), its plan was considered to reflect the representative opinion of shoe retailers. Thus, the Toukutsu Association's course with fewer days and a lower cost than JIF's suggests that shoe retailers wanted a course with lesser burden. Therefore, JIF's shortening of the SF Training Workshop was effective, though JIF believed that even three days were not sufficient ("Shoe fitter" 1988).

5.5 Shoe Retailers' Interpretation of Shoe Fitters

The previous section clarified that JIF's new strategy had a strong beginning. This section will review how shoe retailers interpreted that strategy and how they adopted shoe fitters. It becomes clear that small and medium-sized shoe retailers interpreted shoe fitters as a strategic solution to fierce competition from shoe discount chains, and its interpretation prompted further diffusion of shoe fitters to small and medium-sized shoe retailers.

Figure 5.2 shows the size of the shoe market and the sales trends of two major shoe discount chains. As the market matured in the 1980s, shoe discount chains grew rapidly. A shoe discounter is a retailing format that offers a full line of shoes with self-service at low prices in large suburban stores, which is equivalent to the large mass-market shoe retailers in Table 5.2. Low prices were made possible by mass merchandising, self-service, and low suburban rents. This format flourished in the 1980s (Funabashi 2012; Yahagi 2004). Shoe discount chains took customers away from traditional small and medium-sized retailers that sold shoes at regular prices

[17] The price is calculated based on the dollar-yen rate in 1986.

[18] The price is calculated based on the dollar-yen rate in 1986.

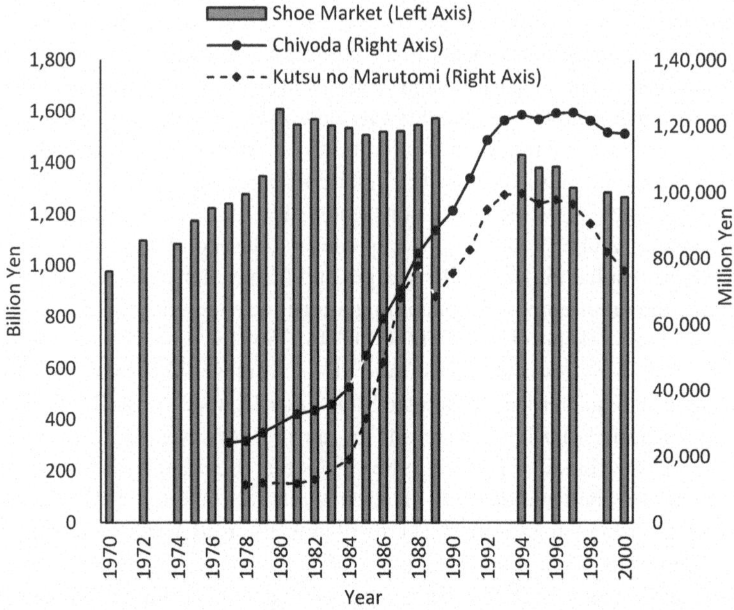

Fig. 5.2 Shoe market scale and shoe discounter sales. *Source* Miura (2019a, Fig. 2, p. 26), translated from Japanese and modified by the author. *Notes* Adjusted for Consumer Price Index (2000 = 1) (Ministry of Internal Affairs and Communications, n.d). Years with no graph had an unknown market size. Chiyoda includes non-footwear sales up to 1984 and up to 1988 for Kutsu no Marutomi

in a town's shopping streets as well as from large high-end shoe retailers that sold expensive shoes in downtown areas.

The frame that highlighted the financial advantages of meeting consumer needs for a shoe fitter's fitting service was appealing to small and medium-sized shoe retailers and large, high-end shoe retailers who were exposed to intense competition from shoe discounters. Shoe retailers who were the first to participate in the SF Training Workshop interpreted the sales method of using shoe fitting services as a strategic solution against suburban shoe discount chains. As shoe discount retailing was based on self-service at large stores, offering shoe fitting services by shoe fitters did not fit their business model, and imitating offering shoe fitting services was difficult for them.

Yoshimura Shōten, a top regional shoe retailer in Gunma Prefecture that corresponds to a large high-end shoe retailer in Table 5.2, sent employees to the SF Training Workshops several times after the first revision of the workshop. According to Hisashi Yoshimura, President of Yoshimura Shōten, this was to ensure that the company would "sell shoes that fit" by "measuring the feet and looking to check" ("Tokushū" 1988, p. 40).[19] Yoshimura stated that this was necessary for the company to survive. He said, "As we became too involved in the design, we forgot about the

[19] Translated from Japanese by the author.

functions of the shoe, and therefore shoes came to be sold in variety stores. If we continued in that manner, shoe stores would decline more and more" ("Tokushū" 1988, p. 40).[20] He stated that "By making it about 'selling health' instead of 'selling shoes,' I think shoe stores will get the approval of society, and we can remain as specialist shops" ("Yoshimura" 1988).[21] Toshiyuki Ozawa, owner of the small shoe retailer Ozawa in Chiba Prefecture, participated in the revised second SF Training Workshop and also believed that fitting services were important for survival. He said, "What is my store for? It should have a proper sense of presence. If you don't have that, and you're just running [a store], you'll be ruined before long."[22] According to him, a sense of presence was "How to fit shoes to satisfy the customer's feet. Ultimately, [it's being able to provide] something that makes walking comfortable and that looks beautiful."[23]

Shoe retailers other than those participating in the SF Training Workshop also believed fitting services by shoe fitters to be an important strategic solution. A letter sent to the organization bulletin of Toukutsu Association, the largest alliance of shoe retailers, stated the following about competition with discount chains: "We've been put in a predicament due to price competition from large stores and the opening of discount stores one after another. We, who really understand shoes, are the ones who should have so-called shoe fitter qualifications, standing in the place of the consumer, and serving them. This is the way to survive" (KKO (Pseud) 1984, p. 3).[24]

5.6 Birth of Certified Shoe Fitters and a Virtuous Circle

Along with how shoe retailers pioneered the model of shoe fittings by shoe fitters as a strategic solution for survival, the attention paid to certified shoe fitters by the mass media boosted the diffusion of shoe fitters among shoe retailers.

In April 1985, 48 certified shoe fitters were introduced for the first time in Japan (JIF 1985b). They were the workshop participants who had completed all the certification steps (written exam, foot shape measurements, and verification of their accuracy). JIF actively promoted this news to shoe-related companies and the media (JIF 1985c; Katō 2002). In 1985, JIF was interviewed by the media at least 27 times, with 70% of those interviews coming from general (rather than trade) media (JIF 1985a, c, d, e, g, h). In addition, JIF published two books on shoe fitting in the 1980s in

[20] Translated from Japanese by the author.

[21] Translated from Japanese by the author.

[22] Toshiyuki Ozawa, Marketing Director of Ozawa Ichiba Ltd. (interview, May 16, 2017). Translated from Japanese by the author. The square brackets were added by the author.

[23] Toshiyuki Ozawa, Marketing Director of Ozawa Ichiba Ltd. (e-mail, June 1, 2017). Translated from Japanese. The square brackets were added by the author.

[24] Translated from Japanese by the author.

Table 5.4 Newspaper articles on shoe fitters

Contents	1985	1986	1987	1988	1989	1990	1991	1992
Explanation of shoe fitters and SF Training Workshop	3	2	2	1	2	0	1	4
Introduction of individual shoe fitters and companies with shoe fitters	0	2	2	2	3	3	2	3
Advice from shoe fitters	0	0	0	0	1	1	2	1
Other	0	1	0	0	0	0	2	0
Total	3	5	4	3	6	4	7	8

Source Prepared by the author based on Miura (2019a, Table 2, p. 28) for *Asahi Shimbun and Nikkei Shimbun,* further adding newly analyzed data for *Yomiuri Shimbun and Mainichi Shimbun.*

response to inquiries from publishers (JIF 1988b; Katō and Yamamoto 1986).[25] The books always included a list of shoe fitters.

Table 5.4 analyzes the content of articles about shoe fitters in four national newspapers: *Asahi Shimbun, Mainichi Shimbun, Nikkei Shimbun,* and *Yomiuri Shimbun.* In addition to articles describing shoe fitters and the SF Training Workshop, it is evident that articles had appeared that refer to shoe fitters or shoe companies having them, introducing them as people and stores that sold shoes with foot health in mind. Exposure of JIF and shoe fitters in the mass media aroused even more consumer demand. The number of articles in Table 5.4 may seem marginal, but even a single mention in the general media sent a rush of consumers to stores expecting shoe fitters to select shoes that fit well.[26] Michiko Kubota, who participated in the first revised workshop from Seibu Department Store, said, "Once such a report in a newspaper was read, customers who had trouble with their feet rushed to the store. So many customers came to the department store that I thought there would be a line."[27]

The book and media coverage were aimed at consumers, but they also had an impact on shoe retailers. The media reported that customer demand for shoe fitters was rising ("Tokyo Fashion" 1987; "Yoshinoya Kutsuten tenchō" 1986, "Yoshinoya Kutsuten no" 1987), that shoe fitters were effectively drawing customers to businesses ("Kutsu no counseling" 1987; "Shoe fitter Kubota" 1986), and that offering shoe fitting services by a shoe fitter was a survival strategy ("Yoshimura" 1988). Exposure to this information raised awareness that shoe fitting was a strategic solution for both small and medium-sized shoe retailers and large high-end shoe retailers facing

[25] JIF continued to self-publish and commercial publish. Two commercially published books were released in the 1990s, one in the 2000s, and two in the 2010s. (FHA 2015, 2017; JIF 1992b, 1995; Katō and Yamamoto 2004).

[26] Miyako Nosaka, Kutsu to Handbag Nosaka (Later Nosaka Kutsuten), a small shoe retailer in Ishikawa prefecture (JIF 1990); and Eizō Murata, owner of Motoyoshi, a small shoe retailer in Tokyo ("'Comfort' ni ikiru senmonten" 1991).

[27] Michiko Kubota, sales consultant at Shoes Frontier (interview, May 15, 2017). Translated from Japanese by the author.

competition from shoe discount chains. As a result, these companies sent participants to the workshops. The high-end service of shoe fitters was already familiar to department stores, and they also sought to acquire certifications (Table 5.2, Sect. 5).

Due to the higher number of applicants for the course, JIF increased the training workshop's capacity since 1985. The capacity of each workshop expanded from 30 to 70 participants. JIF also offered the course more frequently and in venues outside of Tokyo, including Kobe, Fukuoka, and Nagoya (Katō 2002). This expansion led to an increased number of certified shoe fitters, and their activities were covered by the mass media, leading to even more consumer demand and course participants, creating a virtuous cycle.

In 1988, in response to inquiries from certified shoe fitters who wanted to learn more, JIF started an advanced program for these individuals, provided as a 6-month correspondence course with a 2-day workshop.[28] This advanced course was known as the advanced (later, bachelor's) course and has attracted around 20 shoe fitters each year. In 1991, a two-year master's course was launched for people who had completed the advanced course. The master's course had a capacity of 15 people in 1991, and 19 applied.[29]

5.7 Summary of Part II

JIF held the initial two sets of SF Training Workshops in August 1983 and February 1984, and it faced challenges in attracting continued participation for the second workshop. In 1984, JIF gained media attention by publishing a book, which led to the emergence of consumer demand for a shoe fitting service. Learning from this experience and from the responses of companies to the initial SF Training Workshop, JIF narrowed its target audience to shoe retailers, changed the frame of its workshops to tout the economic benefits of shoe fitters for shoe retailers, and modified the qualification requirements to a 3-day program and exam to facilitate the participation of companies. With these revisions, fitting services provided by shoe fitters were accepted as a strategic solution for small and medium-sized shoe retailers and large high-end shoe retailers, which had lost customers to suburban shoe discount chains (large, mass-market shoe retailers). The birth of certified shoe fitters attracted the attention of the mass media and consumers, which increased the number of workshop participants and certified shoe fitters, creating a virtuous cycle. Therefore, JIF succeeded in persuading shoe retailers to have shoe fitters in their stores.

At first glance, this case can be interpreted as one in which an SMO changed corporate behavior through a company's primary stakeholders, as asserted by existing

[28] Tokiko Hasegawa, former JIF office staff member hired in 1985 (interview, February 10, 2016); JIF (1988a).

[29] However, the applicants and instructors did not continue with the program, leading to the discontinuation of the master's course after a single run (Katō 2002). The Master's course was offered again in 2019–2021.

studies (Balsiger 2010; Dubuisson-Quellier 2013; Frooman 1999; Weber et al. 2008). That is, JIF attracted media attention and consumer demand, and shoe fitters spread among small and medium-sized shoe retailers, large high-end shoe retailers, and department stores. However, behind this success was a learning by doing process of JIF. Learning from companies' responses to its initial training workshops and the media and consumer response to its book, JIF changed its strategy: its targets, demand for them, and frame. This strategy change worked, and JIF succeeded in changing shoe retailers' behavior.

JIF modified its strategy through learning by doing, even before it began its SF Training Workshop, as described in Chap. 4. JIF's original strategy was to develop standard shoe lasts and encourage shoe manufacturers to use them to make shoes that fit Japanese feet, with the superordinate goal of improving the health function of shoes and protecting the foot health of the Japanese people. JIF assumed that shoes were supposed to fulfill the health function of supporting walking, and shoe manufacturers should address this. However, JIF unexpectedly discovered the prevalence of foot problems among consumers after taking their foot measurements. JIF also learned about the general indifference to its activities in the 1960s and 1970s and the challenges in pursuing the initial strategy, as JIF failed in its attempt to develop shoe lasts and persuade shoe manufacturers to adopt them. Therefore, JIF modified its strategy to promote the role of shoe fitters. JIF's revised strategy focused on having shoe retailers employ shoe fitters to select well-fitting shoes, with the same superordinate goal of improving the health function of shoes and protecting the foot health of the Japanese people.

Despite being an organization located on the periphery of the industry with scarce and biased resources, JIF succeeded in changing the behavior of shoe retailers because it modified its strategy through a process of learning by doing.

5.8 Discussion of Part II

Existing studies on social movements targeting companies have highlighted the effectiveness of strategies that utilize a company's primary stakeholders as intermediaries (Balsiger 2010; Dubuisson-Quellier 2013; King 2008; Schurman 2004; Weber et al. 2008). However, when there is no interdependence with the company, the SMO is positioned on the periphery of the existing industry, lacking intimate familiarity with the circumstances of the industry. As strategy development depends on an organization's available resources (Freeman 1979), it can be difficult to identify an effective persuasive strategy for an SMO with limited knowledge of the industry. To follow existing studies, SMOs aiming to influence social change by transforming the behavior of companies often experience these difficulties.

The case of JIF suggests that the key to overcoming these challenges is the adoption of a dynamic strategy change model. Even when their strategies are constrained by resource limitations, SMOs can modify their strategy through learning by doing, leading to the emergence of an effective strategy over time. This dynamic strategy change model has been previously explored as an emergent strategy within strategic management theory (Itami and Roehl 1991; Mintzberg and Waters 1985; Sakai 2018). However, it is a perspective that has been overlooked in research regarding social movements that target companies, and this study indicates that the perspective can be applied to research on social movements targeting companies.

JIF's case also implies the need to delve beyond the perspective of SMO's dynamic strategy change model when researching social movements that target companies. A closer examination of the proliferation of shoe fitters in the footwear industry reveals that companies also learned from JIF's strategy. While it was JIF that initially emphasized the economic benefits that the shoe fitting service would bring to shoe retailers, it was the initial shoe retailers who participated in the SF Training Workshop that interpreted it as a way to differentiate themselves from suburban shoe discount chains. Their remarks were picked up by the media, and fitting services were recognized as a strategic solution for the survival of small and medium-sized shoe retailers and large high-end shoe retailers exposed to competition from shoe discount chains. Many shoe retailers adopted this solution, leading to the widespread use of shoe fitters. While JIF's modifications of the frame triggered the spread of shoe fitters, the revised initial workshops were reinterpreted by the first shoe retailers to adopt shoe fitters, which, in turn, encouraged other shoe retailers to implement shoe fitters. This demonstrates how other players learn from the strategic actions of the SMO. If target companies are to learn in the same way as SMOs, research on social movements targeting companies should examine the process by which SMOs and target companies learn from each other and revise their strategies.

Part III
Indirect Effect of Activism: How Unintended Markets Emerged After an SMO's Success

This part of the book addresses the indirect effect of activism, which is the change in society due to the spillover outcome of the direct impact of activism. One of the indirect changes in society brought about by activism is the emergence of new market categories. Several questions are raised in this context. Are the markets that emerge owing to the activities of SMOs always those intended by the SMOs? When the market emergence is unintended by SMOs, specifically one that is inconsistent with the superordinate goals of the SMOs, how does this emergence occur? As the analysis focuses on the consequences of JIF's success, described in Part II, the primary research inquiry revolves around how JIF's successes led to the emergence of the three markets, including the one inconsistent with JIF's superordinate goal. The analysis of the JIF case reveals that the initiatives of SMOs stimulate various consumer needs and company responses, leading to the emergence of markets that either align or do not align with the superordinate goals of the SMO.

Chapter 6
Social Movement Targeting Companies and Market Emergence

The fashion-oriented transparent insole market has grown since the mid-2000s. One example of its success is how fashion-oriented transparent insoles, all in exquisite packaging, lined an entire wall at Sony Plaza Ginza, a variety store in the Sony Building in the high-end shopping district of Ginza, Tokyo.[1] The insoles had their own aesthetic allure; for example, some were rose-shaped and some were glittery.[2] Made with clear gel (elastomer) and millimeters thin, transparent insoles are partial pads that are inserted into the forefoot portions of high-heeled mules, sandals, or pumps to provide shock absorption for comfort without the conspicuous visibility of non-transparent items when shoes are removed.[3] Over time, the products became sufficiently popular to warrant their own displays and racks in a variety stores, drugstores, and other stores (Fuji Keizai 2007).

This was an indirect and unintended effect of the success of JIF's initiatives, which succeeded in popularizing shoe fitters to shoe retailers to protect the health of Japanese feet. The popularization of these insoles was inconsistent with JIF's goal of protecting foot health; the health function of the insole was somewhat questionable, especially given that the insoles were being sold as complementary goods for high-heeled mules, sandals, and pumps, which can inhibit a balanced gait.

How and why did the success of JIF's initiative lead to the creation of a market inconsistent with its superordinate goal? This chapter reviews existing research on market emergence because of SMOs' activities and points out that studies have primarily focused on market emergence intended by SMOs. However, this study assumes that target companies, non-target companies, and consumers that are affected directly and indirectly by the activities of SMOs react in various ways, and suggest

[1] Maeda Tōichirō, President of Arakawa Sangyo Co., Ltd. (interview, May 10, 2021); "Mono" (2009).

[2] "Arakawa Sangyo" (2001); "Mono" (2009).

[3] In Japan, there are many situations in which people need to remove their shoes when they are outside their home, such as in certain restaurants.

S. Miura, *Successful Social Activism and Unintended Market Emergence*,
https://doi.org/10.1007/978-981-99-9291-1_6

that their diverse reactions can create various markets that the SMO did not intend, including the one inconsistent with its superordinate goals.

6.1 Existing Research

SMOs seek to change corporate behavior as their primary goal and thereby change society in the direction they want as a superordinate goal (Snow and Soule 2010). The direct effect of activism is the change in corporate behavior brought about by SMOs, and the indirect effect of activism is the change in society because of the spillover effect from the direct effect of activism (Briscoe and Gupta 2016). One of the changes that occurs in society as the indirect effect of activism is the emergence of new market categories (Briscoe and Gupta 2016).

According to previous research, the following mechanisms are involved in the emergence of markets in response to activism. Social action groups delegitimize existing corporate behaviors and legitimatize new behaviors to realize their ideal society (den Hond and de Bakker 2007). Entrepreneurs who resonate with and see opportunities in this sociocultural change are mobilized and enter the market and provide new goods and services, thereby creating new markets (Sine and Lee 2009). For example, with the contemporary environmental movement, environmental groups, such as the Sierra Club, have identified the high environmental impact of existing power generation methods that use existing oil, natural gas, and coal as a problem, and proposed wind power generation as an alternative power generation method that has low environmental impact. Entrepreneurs who resonated with this value were mobilized and entered the market, resulting in the emergence of the wind power sector in the United States (Sine and Lee 2009).

SMOs also reach out to consumers to promote behavioral changes in companies. As discussed in Part II, SMOs are secondary stakeholders of companies; thus, they have little direct influence on the companies (Stevens et al. 2005; Vasi and King 2012). They attempt to influence corporate behavior by mobilizing consumers, shareholders, and the media, who are the company's primary stakeholders (Balsiger 2010; Dubuisson-Quellier 2013; King and Soule 2007; Miura 2019a; Weber et al. 2008). Consumers are the notable stakeholders in the creation of new markets. SMOs work on consumers to reveal latent demand for new goods and services from companies that adopt new behaviors. The manifestation of that demand promotes behavioral changes in companies (Balsiger 2010; Dubuisson-Quellier 2013; Miura 2019a; Weber et al. 2008).[4]

Through these methods, SMOs attempt to change the values and behaviors of companies and consumers to stimulate the supply and demand of new goods and services, thus creating new markets. Media can also be utilized to further stimulate supply and demand (Weber et al. 2008). Therefore, new markets are born.

[4] Along with this private politics, there is also public politics, which involves influencing corporate behavior legally by appealing to the government (Baron 2003).

6.2 Perspectives Overlooked in Previous Studies

6.2.1 Assumptions of Existing Research

The existing research on the indirect effect of activism targeting companies has generally discussed how the activities of SMOs lead to the emergence of markets that are intended by them, and therefore, consistent with their superordinate goals. A market emerges as a consequence of achieving the immediate goal of changing corporate behavior. For example, entrepreneurs who started a wind energy business mobilized by environmental groups, such as the Sierra Club created the wind energy sector market as an intended and desired consequence of SMOs (Sine and Lee 2009).

The emergence of an intended market consistent with SMOs' superordinate goals assumes three points: (1) the intended target companies of the SMOs will change their behavior according to the SMOs demands; (2) only target companies respond to the activities of SMOs; and (3) consumers also change their awareness and behavior as the SMO intends. Therefore, existing studies suggest that new market categories consistent with the superordinate goals of SMOs emerge. However, these assumptions seem simplistic. To critically examine this issue, this study discusses these assumptions and situates them as invalid.

6.2.2 Diverse Reactions of Target Companies

The target company does not necessarily change its behavior as intended by the SMO (Zald et al. 2005), as the research on the direct effect of activism targeting companies has pointed out. Companies may respond to the demands of an SMO through avoidance (non-reaction), acquiescence, compromise, sidestepping, confrontation, and prevention (Balsiger 2015). Companies find both threats and opportunities in the demands of activists, and they respond and change their behavior according to their own interests (Pacheco and Dean 2015). For example, when MacMillan Bloedel, which is the largest and oldest forestry company in British Columbia, Canada, was criticized by Greenpeace and other environmental groups regarding clearcut logging, the company reframed the problem of ending the practice by arguing that increased regulation would create the problem of job loss to gain support from workers and unions, thereby confronting the demands of the activists (Zietsma and Winn 2008).

The analysis in Part II also indicates that companies may respond to the efforts of SMOs in different ways. The analysis revealed that SMOs learn from environmental feedback and modify their strategies and that the targeted companies also learn from, interpret, and respond to the activism in their own way. Therefore, targeted companies do not always make behavioral changes in line with the will of SMOs.

The findings of previous studies on the direct effect of activism need to be applied to research on market emergence as the indirect effect of activism. Thus, this study assumes that targeted companies do not necessarily implement behavioral changes as demanded by the SMOs, but rather react in diverse ways (Balsiger 2015; de Bakker et al. 2017; den Hond et al. 2010; Gupta and Briscoe 2020; Hiatt et al. 2009; McDonnell and King 2013; Reinecke and Ansari 2021; Yue et al. 2013; Zald et al. 2005; Zietsma and Winn 2008).

6.2.3 Mobilization of Non-Target Companies

Considering that initial target companies as well as other companies are learning entities, the activities of SMOs and their results should impact a wide range of companies beyond their initial targets. Research on the direct effect of social movements targeting companies has indicated that non-targeted companies learn environmental threats and opportunities from SMOs' initiatives directed at target companies and those companies' responses to them, thereby changing their behavior (den Hond et al. 2010; Hiatt et al. 2009; Yue et al. 2013). For example, in the sports apparel industry, Nike was heavily attacked by the anti-sweatshop movement. Seeing this, Reebok took steps toward improving working conditions in its Indonesian factories, although not under direct pressure (den Hond et al. 2010).

Research dealing with the indirect effects of activities also points to the mobilization of non-target firms (Hiatt et al. 2009). The Woman's Christian Temperance Union delegitimized alcohol consumption, which resulted in the decline of breweries (Hiatt et al. 2009). This created more demand for soft drink beverages as alternatives, and entrepreneurs who saw the opportunities expanded their production of soft drinks, thereby expanding the soft drink market. Thus, companies that are not targeted may still find opportunities in social movements and accordingly change their behavior in ways that yield new markets.

6.2.4 Diverse Reactions of Consumers

If SMOs and companies are learning entities, then consumers are also learning entities. Therefore, consumers are not necessarily mobilized in line with SMOs' superordinate goals. However, existing research on social movements targeting companies has not addressed how consumers are not always mobilized as intended by SMOs. According to marketing research, "buyers in any market differ in their wants, resources, locations, buying attitudes, and buying practices" (Kotler and Armstrong 2012, p. 214). Therefore, when consumers encounter the claims made by SMOs, they will have different responses; for example, they may strongly or weakly resonate with, oppose, or be uninterested in the claims. The work by Weber et al. (2008) on new market category emergence in the context of the movement for grass-fed meat and dairy products found that the mobilized consumers were from a specific segment; specifically, they reported that "Much of the demand for grass-fed products is in the politically more liberal, affluent urban population centers inhabited by 'sophisticated consumers' of specialty and alternative food products" (Weber et al. 2008, p. 552). This previous finding suggests that not all consumers will respond equally.

The discussion about consumer responses can be taken one step further. The spread of premium-priced grass-fed products could reveal consumers who cannot afford such expensive products, but want to eat products that are healthy and environmentally responsible. In response to such demand, producers who produce quasi-grass-fed products instead of following the strict grass-fed production guidelines that take more time and effort may emerge and offer products at relatively low prices. This change in consumer and producer behavior and the resulting market are not desirable for SMOs that want to promote grass-fed production.

The changes in consumer awareness and behavior created by the claims of SMOs can be diverse; therefore, diverse business opportunities and diverse markets can emerge. Although the above example considers a downgraded version of the market in terms of SMOs' goals, an upgraded market could emerge. That is, markets that do not follow the superordinate goals of SMOs may emerge, and markets that pursue their goals more strictly may also spring up.

6.2.5 Unintended Market Emergence

In summary, target companies do not necessarily change their behavior in line with the superordinate goals of SMOs. Non-targeted companies also react in various ways to the SMOs' initiatives. Consumers also react in various ways. Reactions to the actions of SMOs from each actor can be diverse. Therefore, diverse markets—including markets that do not align with or that strictly pursue SMOs' superordinate goals—can emerge when the diverse behavioral changes on the supply side are combined with the emerging diverse needs on the demand side. However, previous research on social movements with market emergence as the outcome variable implicitly makes three assumptions: (1) the intended target companies of the SMOs will change their behavior according to the group's demands; (2) only target companies respond to the activities of SMOs; and (3) consumers also change their awareness and behavior as the SMO intends. However, these assumptions seem simplistic. While existing research has suggested that markets will emerge in line with the superordinate goals of SMOs, it has not adequately discussed the emergence of unintended markets inconsistent with SMOs' superordinate goals (Hiatt et al. 2009).

This lack of research does not negate the emergence of unintended markets or the importance of studying their mechanisms. In research on social movements against the state (political context), the ultimate impact on society has been an important question, and efforts have been made to elucidate the long-term and diverse consequences of social activism and the mechanisms behind them (Bosi et al. 2016; Giugni 1998; Tilly 1999). This question is equally important for social movements that target companies. In particular, when the activities of the SMOs lead to inconsistent markets with the SMOs' superordinate goals in the long term, research on how such phenomena occurred needs to be accumulated.

The expansion of the fashion-oriented transparent insole market by insole manufacturers is a case in which companies that were not targeted by JIF and consumers changed their behavior inconsistent with the superordinate goal of JIF. Therefore, clarifying how this happened is meaningful in elucidating the process and mechanism by which the activities of SMOs indirectly and unintentionally created markets inconsistent with SMOs' superordinate goals.[5]

6.3 Perspectives of This Research

This study assumes that target companies, non-target companies, and consumers who are affected directly and indirectly by the activities of SMOs can learn. Thus, this study assumes that (1) targeted companies do not necessarily implement behavioral changes as demanded by the SMOs, but rather react in diverse ways (Balsiger 2015; de Bakker et al. 2017; den Hond et al. 2010; Gupta and Briscoe 2020; Hiatt et al. 2009; McDonnell and King 2013; Yue et al. 2013; Zald et al. 2005; Zietsma and Winn 2008); (2) both companies that are intentionally targeted by SMOs and non-targeted companies react to the efforts of SMOs (den Hond et al. 2010; Hiatt et al. 2009; Yue et al. 2013); and (3) consumers do not necessarily change their behavior in line with SMOs' superordinate goals—rather, they exhibit diverse responses (notably, the diverse responses of consumers have been overlooked in existing research on social movements that target companies). These diverse reactions of companies and consumers can create various markets that the SMO did not intend.

Markets that possibly emerge as indirect effects of activism can be organized into intended and unintended markets. Intended markets align with SMOs' superordinate goals. Unintended markets may be diverse—some may not follow the superordinate goals of SMOs and some may strictly pursue them.

The subsequent chapters present the various markets that emerged as a result of JIF's successful shoe fitter diffusion strategy and analyze their emergence mechanisms with a focus on the reactions of the targeted and non-targeted companies and consumers. As a result of JIF activities, the comfort shoe market, the European comfort shoe market, and the fashion-oriented transparent insole market emerged (Fig. 6.1). Chapter 7 analyzes how the comfort shoe market emerged; this market was JIF's intended market and it emerged as a result of the popularization of shoe fitters. Chapter 8 explains how the European comfort shoe market emerged; this market was unintended but in line with JIF's superordinate goal. Chapters 9–10 describe how the fashion-oriented transparent insole market emerged; this market was unintended and inconsistent with JIF's superordinate goal. Chapter 10 also presents the conclusions and discussion of this study on market emergence as an indirect effect of activism.

[5] Although not related to social movements, for an exploration of unintended consequences found in corporate environments, see Numagami (2000) and Shimamoto (2020).

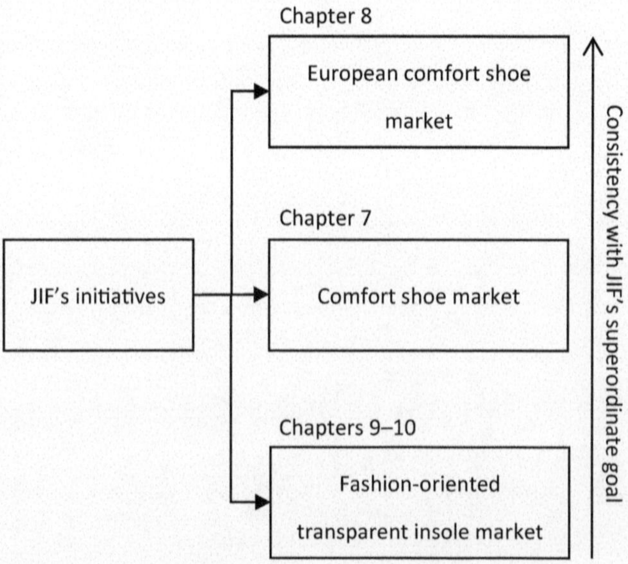

Fig. 6.1 Market emergence as an indirect effect of JIF's initiatives

Chapter 7
The Comfort Shoe Market and Changes in Consumer Awareness

This chapter examines how JIF's activities targeting shoe retailers that caused the spread of shoe fitters changed the awareness of foot health in Japan and gave rise to the comfort shoe market. Section 7.1 describes that the activities of JIF increased foot health awareness among consumers and in the footwear industry. Section 7.2 discusses how the changed context gave birth to the comfort shoe market—this was an intended and indirect consequence of JIF's activities. Section 7.3 shows that, despite these consequences, not all foot health problems can be solved. The system of shoe fitters encountered challenges, and it became evident that shoe fitters were unable to meet certain consumer needs. This situation provided the backdrop for the unintended market emergence described in Chaps. 8–10.

7.1 Improvements in Foot Health Awareness

Among health consciousness, which is an awareness of preventing and treating ailments throughout the body, foot health especially began to draw significant attention in the mid-1980s in Japan. As a result of JIF's activities, shoe fitters became widespread in the footwear industry, and consumer awareness of foot health improved. Improvement in consumer awareness of foot health is evident in the increased number of newspaper articles that referred to bunions (hallux valgus), the most well-known foot disease, since the mid-1980s. In 1987, *Yomiuri Shimbun*,

---

This chapter consists of restructured and revised version of Miura, S. (2020). Naze eranda kutsu de ashi o itameru noka: Shijō deno kutsu erabi no muzukashisa o saguru [Why do we have trouble with the shoes we wear?: The difficulty of finding shoes that fit in Japan]. *Gakuen*, (958), 16–36. https://swu.repo.nii.ac.jp/records/7011; and Miura, S. (2021). The developmental history of the insole market in Japan: Rising health consciousness and an unintended shift toward fashion (1984–2010). *Japanese Research in Business History, 38*, 43–61. https://doi.org/10.5029/jrbh.38.43.

S. Miura, *Successful Social Activism and Unintended Market Emergence*,
https://doi.org/10.1007/978-981-99-9291-1_7

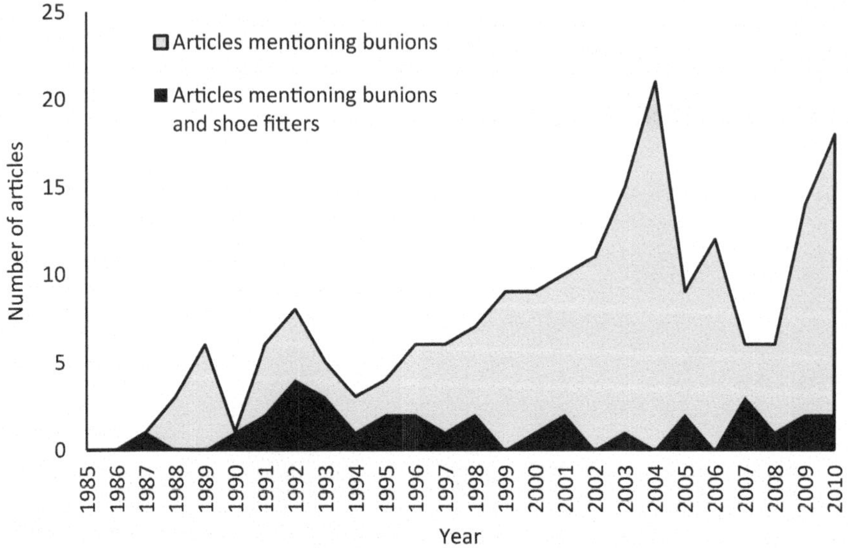

Fig. 7.1 Number of articles mentioning bunions and shoe fitters. *Source* Miura (2021, Figure 1, p. 47), modified by the author

the newspaper with the largest circulation, started publishing articles mentioning bunions more frequently, as shown in Fig. 7.1. Figure 7.1 also shows the number of articles that mentioned bunions and shoe fitters. Bunion-related articles mentioning shoe fitters were constantly published from 1987 to 2010, with the highest percentage occurring between 1987 and 1995. This suggests that shoe fitters played a significant role during the early years of growing public awareness about foot problems and health. These articles introduced shoe fitters as professionals who could treat foot problems by selecting shoes that best fit the consumer's feet. One article stated that "foot problems include shoe sores, bunions, inward bending of the big toe, and hammertoes, deformities of nail and bone. Shoe fitters are technicians and counselors who prevent these problems and ensure that the shoes fit properly to your feet" ("Anata no sentaku ketsudan" 1992).[1]

Additionally, owing to the initiatives by JIF and the spread of shoe fitter, people in the footwear industry and the medical community began taking an increased interest in the relationship between shoes and foot health and began disseminating their knowledge. Figure 7.2 shows the number of books published on the subject of shoes and their relationship with foot health, and the number of books by JIF among them. Since the publication of JIF's *Itai Kutsu wa Mō Hakanai* in 1984 (JIF 1984h), and the birth of the first certified shoe fitters in 1985, publications have increased. Figure 7.2 is based on data from CiNii Books, a cross-search database of

[1] Translated from Japanese by the author.

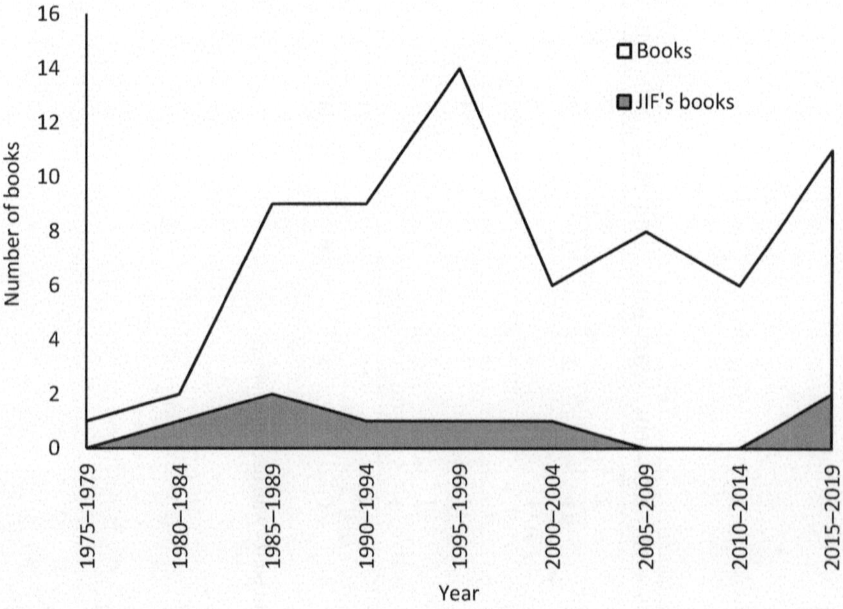

Fig. 7.2 Number of books published about shoes and health. *Sources* Prepared by the author based on Miura (2020) and CiNii Books

books held in Japanese university libraries.[2] CiNii Books does not cover all books published in Japan. However, as the books held by university libraries are expected to be of a certain quality, this database is well-suited to capture the most relevant books on foot health.[3] Table 7.1 lists the authors of these books, which include JIF, shoe-related companies, medical professionals, and researchers in home economics and developmental studies.

Given JIF's advanced nature, its initiatives were the starting point in improving awareness about foot health among consumers and experts in the footwear industry and medical community. As confirmed in Chap. 2, in the 1970s, research about

[2] Searching CiNii Books using "shoes" as the keyword showed 1,665 results, and they were narrowed down to 66 books related to shoes and foot health through Steps 1–5. 1. Exclude books with unknown year. 2. Exclude prewar and wartime books, i.e., books published before August 1945. 3. Exclude books thought to be unrelated to the footwear industry/shoe market based on the title (mainly literary works). 4. Exclude books that fall under (a) or (b) below based on the title. (a) Books unrelated to shoes and health: shoe directories introducing brand shoes, books on shoe care and polishing, books for footwear industry managers (management guidebooks, etc.), various surveys, research, and reports, etc. (b) Books related to shoes and health but not for the general public: books for medical and welfare workers, books devoted to sports, books devoted to children's shoes, etc. 5. Confirm whether the contents of the remaining books correspond to Steps 3 or 4 above, and narrow the remaining books down to those related to shoes and foot health.

[3] The search results for books belonging to the National Diet Library, which has the largest collection of publications published in Japan, are also consistent with Fig. 7.2, although the library has two books between 1945 and 1974, one in 1963 and one in 1971.

Table 7.1 Classification of book authors

	1975–1979	1980–1984	1985–1989	1990–1994	1995–1999	2000–2004	2005–2009	2010–2014	2015–2019
JIF associates		1	2	1	1	2			2
Shoe-related companies[a]			1	3	6	1	2	3	3
Medical associates[b]		1	4	5	6	1	6	4	5
Non-medical researchers[c]	1		1	1	2			1	
Journalists/writers				2	1	2			1
Other			1		2	1	2	1	
Unknown			1			1	1		
Total number of authors	1	2	10	12	18	8	11	9	11
Total number of books	1	2	9	9	14	6	8	6	11

Source Prepared by the author based on the same data as Fig. 7.2.
Notes Categorized according to colophons. The total numbers may not match Fig. 7.2 due to books with multiple authors
[a] Shoe manufacturing, wholesale, retail, materials, etc.
[b] Physicians, physical therapists, judo therapists, foot care specialists, etc.
[c] Researchers of home economics, developmental studies, leather, etc.

shoe and foot health was virtually non-existent, both in the footwear industry and at the university level, and a systematic framework of related knowledge had yet to take shape (Sugano 1975). There were also no foot-disorder specialists in the medical field at that time (Ōtsuka and Abe 1990). While there were orthopedists and prosthetists and orthotists (POs) in practice, they dealt with the entire body and did not necessarily have specific expertise in foot afflictions. Medical doctors established the Japanese Society for Medical Study of Footwear in 1987, 4 years after JIF's original SF Training Workshop and 2 years after the first certified shoe fitters. Therefore, JIF's initiatives prompted consumers and experts in the footwear industry and medical community to pay attention to foot health. A reciprocal cycle of influence then ensued. An increase in the number of shoe fitters in shoe stores led to more consumers and experts becoming aware of foot health, which encouraged more shoe retailers to employ shoe fitters. Thus, Japanese people became more aware of foot health.

7.2 Emergence of the Comfort Shoe Market: Intended Consequence of JIF's Initiatives

The increase in the number of shoe fitters in shoe stores and the improved consumer awareness about foot health gave rise to the comfort shoe market. Shoe manufacturers and shoe retailers saw a business opportunity in these changes and started to make and sell comfort shoes.

Today, the comfort shoe is a category in the Japanese shoe market. Although there is no clear definition of comfort shoes, shoes marked as comfort shoes claim to be good for foot health and typically have a low heel and wide toe. The players in the market category included manufacturers and wholesalers of shoes that consider foot health; retailers that carry such products, perform fittings, and provide shoes that fit each foot; and the consumers who seek shoes that fit them to address their foot problems. Since the mid-1980s, the footwear industry trade magazine, *Footwear Press,* has regularly featured the comfort shoe market.[4] The comfort shoe market was not affected by the collapse of the bubble economy in the 1990s; it was considered to be recession-proof ("Tokushū fukyō" 1992), and it continues to occupy a corner of the footwear industry.

Although comfort shoes did exist prior to shoe fitters, it was only after the shoe fitters became common that comfort shoes sold well and manufacturers began to make more comfort shoes (Takesawa 2005; "Zadankai" 2003). Making comfort shoes was attractive to manufacturers because the shoes sold well at high prices as a high-health-performance product owing to shoe fitters' services and consumers' growing interest in foot health. For example, comfort shoes priced from ¥10,000 (US$78)

[4] *Footwear Press* has repeatedly featured the comfort shoe market since February 1988 (e.g., "Item-betsu" 1988; "Item-betsu" 1994; "Tokushū comfort" 1988; "Tokushū fukyō" 1992; "Tokushū sonogo" 1991; "Zone" 1992).

to ¥20,000 (US$156) were listed in the comfort shoe purchasing guide for shoe retailers in 1988 ("Shiire" 1988).[5] Selling comfort shoes was attractive to small and medium-sized shoe retailers looking for a way to survive in the face of competition from shoe discount chains, as the shoes sold well at high prices based on shoe fitters' recommendations. Therefore, as the number of shoe retailers with shoe fitters (henceforth referred to as SF retailers) increased, shoe manufacturers increased their production of comfort shoes, and as the production of comfort shoes increased, the number of SF retailers and their comfort shoe offerings increased.

The main customers in the comfort shoe market are women in their 40s and older (Maeda 2003). Women often are less muscular than men, and they wear high-heeled pumps that do not support the instep; thus, their feet tend to get injured over time. Therefore, women are prone to foot problems as they age (Kobayashi 2017). If they have sufficient muscle strength for support, then they can wear shoes that are somewhat ill-fitting; otherwise, their shoes need to fit well, that is, they require shoes with a precise fit. Therefore, women who were middle-aged or older and had foot problems became customers of SF retailers. They bought comfort shoes, even at prices higher than for other shoes, because they wanted to solve their foot problems.

The emergence of the comfort shoe market was the indirect and intended consequence of JIF's initiatives. JIF successfully compelled shoe retailers to house shoe fitters, which led shoe manufacturers to produce comfort shoes. Therefore, JIF eventually succeeded in getting manufacturers to make shoes that emphasized health over fashion, which was its original objective.[6]

7.3 Insufficient Skills and Unmet Needs

This section discusses some of the problems with the shoe fitter system and unmet consumer needs. JIF popularized the shoe fitter to the footwear industry, which led to the emergence of the comfort shoe market. However, this did not solve all foot health problems.

Great expectations were placed on shoe fitters as foot health professionals by consumers who had increased foot health awareness. However, their techniques did not fully meet the needs of consumers: who wanted shoes that fit their feet with difficult problems, and sought trendy and fashionable options without enduring discomfort.

Although shoe fitters were recognized as shoe-fitting specialists by consumers, they also received criticism. Some journalists believed that the training offered was insufficient for shoe fitters to be considered specialists (Ōtsuka and Abe 1990; Ōya 1988). They also noted that a lack of expertise among shoe fitters would lead to inadequate services that could disappoint or even harm consumers (Ōtsuka and Abe

[5] The prices are calculated based on the dollar-yen rate in 1988.

[6] See Chaps. 4 and 5 on the transition of JIF's strategy.

1990). Some shoe fitters themselves recognized their lack of expertise ("Kouriten ni Interview" 1988; "Kouriten ni Kiku" 1988; Ōtsuka and Abe 1990).

However, JIF believed that shoe retailers were to blame for the lack of adequate training. JIF criticized trainees for not seeming eager to learn and only attending the SF Training Workshop to receive the certification (Ōya 1988). JIF believed that at least one week of training was necessary; however, shoe retailers argued that they could not leave their stores for that long. Therefore, JIF had to shorten the training program to 3 days.[7]

To address the training problems, JIF responded to requests from some diligent shoe fitters. However, the number of dedicated shoe fitters remained limited. JIF introduced a six-month advanced course in 1988 (Ōtsuka and Abe 1990). In 1992, out of 1,380 qualified shoe fitters, only 126 (9%) had completed the advanced course (JIF 1992a). In 1991, the two-year master's course was implemented for people who had completed the advanced course with 19 participants, exceeding the planned limit of 15. However, the applicants did not continue with the program, and the master's course ended after one run (Katō 2002).[8] Ultimately, only a few shoe fitters were eager to improve their skills as professional shoe fitters. Therefore, although shoe fitters were considered foot health professionals, in reality, they had limited expertise and skills. Thus, it is difficult to assume that all shoe fitters had strong technical abilities.[9]

Although inadequate shoe fitter education was one reason for customer dissatisfaction, from the perspectives of the shoe fitters, the customer's own misunderstandings also contributed to their dissatisfaction. Consumers mistakenly believed that shoe fitters could select shoes that would fit any foot, relieve pain completely, and solve any foot problem. More specifically, these misconceptions can be divided into two main types. First, customers sometimes came with serious problems ("Kouriten zadankai" 1988). As confirmed in Chap. 2, when an individual has serious foot problems, it becomes difficult to select a shoe that fits their foot perfectly. Asking shoe fitters to select a shoe that fits the foot and does not hurt, despite these constraints, was sometimes an unreasonable request because it was beyond the abilities of even decently skilled shoe fitters.

Second, some customers asked shoe fitters to find comfortable yet fashionable and trendy shoes. For example, some customers wanted shoe fitters to select high-heeled shoes that would not hurt their feet after wearing them all day ("Professional" 1988). However, wearing high-heeled shoes for prolonged periods can hurt the feet, even if the shoes fit properly. Therefore, JIF had consistently recommended that people vary their footwear according to setting and situation owing to the added load on the foot caused by wearing high-heeled shoes for extended periods of time (JIF 1988b, 1992b). When consumers asked for high heels that were comfortable and would not hurt their feet after long periods of wear without considering the use of other shoes in conjunction, shoe fitters could not satisfy their needs.

---

[7] Hiromu Yamamoto, former JIF executive director (interview by phone, December 8, 2015).

[8] The master's course was held again in 2019–2021.

[9] I do not deny the existence of shoe fitters who did not attend advanced courses but improved their skills through practice, self-study, or learning from other sources.

Together, shoe fitters' lack of skills and excessive consumer expectations make some consumers dissatisfied with the shoe fitters' services. Specifically, as established above, shoe fitters lacked the skills to deal with consumers who had major foot concerns and could not deal with consumers who wanted to wear fashionable and trendy high heels without pain.

Chapter 8
The European Comfort Shoe Market: Seeking Further Health Functions

This chapter describes and analyzes the emergence of the European comfort shoe market in Japan as one of the consequences of JIF's success. Comfort shoes imported from Europe were foreign to the Japanese shoe market and did not sell well at first. Although these shoes were good for foot health, they were unfashionable and expensive. However, demand for European comfort shoes began in the mid-1980s and the European comfort shoe market began to expand in the mid-1990s. Why and how did the European comfort shoe market emerge and expand?

This chapter responds to this question by clarifying the following points. Wholesalers importing comfort shoes from Europe thought that the shoes were of high quality for health purposes, but struggled to secure business partners. Therefore, the wholesalers invited an *orthopädieschuhmacher-meister* (master orthopedic shoemaker)[1] from Germany and other European countries to hold a seminar on how to adjust European comfort shoes to fit customers' feet by modifying the shoes and insoles. Some shoe retailers responded to this and became shoe adjuster (SA) retailers. The driving force behind shoe retailers was the presence of consumers with difficult foot problems that shoe fitters' techniques could not address. SA retailers wanted to improve their ability to address these concerns. As a result, the European comfort shoe market emerged.

The emergence of this market was an indirect effect of JIF's initiatives and their unintended consequence; however, while its emergence was unintended, the market still strictly pursued JIF's superordinate goal of foot health.

---

[1] The English translation is based on Baumgartner (2016).

This chapter is restructured and revised version of Miura, S. (2023). *Retail format innovation and survival of small stores: Evidence from the Japanese shoe trade, 1974–2022*. Institute of Current Business Studies of Showa Women's University Working Paper, (7), 1–34. http://swubizlab.jp/wp/wp-content/uploads/2023/03/2023miura.pdf.

S. Miura, *Successful Social Activism and Unintended Market Emergence*,
https://doi.org/10.1007/978-981-99-9291-1_8

8.1 Expansion of the European Comfort Shoe Market

There are no statistical materials that directly indicate the size of the European comfort shoe market in Japan. However, it is evident that import from Germany gradually increased after 1986 into the 1990s and experienced rapid growth from 1994 to 1999 (Fig. 8.1). Shoe imports from Germany can be as used an approximation of the European comfort shoe market in Japan. Germany established itself as a leader in foot health because of its extensive experience with injuries from World War I (Kuze 1999; Makiya 1997; Shimizu 1995).[2] Not all shoes imported from Germany are comfort shoes, while women's fashionable shoes, such as high heels, are imported mainly from France and Italy, and men's dress shoes are imported mainly from England and Italy; therefore, the shoes imported from Germany are primarily comfort shoes. Though comfort shoes were also imported from other countries, such as Switzerland, European comfort shoes primarily comprised of German comfort shoes. SA retailers have stated that European comfort shoes sold well from around the mid-1990s,[3] and the statements are consistent with the German shoe import value trends in Fig. 8.1. The European comfort shoe market can therefore be estimated to have generally expanded from the mid-1980s, with a rapid expansion in the mid- to late-1990s.

Although one reason for this growth was the deregulation of leather shoe imports, it alone cannot explain it. The number of imported leather shoes had been restricted by the import quota (IQ) system, but in April 1986, the tariff quota (TQ) system was implemented, and the number limit was removed. This allowed any quantity of imports if the tariff was paid—though the tariff rate was high (Appendix 3). However, the growth from the mid-1980s to the 1990s cannot be explained by the deregulation of leather shoe imports. During this time, the growth of imported German shoes increased even faster than the import of shoes overall, as shown in Fig. 8.2. Germany's share of the total value of shoe imports increased from 0.5% in 1985 to 1.5% in 1999.[4]

8.2 Features of European Comfort Shoes

European comfort shoes had such high functionality and quality that they were the model for Japanese comfort shoes. Typical European comfort shoes have a wide toe box that does not constrict the toes (Fig. 8.3). Additionally, the insole is shaped such

[2] As Germany is an advanced country in foot health (Kuze 1999; Makiya 1997; Shimizu 1995), many Japanese learned the technology in Germany and made domestic comfort shoes. For example, Pedx is a shoe brand that was developed by Yūichirō Suzuki, who was qualified as a master shoemaker in Germany ("Meister technology" 1992).

[3] Abe Kaoru, Professor at the Graduate School of Niigata University of Health and Welfare (interview, March 25, 2017); Shigehiro Sakata, owner of Shoe Laboratory Condor (email, June 25, 2019).

[4] Calculated by the author based on the same sources used for Fig. 2.11.

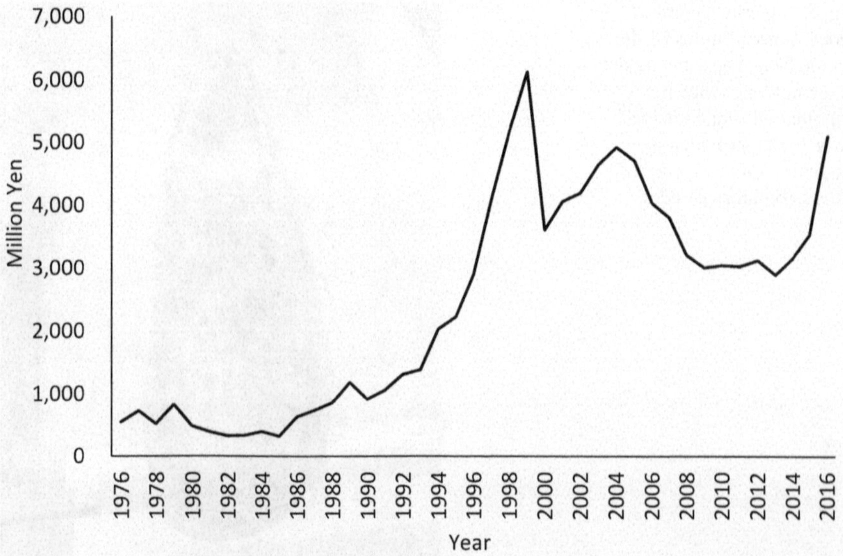

Fig. 8.1 Import value of shoes from Germany. *Source* Prepared by the author based on the same sources used for Fig. 2.11. *Note* Adjusted to real values as in Fig. 2.11, with 2010 = 1

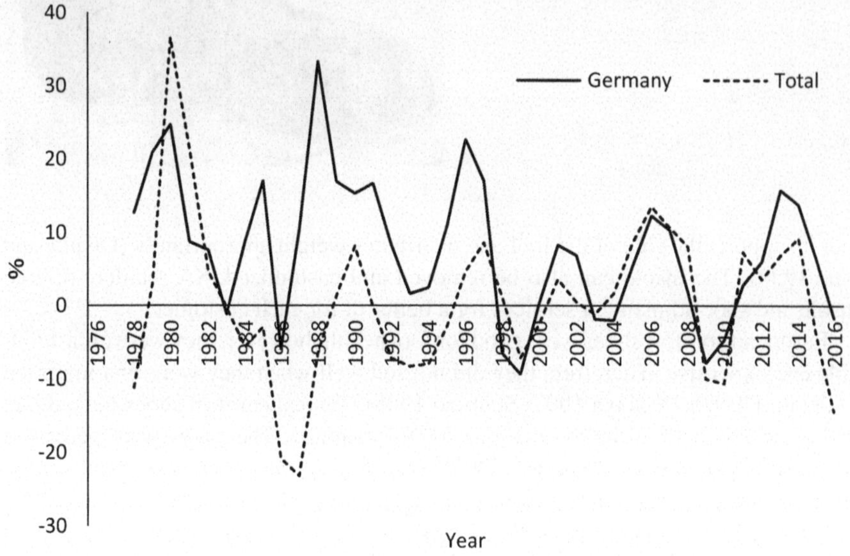

Fig. 8.2 Three-year compound annual growth rates of German shoe imports and total shoe imports. *Source* Prepared by the author based on the same sources used for Fig. 2.11. *Note* Adjusted to real values as in Fig. 2.11, with 2010 = 1

Fig. 8.3 German comfort shoes. *Source* Photos by the author. *Note* The same model as the first one Alice Inc. imported into Japan in the early 1980s, provided by Shigehiro Sakata, owner of Shoe Laboratory Condor

that it supports the sole of the foot and distributes weight appropriately (Ōtsuka and Abe 1990). The insole can also be removed and customized. SA retailers offered insole and shoe adjustment services for a better fit for each customer.

European comfort shoes were good for foot health; however, they were unfashionable and expensive. Therefore, they did not sell well when they were first imported in the mid-1980s (Makiya 1997; Shimizu 1995). Typical comfort shoes looked odd to Japanese people at the time (Fig. 8.3); for example, The shoes were perceived as looking like catfish ("Endoh" 2005). One female customer, who tried on the shoes at the Foot and Shoe Science Institute's store (an SA retailer) stated, "I'd rather die! I'm so embarrassed that I can't go to work [wearing these shoes]. I'd rather put up with pain" (Shimizu 1995, p. 153).[5] In addition, as these shoes were priced at around ¥30,000 (US$237), they were more expensive than Japanese comfort shoes, which were already considered expensive at approximately ¥20,000 (US$158)

[5] Translated from Japanese by the author. The square brackets were added by the author.

("Zone" 1992).[6] Kaoru Kuribayashi, President of Footmind, which later became an SA retailer, said, "imported shoes were about 30,000 yen (US$237)–40,000 yen (US$316) in monetary terms, and I had a hard time trying to find out who would pay 30,000 yen for badly shaped shoes" ("Zadankai" 2003, p. 23).[7]

Thus, it was impossible to sell these shoes unless retailers had the knowledge and skills that could help consumers understand their benefits. However, few such skillful shoe retailers existed, and few shoe retailers were willing to purchase shoes that were difficult to sell ("Endoh" 2005; "Interview Fuss und Schuh Institut" 1999; Shimizu 1995). Sumiko Tanaka of Schöne, which later became an SA retailer, said that she tried to stock European comfort shoes at the time, but she was unable to sell them well because she lacked knowledge about them.

> Even if we had Ganter shoes from Van San-Sho or something like that, they didn't sell well. We didn't even know how to sell them. Until then, the most expensive shoes we'd ever sold were around 30,000 yen (US$237), and the best-selling shoes were around 9,800 yen (US$77); that's about the range of shoes we sold. When you think about it, we were a store that sold *chemical shoes* (shoes made of artificial leather) that were cheaper, like at 4,000 (US$32), yen or 5,000 yen (US$39). We did not even know the features of those [European comfort] shoes. We were doing it, but they wouldn't sell, and we didn't put much effort into it.[8]

In this way, as European comfort shoes were initially a foreign presence in the Japanese shoe market, neither shoe retailers nor consumers paid much attention to them.

8.3 Import of German Comfort Shoes

Alice Christians was the first person to continuously and systematically import European comfort shoes to Japan. Christians, originally from Germany, taught German at Kobe Medical College (now Kobe University Graduate School of Medicine) in Kobe City, Hyogo Prefecture. Professor Daiji Kashiwagi, founder of the Division at Orthopedics of the college, asked Christians whether there were any good German shoes for his patients ("Interview, sōgyō" 1999).[9] Unable to find good shoes ideal for foot health in Japan, she established Alice Inc. in 1984 to import German comfort shoes ("Interview, sōgyō" 1999). She opened a small store to sell these shoes and

[6] The prices are calculated based on the dollar-yen rate in 1989. European comfort shoes were expensive even in their home countries because of their quality, and in addition, wholesalers had to pay high tariffs to import them into Japan ("Tokushū" 1988). See Appendix 3 for tariff rates on footwear.

[7] Translated from Japanese by the author. The parentheses were added by the author. The prices are calculated based on the dollar-yen rate in 1992.

[8] Sumiko Tanaka, former owner of Schöne (interview, January 15, 2020). Translated from Japanese by the author. The parentheses and square brackets were added by the author. The prices are calculated based on the dollar-yen rate in 1992.

[9] Mitsuko Makiya, former owner of Maki no Kutsu (interview, October 1, 2017).

started a small wholesale business. In 1987, she invited a master orthopedic shoemaker, Karl Heinz Schott, to offer comfort shoe- and insole-adjustment services both in her shop and for shoe retailers that stocked comfort shoes from Alice Inc. ("Interview, sōgyō" 1999). The title of master orthopedic shoemaker is a national qualification in Germany and German-speaking countries and is obtained by passing an examination after 7–8 years of classroom and practical training in shoemaking and orthopedics. Master orthopedic shoemakers craft orthopedic shoes and foot orthoses under a doctor's prescription.

Following Christians, some wholesalers started to import comfort shoes. Table 8.1 lists companies that began to import European comfort shoes by 1990. Although each company had a reason to start importing, they all recognized the high quality of German and other European comfort shoes that were different from Japanese shoes and saw them as a business opportunity. Other than Samco Sanei, all these companies were small and were either established specifically to import European comfort shoes or were only a few years old when they started importing them.

8.4 Start of Orthopedic Shoe Technique Seminars

Although the wholesale importers of European comfort shoes recognized the quality of European comfort shoes, the shoes did not sell well at first (Makiya 1997; Shimizu 1995). To sell European comfort shoes, import wholesalers started exhibitions, Comfort 21, in 1991 with Japanese comfort shoe manufactures and held it in Tokyo twice a year through the 1990s ("Kaitekigutsu o teiansuru" 1991; "Seikyōdatta 'comfort 21'" 1993; "Hitotsu ue" 1991; "Orthopedic shoes" 1994; "Dai 8-kai" 1995; "Dai 9-kai" 1995; "Dai 10-kai" 1996; "Dai 11-kai" 1996; "Dai 12-kai" 1997; "Dai 13-kai" 1997; "Dai 14-kai" 1998; "Dai 15-kai" 1998; "Dai 16-kai" 1999; "Dai 17-kai" 1999; "Dai 18-kai" 2000; "Dai 19-kai" 2000; "Dai 20-kai" 2001; "Dai 21-kai" 2001; "Dai 22-kai" 2002). In 2002, Comfort 21 was combined with the Import Shoes Fair ("ISF de" 2002).

Several European comfort shoe import wholesalers took further steps. Shimizu's Foot and Shoe Science Institute, Kuze's Schritt, and Endoh's Van San-Sho started orthopedic shoe technique seminars for shoe retailers. They wanted to build strong relationships with retail partners from both a commercial and moral standpoint. Commercially, a certain sales scale was necessary to sustain their European comfort shoe import business, as they were small importers (Kuze 1999).[10]

Morally, they wanted to help people with foot problems.[11] The diffusion of shoe fitters raised awareness of foot health; however, it revealed consumer needs that could not be met by shoe fitters. Some people had difficult foot problems beyond the

[10] Shōichi Shimizu, Director of Foot and Shoe Science Institute Co. Ltd, (interview, December 14, 2017).

[11] Paige and Littrell (2002) also found that the objectives of small retailing are not only commercial but also cultural or moral, based on the analysis of small craft retailers.

Table 8.1 European comfort shoe import wholesalers

Company	Founder	Year founded	Year European comfort shoe imports started	Reasons for starting to import European comfort shoes
Alice[a]	Alice Christians	1983	1983	She thought there were no good shoes in Japan, and a co-worker at Kobe Medical College, where she was teaching German, asked whether there were any good shoes in Germany for patients. She started to import **Solidus**
Samco Sanei[b]	Sanei Corporation	1975	1985	Sanei Corporation was founded as an export trading company of miscellaneous goods to Europe in 1946. Sensing the potential of **Birkenstock**, Samco Sanei, a subsidiary, became its sole Japanese distributor in 1985
Van San-Sho[c]	Michio Endoh	1981	1987	The company's shoe export business was ruined by the strong yen after the Plaza Accord in 1985. He found **Ganter** shoes comfortable at the Tokyo Shoe Fair in January 1987 and started importing them
Foot and Shoe Science Institute[d]	Shōichi Shimizu	1988	1988	The predecessor company had closed due to over-investment in the health-conscious shoe business. After meeting a master orthopedic shoe maker Karl Heinz Schott at Alice in 1987, Shimizu was impressed and invited him to restart the comfort shoe business together. Shimizu and Schott developed **Schott Shoes**

(continued)

Table 8.1 (continued)

Company	Founder	Year founded	Year European comfort shoe imports started	Reasons for starting to import European comfort shoes
Ōbāmain Japan[e]	Unknown	1988	1988	Sensing the opportunity for **Jacoform**, the founder quit a major domestic spinning company and started to import its shoes
Schritt (Alka)[f]	Yasuo Kuze	1990	1989	At Alka, a shoe retailer, Kuze, offered high-quality European shoes; however, they did not sell well. He knew that Germany was a leader in comfort shoes; therefore, he went there in 1987 and was impressed by its comfort and the master orthopedic shoe makers. He started importing comfort shoes, including **Spiess**, and founded Schritt as an import company

Sources Prepared by the author based on comfort shoes brand features and their exhibition features as published in *Footwear Press* between 1988 and 1992 ("Buying box" 1991; "Comfort shijō o semeru" 1989; "Comfort yūryoku, chūmoku brand" 1992; "Dakara kono brand wa" 1988; "Kaitekigutsu o teiansuru" 1991; "PR Special" 1988; "Shiire guide" 1988), and interviews

[a] Mitsuko Makiya, former owner of Maki no Kutsu (interview, October 1, 2017); "Interview, sōgyō" (1999)

[b] "Buyer's guide" (1990): "Comfort ni ikiru: Sapporo" (1991)

[c] "Buyer's guide" (1990); "Endoh Michio" (2005); "Tokyo" (1987)

[d] Shimizu (1995)

[e] Shigehiro Sakata, owner of Shoe Laboratory Condor (email, June 25, 2019)

[f] "Buyer's guide" (1990); "Interview hassō no genten" (2001); Mizuho Sōgō Kenkyūjo (2002); Ōya (1996a)

Note Brands in bold

ability of shoe fitters to solve and wanted the problem to be solved. Such dissatisfied consumers came to retail stores of European comfort shoe importers or inquired about the shoes from all over the country. Although European comfort shoe importers wanted to help solve consumers' problems, it was beyond their capacity to handle everything. They could not afford to open retail stores across the country. Therefore, they wanted retail partners with knowledge and skills to address the foot problems around the country (Kuze 1999; Shimizu 1999). Additionally, by having partners, they ultimately aimed to raise the awareness level among the Japanese regarding the functionality of these shoes and their benefits to foot health ("Interview" 2001; Kuze 1999; Mizuho Sōgō Kenkyūjo 2002; Shimizu 1999; Ōya 1996a).

To build strong relationships that would sustain their import business and address foot problems, Shimizu, Kuze, and Endoh viewed the master orthopedic shoemakers' knowledge and skills as ideal. With the necessary knowledge and skills, shoe retailers could sell European comfort shoes and address consumers' foot problems. Therefore, they began to offer orthopedic shoe technique seminars to shoe retailers, which were led by European master orthopedic shoemakers. To encourage shoe retailers to participate, importers praised the seminars as authentic and explicitly or implicitly distinguished them from shoe fitter training by saying that small participant groups received practical training from the masters through a course that took at least two years to complete ("Fukyō" 1995; Ōtsuka and Abe 1990). Most of the workshops were designed to last for several days each month. In between workshops, the participants learned on the job at their own stores, and their questions and concerns were addressed at the next seminar.

Specifically, Shimizu and Kuze were active in holding seminars from the beginning. They began orthopedic shoe technique seminar in 1989 (Shimizu 1995) and 1992 ("Schritt" 1992; "Wadai" 1994), respectively. Endoh started a short-term orthopedic shoe technique seminar in 1993, as he was initially cautious about holding an intensive orthopedic shoe technique seminar that had some medical aspects ("Interview" 1996). However, he began holding full-scale long-term seminars in 1997 ("Interview Fuss und Schuh Institut" 1999). Endoh said that studying orthopedics was necessary to deal with people whose concerns could not be addressed by shoe fitters.

> The fitting work of choosing the shoes that suit you from inventory is necessary for selling comfort shoes, but what happens to those who actually have foot problems? Instead of "we don't have shoes that fit," if you want to deal with it somehow, you need orthopaedic [knowledge and skills]. …We thought that, unlike shoe fitting, we should also study medical science. We thought it was necessary to create training opportunities for this and to study together, and started [the orthopedic shoe technique seminars] ("Zadankai" 2003, p. 24).[12]

8.5 Birth of SA Retailers

Some small and medium-sized shoe retailers perceived obtaining shoe- and insole-adjustment skills at the orthopedic shoe technique seminars held by wholesalers as opportunities. They searched for breakthroughs for both commercial and moral reasons. For commercial reasons, they viewed honing their shoe- and insole-adjustment skills and offering better-fitting shoes as ways to differentiate themselves from shoe discount chains and SF retailers. In the 1990s, SF retailers faced mounting competition. As described in Table 5.2, shoe fitters could be found in department stores as well as in small and medium-sized shoe retailers. The comfort shoe assortment was also being imitated by department stores. In addition, shoe discounters started to offer lower-priced versions of shoes that claimed to be comfortable ("Ryōhanten" 1989). In the face of this, some small and medium-sized shoe retailers joined orthopedic shoe technique seminars because they believed that while the shoe fitter certification and shoe assortment could be imitated, the higher skills could not (Joyochiiki Kenkyū Center 2009; Ōya 1996b).

For moral reasons, some small and medium-sized shoe retailers wanted to improve their skills to help customers who had difficult foot problems that shoe fitters could not

[12] Translated from Japanese by the author. The square brackets were added by the author.

address (Makiya 1997; Ōya 1996c). Solving customers' problems was their reward. Tanaka, the former owner of Schöne, an SA retailer, strove to acquire shoe- and insole-adjustment skills through trial and error both at seminars and outside of seminars because she believed helping customers with foot problems was meaningful. She stated:

> Ultimately, when someone says it hurts somewhere, I do my best, even just a little. I have built trust in this way. …I'd do this, and my customers would actually really appreciate it. …. It was a rewarding feeling, like my work was really useful to people.[13]

Michiko Kida, President of Alpha Miki, an SA retailer, also said that she had been studying to provide useful services to customers with serious foot problems.[14]

Because of these commercial and moral reasons, some small and medium-sized shoe retailers became SA retailers, even at great cost. The investment burden, including the cost of the orthopedic shoe technique seminars, European comfort shoe inventory, and adjustment equipment, was substantial.[15] Two SA retailers said that they had invested enough to build a house ("Kenkō" 2015).[16] However, these retailers devoted themselves to incorporating the orthopedic shoe technique and equipping it in their stores ("Kenkō" 2015). Through their studies, they became SA retailers with an assortment of European comfort shoes, not only offering shoes based on size, but also adjusting shoes and insoles as needed.

8.6 Growth of SA Retailers

The number of shoe retailers who had studied those skills for more than two years—that is, the number of SA retailers—in the 1990s was estimated to be between 50 and 70.[17] As the number of SA retailers increased and each increased their sales, import

[13] Sumiko Tanaka, former owner of Schöne. (interview, January 15, 2020). Translated from Japanese by the author.

[14] Michiko Kida, President of Alpha Miki (interview, October 4, 2018).

[15] Akiko Yoshiki and Hidetoki Yoshiki, owners of Alkomeister (interview, November 30, 2019); Kunihiko Tatesaka, President of Grace Co., Ltd. (interview, October 26, 2021); Mitsuko Makiya, former owner of Maki no Kutsu (interview, October 1, 2017); Takayuki Igari, former owner of Catch Ball (interview, November 29, 2019).

[16] Kunihiko Tatesaka, President of Grace Co., Ltd. (interview, October 26, 2021).

[17] The author estimated the number of retailers who had finished one or more orthopedic shoe technique seminars lasting for two or more years based on books and interviews (Kaoru Kuribaayshi, President of Footmind, interview, January 31, 2019; Kayo Kubota, Schritt, email, September 14, 2022; Kyoto University Hospital Kango Jissen Kaihatsu Center 2004; Masateru Teramoto, President of Monet Teramoto, interview, February 1, 2019; Sadayoshi Asahi, president of Kutsu no Asahiya, interview, November 8, 2021; Shimizu 1999; Yasuo Kuze, President of Alka and Schritt, interview, March 9, 2018; Van San-sho n.d). This is consistent with the documentation that about 50 shoe retailers participated in the IVO (International Association for Orthopaedic Shoe Technicians) World Congress 2000 in Friedrichshafen, Germany (Kaoru Kuribayashi, President of Footmind, interview, January 31, 2019).

sales increased, and Kuze's Schritt and Endoh's Van San-sho, the leading European comfort shoe import wholesalers, increased their sales. Total sales of Schritt and Van San-sho quadrupled from ¥550 million (US$4.3 million) in 1992 to ¥2.6 billion (US$24 million) in 2004 (Yano Research Institute 2009).[18] SA retailers and European comfort shoe import wholesalers grew the European comfort shoes market together. For consumers with difficult foot problems, small wholesalers provided European comfort shoes and the knowledge and skills of orthopedic shoe techniques, and the small shoe retailers attended the seminars and sold the shoes using acquired knowledge and skills at the seminars.

SA retailers tended not to be large-scale shoe retail chains, but were mostly small and medium-sized shoe retailers (Miura 2023). Their outstanding technical skills despite their small size are expressed by the fact that 30 SA retailers were recognized by nurses at Kyoto University Hospital Kango Jissen Kaihatsu Center as "retailers that you can consult about your foot problems" in a medical book (2004, p. 130).[19] The list of these 30 retailers is shown in Table 8.2.

Although the wholesalers' sales grew, they could not control or restrict the retailers. Retailers joined various wholesalers' orthopedic shoe technique seminars and purchased European comfort shoes from different wholesalers. Instead, SA retailers organized themselves; one of the most recognizable groups was German Orthopaedic Shoe Research (GOSR), which was founded in 1999 with 25 members ("Doitsu" 1999; Miura 2023). Those who had studied at orthopedic shoe technique seminars for more than two years could join GOSR. Members sometimes made joint purchases from wholesalers and foreign manufacturers. In addition, they continued to learn together from master orthopedic shoemakers, orthopedists, sports physicians, and other shoe, foot, or health experts and attended various medical conferences (German Orthopaedic Shoe Research, n.d.; Monet Teramoto, n.d.).

Although changes in membership have occurred, GOSR still continues these activities, and members still hone their skills through learning. According to Mutsuko Nishiyama, president of GOSR, shoe- and insole-adjustment techniques have been updated and differ from those during the time of its founding.[20] Members kept learning because the relationship between the foot and the shoe is inherently difficult and requires constant study, as seen in Chap. 2, and it is necessary to incorporate a variety of globally advancing techniques and knowledge in order to address customer concerns. Tanaka, the former owner of Schöne, said, "The more I do it, the deeper I go. At first I did it lightly, just enough to deal with the problem of bunions, but gradually I started getting more and more consultations for really difficult feet."[21] Further, Alpha Miki's Kida stated:

> It's that we're doing something that cannot be found anywhere else. …The more you do it, the more you get deeper into it, and the more you find that you don't know. Among these vague

[18] The prices are at the dollar–yen rate in 1992 and 2004, respectively.

[19] Translated from Japanese by the author.

[20] Mutsuko Nishiyama, Director of Kinboshi Shōten Co. Ltd. (interview, August 30, 2022).

[21] Sumiko Tanaka, former owner of Schöne (interview, January 15, 2020). Translated from Japanese by the author.

Table 8.2 SA retailers listed in Kyoto University Hospital Kango Jissen Kaihatsu Center (2004)

No	Name	Location
1	Alpha Miki	Sapporo, Hokkaido
2	Grace	Hachinohe, Aomori
3	Wohlsein	Yamagata, Yamagata
4	La Moustache	Shiogama, Miyagi
5	Catch Ball	Hitachinaka, Ibaraki
6	Hoshino Seika	Omama, Gunma
7	Schöne	Kuki, Saitama
8	Shoe Fit Sekine	Siki, Saitama
9	Danī Shoes	Yotsukaido, Chiba
10	Gluch	Koto-ku, Tokyo
11	Shoes Shimura	Setagaya-ku, Tokyo
12	Kurantsu	Nakano-ku, Tokyo
13	Alka	Toshima-ku, Tokyo
14	Shoe Shop Iwasaki	Katsushika-ku, Tokyo
15	Ortho Fits	Musashino, Tokyo
16	Profit Iijima	Yokohama, Kanagawa
17	Wakamatsu Kutsuten	Yokosuka, Kanagawa
18	Nosaka Kutsuten	Kanazawa, Ishikawa
19	Kutsu no Asahiya	Nagano, Nagano
20	Alkomeister	Nagoya, Aichi
21	Foot and Shoe Science Institute	Nagoya, Aichi
22	Foot Balance	Anjo, Aichi
23	Comfort Shoes Frau	Kyoto, Kyoto
24	Foot Create	Kyoto, Kyoto
25	Room-9 Nishiyama Kutsu Kenkyūjo	Ikeda, Osaka
26	Monet Teramoto	Osaka, Osaka
27	Matsuya	Wakayama, Wakayama
28	Spross Mikki Dō	Mihara, Hiroshima
29	Nakamura	Fukuyama, Hiroshima
30	Maki no Kutsu	Naha, Okinawa

Source Kyoto University Hospital Kango Jissen Kaihatsu Center (2004, pp. 130–131), translated and modified by the author

areas, if you do not make at least part of this something you know, then I think customers also won't feel relieved, and I would feel worried, and I can't do something that sloppy. So, I do it in my own way. There really are so many things that I don't know. …Ultimately, it feels like there is the beginner, intermediate, and advanced levels, and once the master [orthopedic] shoemaker seminars are over, the question is what to do afterwards. But the world keeps on moving forward, and various things are happening, and if it ends with just that, then it feels a bit grim.[22]

The nurses at Kyoto University Hospital discovered GOSR in the process of searching for reliable shoe retailers for their patients, and consequently, 30 shoe retailers, comprising 26 GOSR members and four other shoe retailers, were listed in the medical book as SA retailers (Kyoto University Hospital Kango Jissen Kaihatsu Center 2004), as shown in Table 8.2.

8.7 Customers of SA Retailers

Despite having an assortment of mainly European comfort shoes and offering advanced adjustment techniques in common, the individual SA retailers and their customers were diverse. However, their most common customers were women in their 40s and older.[23] Just as SF retailers had a customer base of middle-aged and older women who tended to have foot problems due to aging (Kobayashi 2017; Maeda 2003; Takesawa 2005; "Zadankai" 2003), the same was true for SA retailers. Put differently, SA retailers served middle-aged women with difficult foot problems that shoe fitters were unable to address.[24] Additionally, a certain number of people experience heavy foot deformities and heavy pain regardless of age or gender. SA retailers have also responded to such people, sometimes in collaboration with medical doctors (Kyoto University Hospital Kango Jissen Kaihatsu Center 2004; Monet Teramoto n.a.; Zadankai 2003).[25]

[22] Michiko Kida, President of Alpha Miki (interview, October 4, 2018). Translated from Japanese by the author. The square brackets were added by the author.

[23] Akiko Yoshiki, Alkomeister (interview, November 30, 2019); Shigehiro Sakata, owner of Shoe Laboratory Condor (interview, September 28, 2019); Sumiko Tanaka, former owner of Schöne (interview, January 15, 2020); Wataru Tatesaka, President of Grace (interview, October 26, 2021).

[24] In Japan, POs have also been refining their skills related to orthopedic footwear and foot orthoses based on the techniques of master orthopedic shoemakers (Madono 2002). However, the introduction of master orthopedic shoemakers' technology to POs was later than to shoe retailers (Kaoru Abe, interview, March 25, 2017). Orthopedic shoe technique seminars by European comfort shoe importers for retailers were first started by Shimizu in 1989, but it was not until 1994 that the first workshop specializing in orthotic footwear was held by the Japan Orthotics Prosthetics Association. By 2002, more than 80 people had completed the course. However, this was only 7% of the total number of 1,122 POs as of 2002 (Association for Technical Aids n.d.). Furthermore, only a limited number of those POs specialize in orthotic footwear, less than 1% of the total POs (Madono 2002). In other words, while the medical field had been inadequate in dealing with foot problems, SA retailers had addressed such problems (Ōya 1996b).

[25] Michiko Kida, President of Alpha Miki (interview, October 4, 2018).

8.8 Summary

8.8.1 Rise of the European Comfort Shoe Market

This chapter described how and why the spread of shoe fitters to shoe retailers by JIF's activities and the emergence of the domestic comfort shoe market contributed to the rise of the European comfort shoe market in Japan. JIF's initiatives increased the Japanese people's awareness of foot health, but the skills of shoe fitters were not fully developed. This gave rise to a consumer need for a solution to a difficult foot problem that could not be solved by the shoe fitter's technique.

Wholesalers saw an opportunity in European comfort shoes and started importing them. However, although European comfort shoes were of high quality for health, they were not fashionable and they were expensive; therefore, they did not sell immediately. Selling European comfort shoes required knowledge and skill. As a result, some import wholesalers invited master orthopedic shoemakers from Europe to hold seminars on orthopedic shoe techniques.

Some small and medium-sized retailers saw an opportunity here. It had become difficult to differentiate simply by acquiring the shoe fitter certification and stocking Japanese-made comfort shoes, so improving skills and handling European comfort shoes were the means of differentiation. These approaches were also a way to assist people who were not satisfied with shoe fitters. They learned at the orthopedic shoe technique seminars. Thus, SA retailers were born.

The combination of consumer needs and the activities of European comfort shoe importers and SA retailers led to the emergence of the European comfort shoe market.

8.8.2 The Market Unintended by JIF but Rigorously Pursuing Foot Health

The change in behavior of shoe retailers becoming SA retailers was not what JIF had demanded of shoe retailers. JIF wanted shoe retailers to acquire shoe fitter certifications in the SF Training Workshop and provide fitting services at stores. However, some small and medium-sized shoe retailers desired to enhance their skills and knowledge beyond those of shoe fitters. In response, they attended orthopedic shoe technique seminars and became SA retailers, offering shoe- and insole-adjustment services in addition to shoe selection services. JIF did not ask shoe retailers to become SA retailers; however, this shift was consistent with JIF's superordinate goal of protecting the health of Japanese feet. That is, this shift reflected an unintended behavioral change among shoe retailers, which were JIF's target companies, but the result was consistent with JIF's superordinate goal.

JIF also did not intend to encourage awareness and behavioral changes among consumers who became customers of SA retailers. JIF's assumption was that consumers would become aware of foot health and would then choose shoes that fit their feet at stores with shoe fitters. JIF did not expect that some consumers would be dissatisfied with the selection of shoes by the shoe fitters and would seek advanced solutions. However, these changes in consumer needs and behaviors were triggered by JIF initiatives, and although they were not what JIF intended, they were consistent with JIF's superordinate goal of protecting foot health.

SA retailers and consumers were connected with European comfort shoe importers to create the European comfort shoe market. This market, in which SA retailers with advanced shoe- and insole-adjustment skills cater to consumers with difficult foot problems, was not what JIF intended. However, when considering JIF's superordinate goal of protecting foot health, the market was in line with the superordinate goal.

The case of the European comfort shoe market shows that influenced by the success of the SMO's initiative, target companies and consumers respond in their own way—a shift that the SMO did not intend—and their behavior results in the emergence of a new market category. The case demonstrates that despite not being intended by the SMO, the market category rigorously pursuing the SMO's superordinate goals may emerge.

Chapter 9
The Walking Support Insole Market: Moving Toward Walking Support

This chapter and the next analyze the impact of the success of JIF's activities on the insole market.[1] The heightened interest in foot health, triggered by the spread of shoe fitters, led to behavioral changes among insole manufacturers, who were beyond JIF's initial target of shoe retailers, and consumers. Due to their chain of actions, the insole market shifted in a direction consistent with JIF's superordinate goal—foot health—in the late 1990s, and the market gradually changed its path and became oriented toward a direction—fashion—that was inconsistent with JIF's superordinate goal in the 2000s.

This chapter deals with the period from the establishment of the insole market in the 1970s in Japan to the establishment and growth of the walking support insole category in the late 1990s. The market's focus shift from hygienic insoles to walking support insoles is discussed and the reasons behind this shift are analyzed. In summary, as the hygienic insole market peaked in the 1990s, insole manufacturers launched walking support insoles for women as alternatives to hygienic insoles for men, and the walking support insole category was established. Behind the success of walking support insoles among women was the heightened awareness of foot health, which was triggered by JIF and shoe fitters. This, in turn, boosted the establishment and growth of the overall walking support insole market category.

[1] Insoles refer to inserts added to finished shoes, not inserts sewed to the upper leather during the manufacturing process.

This chapter is restructured and revised version of Miura, S. (2021). The developmental history of the insole market in Japan: Rising health consciousness and an unintended shift toward fashion (1984–2010). *Japanese Research in Business History*, *38*, 43–61. doi:https://doi.org/10.5029/jrbh.38.43.

S. Miura, *Successful Social Activism and Unintended Market Emergence*,
https://doi.org/10.1007/978-981-99-9291-1_9

9.1 Insole Market Change in Terms of New Product Introductions and Market Size

The mainstream focus of the insole market changed from hygienic insoles to walking support insoles in the late 1990s. Changes in the market are confirmed based on the number of new insole products that were introduced. A new product database was created from insole articles published in three major economic newspapers, the *Nihon Keizai Shimbun*, *Nikkei Ryutsu Shimbun (Nikkei MJ)*, and *Nikkei Sangyo Shimbun*. Based on the database, the new products were classified by function (Table 9.1). Various companies introduced various insoles; therefore, it is unlikely that these newspapers covered all the new products. However, this database is sufficiently useful for identifying long-term trends in the insole market for two reasons. First, owing to their focus on economics-related content, these publications should offer more comprehensive coverage of new insole products than other newspapers. Second, the listed products were noteworthy and suitable for the limited space available; thus, determining trends in the insole market should be possible.

Table 9.1 shows that new mainstream products changed from hygienic insoles to walking support insoles. In the 1970s and 1980s, insoles with hygienic functions were the most common new product, with functions such as eliminating odor or increasing breathability by using deodorizing, antibacterial, or breathable materials. Beginning in the mid-1990s, the number of insoles with walking support functions increased and in the 2000s, the number of new walking support product introductions exceeded those of hygienic insoles. Walking support insoles emphasize walking support through shock absorption, pain-mitigating functions, and/or improved walking balance using shock-absorbing materials and insoles molded to match the bottom of the wearer's foot. Insoles with cold-resistant and relaxation functions were introduced in small numbers but steadily in each period. Cold-resistant insoles generate heat using far-infrared rays or have a heat-retaining function derived from their wool or cashmere materials. Insoles with relaxation functions improved circulation by applying pressure to specific points or using far-infrared rays.

The expansion of the walking support insole category can be confirmed even on a monetary basis (Fig. 9.1), although the size of the market before 1995 is unknown. As the overall insole market shrank, the market for women's insoles grew. This category saw its market share rise from 14% in 1995 to 33% in 2010. This growth was brought about by walking support insoles that eliminate problems that occur while walking (Fuji Keizai 1999, 2000, 2001, 2002, 2003, 2006, 2007, 2010; "Hīrugutsu" 2006).

9.2 Hygiene Insoles: Birth of the Insole Market

In postwar Japan, the insole was not a product but rather an ancillary service of shoes. Shoe retailers offered insoles to customers buying dress shoes as free add-ons for making size and fit adjustments easily (Fuji Keizai 2002, 2003). Shoe care and shoe-related material manufacturers, such as Morito, Columbus, and Kihara Sangyo,

Table 9.1 Number of new insole products by function

Function	1975–1979	1980–1984	1985–1989	1990–1994	1995–1999	2000–2004	2005–2009	2010–2014	2015–2019
Hygiene	9	6	27	15	21	11	7	6	4
Cold resistance	2	3	5	7	3	1	2	1	0
Walking support	0	0	6	5	17	27	32	21	13
Relaxation	0	2	1	4	6	4	4	1	0
Others	0	0	0	1	3	7	3	3	3
Unknown	2	1	1	0	0	1	0	0	0
Total	13	12	40	32	50	51	48	32	20

Source Prepared by the author based on *Nihon Keizai Shimbun*, *Nikkei Ryutsu Shimbun* (*Nikkei MJ*), *Nikkei Sangyo Shimbun*, and Miura (2021, Table 1, p. 51)
Note A total of 1,679 articles were searched for *nakajiki* (shoe insert) or *insōru* (insole) on Nikkei Telecom, the database of *Nikkei* newspapers, and those that were not newly launched insoles were excluded. Duplicates were also excluded. For products that featured multiple functionalities, the main function was identified based on the title and text of the article(s)

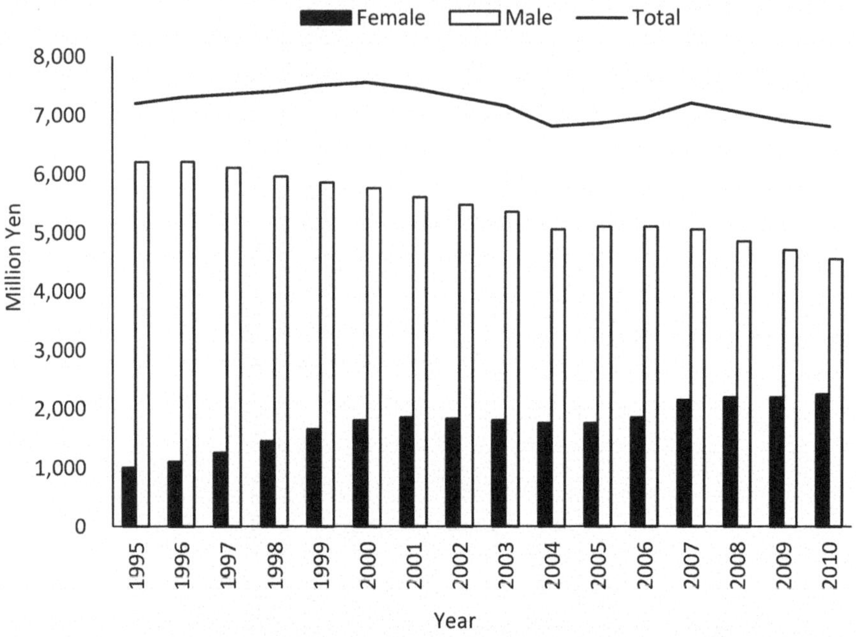

Fig. 9.1 Trends in insole market size. *Source* Miura (2021, Fig. 2, p. 50), modified by the author

sold them wholesale to shoe specialty stores and shoe sections of department stores (Fuji Keizai 2002, 2003).

However, the dynamics changed in the mid-1970s when Chūō Bussan began selling "Odor-Eaters" (manufactured by Combe Incorporated, a US company) in 1976 and a separate market for insoles was born ("Chūō Bussan" 1976; Fuji Keizai 1999). In the 1980s, Odor-Eaters became more visible when Kobayashi Pharmaceutical, a health and medical sundries manufacturer, took over the brand and ran a string of TV commercials advertising the products (Fuji Keizai 2000). Kobayashi Pharmaceutical's close relationships with general merchandise stores, supermarkets, drug stores, and home improvement centers led to the corporation's products spreading to their sales floors.

With the success of Odor-Eaters, various companies developed hygienic insoles ("Kutsu no nakajiki" 1990) and the number of new products increased in the late 1980s, as shown in Table 9.1. For example, Kobayashi Pharmaceutical launched Combe's "Odor-Eaters Kawa-Shibo" (Odor-Eaters leather texture) in 1986 ("Kutsu no nakazoko" 1986). This hygienic insole used a material that looked like leather to hide the fact that it was a deodorant insole. Shoe-related material companies also introduced hygienic insoles. In 1986, Morito released the "Saran Insole Leather Type," which had a leather-like surface ("Kutsu no nakajiki" 1990). In 1987, Columbus launched "Fragrant," which had antibacterial properties and a pleasant smell ("Hana" 1987). Hence, hygienic insoles for men's dress shoes became the dominant product category in the market in the 1980s and the 1990s.

9.3 Walking Support Insoles: Savior of the Mature Market

In the early 1990s, the insole market was mature and insole companies began to explore new directions ("Kutsu no nakajiki" 1990). Kobayashi Pharmaceutical launched its first walking support insole in 1992. This was the "Odor-Eaters Yōtsū Taisaku" (Odor-Eaters countermeasure for lower back pain), which absorbed heel impact when walking to relieve lower back pain ("Shōgeki" 1992). Kobayashi Pharmaceutical's insoles had specialized in products for businessmen; therefore, the insole was for men. It subsequently developed the walking support insole for women in 1993—"Odor-Eaters Gaihanboshi Taisaku" (Odor-Eaters countermeasure for bunions) ("Biyō" 1994; "Kobayashi" 1994). Kobayashi Pharmaceutical was concerned because of its relative lack of experience with insoles for women; however, the insoles sold surprisingly well. Over 130,000 insoles were sold in one year, within four months of the release.[2] Bunions are when the big toe turns outward (toward the other toes) and causes pain. This insole had a partially protruding shape to maintain the position of the foot bone and avoid excessive pressure on the big toe.

Because of this success, various companies found business opportunities in insoles that provided walking support for women (Fuji Keizai 1999; Sugawara 1999), and the number of new products increased in the late 1990s, as shown in Table 9.1. For example, in 1994, Scholl Japan, which sold sanitary and medical sundries, released "Back Ease," an insole designed to prevent back pain by absorbing the impact on the heel when walking ("Nakajiki tsukai" 1994).[3] In 1996, Kobayashi Pharmaceutical launched "Odor-Eaters Hizatsū Taisaku" (Odor-Eaters knee pain prevention), which slightly raised the outside of the foot to keep the knee straight to reduce knee pain caused by bowed legs ("Nakajiki" 1996). Shoe-related companies also introduced walking support insoles. For example, Columbus introduced the "Shoe Fitter Insole" in 1995 to make the shoe size fit perfectly ("Ashi ni au" 1995), and the "Shoe Fitter Sandal Yō" (an insole for sandals named Shoe Fitter) in 1997 to prevent the foot from slipping forward in high-heeled shoes ("Sandal to ashi" 1997). In 1999, Morito launched "Comfort Zone," which allowed wearers to mold their own insoles to fit their feet ("Kutsu no nakajiki" 1999).

Futoki Yabuki, Director of customer service operations at Morito, which was the top insole manufacturer in Japan at the time, noted the company's product

[2] Calculated by the author based on "Gaihanboshi" (1993) and "Kutsu no nakajiki" (1990).

[3] Scholl Japan has undergone several name changes as the result of mergers and acquisitions of its parent company. The organization was established as Scholl Japan in 1988 and it has been called Seton Scholl Japan (from 1998 to 2000), SSL Healthcare Japan (from 2000 to 2010), and Reckitt Benckiser (from 2010 to current). For the sake of simplicity, I use the name Scholl Japan to refer to the organization throughout the book. For the history of Scholl, see Hensmans et al. (2013).

diversification outlook and growth expectations for the insole market in 1999, as follows:

> It is not possible to meet the diversification of demand without having abundant item-s…Although the size of the market is not comparable to that of the shoe market, the demand is rapidly increasing and we have high expectations for the market to continue to grow (Sugawara 1999, p. 145).[4]

Though not included in this statement, the corporation's hit products at the time were walking support insoles. Specifically, these included "Foot Assist" for blisters, calluses, and shoe sores, "Foot Support" for shock-absorbing pads, and "Foot Helper" for hallux valgus and metatarsal bone placement (Sugawara 1999). Morito, therefore, planned to enhance its products in anticipation of the expansion of the walking support insole market.

SF and SA retailers as well as large variety store chains, such as Tokyu Hands and Loft, actively stocked and sold walking support insoles from the outset (Sugawara 1999). While a large variety store chains sold insoles with self-service, the SF and SA retailers selected insoles and processed them according to the customer's foot problems (Sugawara 1999). These stores sold insoles and made adjustments because they believed that adjusting insoles in addition to selecting comfortable shoes could solve foot problems, and it would be an effective way to differentiate themselves from other shoe stores (Asahara 2004; "Insole hanbai" 2006; "Kyakutanka" 2009; Sugawara 1999). Some insole manufacturers based in the footwear industry offered training workshops on insoles for shoe retailers for the proper use of their insoles (Fuji Keizai 2000; "MD guide" 2003). Many consumers did not know which insole to choose to alleviate their foot problems from various products (Aasahara 2001). Therefore, recommendations by SF and SA retailers helped customers' and thus they encouraged the emergence of the walking support insole market.

9.4 Tailwind of Growing Foot Health Awareness

The establishment of the walking support insole market in the 1990s was supported by the growing interest in foot health (Fuji Keizai 1999, 2000, 2001, 2002, 2003, 2006, 2007, 2010). In the late 1980s and 1990s, consumers' awareness of foot health grew, as discussed in Chap. 7. With JIF's activities and the resulting shoe fitter as a trigger, the latent needs for foot health of the consumer became apparent. Women began to want to walk comfortably and seek out ways of eliminating, and not simply tolerating, foot pain, trouble, or fatigue (Asahara 2001; "Item-betsu" 2010). The following fact supports this observation. Kobayashi Pharmaceutical's "Odor-Eaters Gaihanboshi Taisaku" (Odor-Eaters countermeasure for bunions), which was introduced for women in 1993, triggered the establishment of the walking support insole market; however, Kobayashi Pharmaceutical was not the first company to introduce

[4] Translated from Japanese by the author.

insoles with walking support functions in Japan. Scholl Japan was the pioneer of walking support insoles in Japan and had been marketing these products since the 1980s ("MD guide" 2003; Sugawara 1999). However, it was only in the 1990s that walking support insoles were established as a market category and expanded, as shown in Table 9.1. Thus, walking support insoles have sold well since foot health awareness was raised by JIF's initiatives.

Beyond middle-aged and older women, who often suffered from foot problems due to weakened muscles, young women in their teens, 20s, and 30s became interested in foot care, including insoles that enabled comfortable walking (Asahara 2001, 2002; Sugawara 1999). For example, Hiroshi Yoshino, the manager of Ortho Fits, an SA retailer, described changes in the customer base, "People who look at care products with interest and buy them quickly and easily are young women" (Sugawara 1999, p. 143).[5] Ayako Konuma, who was in charge of sales in the women's shoes section of Nihonbashi Takashimaya, a department store, indicated that both old and young people came to buy insoles, saying, "young people often come to buy single items, and older people tended to come to buy them saying that they were tired after walking" (Asahara 2002, p. 87).[6] Although newspapers and magazines did not mention it much, the low price of insoles, from a few hundred to a thousand yen, was another reason for the entry of young women into the walking support insole market. In response to the growing awareness of foot health, walking support insoles emerged as products that young women could afford. As young women have less trouble with their feet than middle-aged and older women, they have no reason to pay high prices for expensive European and domestic comfort shoes with higher health benefits. Insoles offered them reasonable comfort at a low price.

Sensing the growing demand from women for foot comfort, insole manufacturers anticipated strong sales and introduced new walking support insoles and large variety store chains and SF and SA retailers promoted the products (Sugawara 1999; Asahara 2001). The increased insole varieties attracted consumers and ensured strong sales, which led manufacturers to ramp up the introduction of more products (Asahara 2002; "MD-guide" 2003) and retailers to stock and sell the products (Asahara 2001). Hence, given the virtuous cycle of supply enhancement and demand stimulation, the walking support insole market expanded (Asahara 2001, 2002; Sugawara 1999).

9.5 Summary

This chapter elucidated that there was a change in the mainstream trend of the insole market in terms of product functionality. The emergence of hygienic insoles established an independent insole market in the 1970s, making them a mainstream product.

---

[5] Translated from Japanese by the author.

[6] Translated from Japanese by the author.

Walking support insoles have grown as a new category since the mid-1990s. As the insole market matured in the 1990s, women's walking support insoles were discovered by insole manufacturers seeking new product directions. Walking support insoles sold well among women, and manufacturers and retailers saw this as an opportunity, resulting in an increase in the number of products. The heightened awareness of foot health, triggered by JIF's activities, supported the emergence of the walking support insole market.

JIF did not intend to give rise to the walking support insole market; however, it emerged as a result of the indirect effect of JIF's initiatives. JIF did not aim for its target companies, shoe retailers, to carry walking support insoles, and it did not target insole manufacturers and variety stores. However, these behavioral changes in the target and non-target companies emerged in response to consumers' growing health consciousness, which was triggered by JIF. The walking support insole market category was consistent with JIF's superordinate goal of protecting and promoting foot health. It had evolved as a complementary goods market to the shoe market to make shoes fit better.

However, since 2000, walking support insoles have become a fashion accessory that prioritizes fashion over health (Miura 2021). The next chapter confirms this change and discusses how it occurred.

Chapter 10
The Fashion-Oriented Transparent Insole Market: Fashioning Walking Support Insoles

The previous chapter discussed how the insole market shifted in the direction of foot health in the late 1990s. However, since 2000, there has been an increase in walking support insoles that emphasize fashionable qualities while promoting comfort (Miura 2021). This chapter explains this transformation. Insole manufacturers that had been making walking support insoles developed transparent insoles to solve the problem of shoe sores and blisters that occur when wearing trendy shoes, such as high-heeled mules, which had become very popular among young women. When transparent insoles became popular, beauty, health, and hygiene goods suppliers found an opportunity to enter the market. Consequently, the number and variety of fashionable insoles increased. Variety stores and drugstores were also highly motivated to supply them because they felt that there was a growing demand for them among young women who wanted to wear fashionable and trendy high-heeled shoes without enduring pain. The fashion-oriented transparent insole market was formed by these beauty, health, and hygiene goods suppliers, variety stores and drugstores, and young women.

The emergence of the fashion-oriented transparent insole market as an indirect and unintended effect of JIF's initiatives was inconsistent with JIF's superordinate goal. The market dealt with insoles that were somewhat questionable in terms of their health function, particularly because the market served as the complementary goods market for high-heeled mules, sandals, and pumps, which prevent a balanced gait.

This chapter also summarizes the discussion developed in Part III on the emergence of three markets as indirect effects of JIF's success, clarifies the contributions

---

This chapter is restructured and revised version of Miura, S. (2021). The developmental history of the insole market in Japan: Rising health consciousness and an unintended shift toward fashion (1984–2010). *Japanese Research in Business History*, *38*, 43–61. doi:https://doi.org/10.5029/jrbh.38.43.

S. Miura, *Successful Social Activism and Unintended Market Emergence*,
https://doi.org/10.1007/978-981-99-9291-1_10

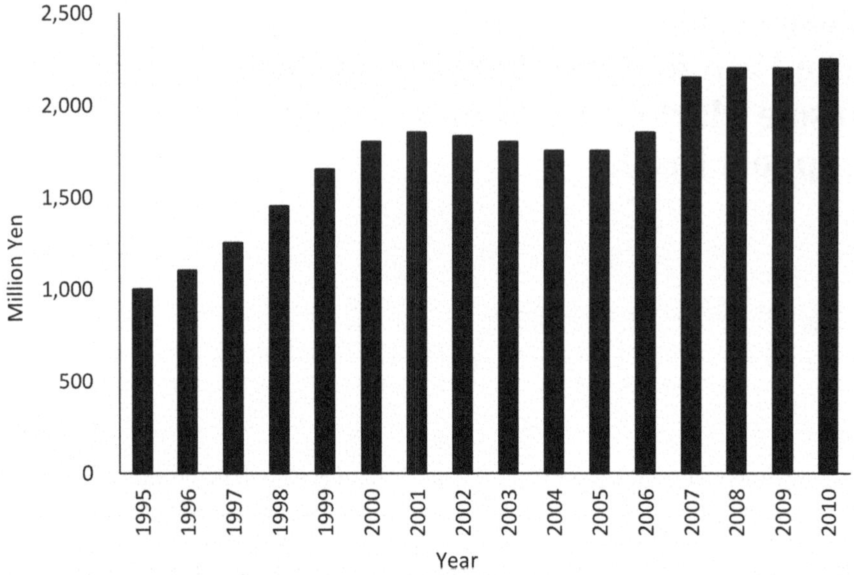

Fig. 10.1 Trends in female insole market size. *Source* Same as Fig. 9.1

of this study, and discusses the research implications on the indirect effect of activism targeting companies.

10.1 Fashion-Oriented Transparent Insoles Revitalize the Market

The market research firm Fuji Keizai points out that the abundance of fashion-oriented transparent insoles reignited and sustained momentum in the women's insole market that had been stagnant since the turn of the century, as shown in Fig. 10.1 (Fuji Keizai 2007, 2010; "Mono" 2009). A vivid example of its success is how the transparent insoles, all in exquisite packaging, lined an entire wall of Sony Plaza Ginza, a variety store in the Sony Building in Ginza, Tokyo, the most high-end shopping district in Japan in the late 2000s ("Mono" 2009).[1] The number of products introduced indicates that the number of transparent insoles increased in the 2000s. Table 10.1 shows the number of new transparent insole products among walking support insole products. As already mentioned in Chap. 9, the new products mentioned in the three *Nikkei* newspapers did not cover all the new insoles launched; however, the trend of increasing numbers of transparent walking support insoles can be implied by the results.

[1] Tōichirō Maeda, President of Arakawa Sangyo Co., Ltd. (interview, May 10, 2021).

Table 10.1 Number of new transparent insole products among walking support insole products

	1980–1984	1985–1989	1990–1994	1995–1999	2000–2004	2005–2009	2010–2014	2015–2019
Walking support	0	6	5	17	27	32	21	13
Transparent (%)	0 (0)	0 (0)	0 (0)	2 (12)	6 (22)	8 (25)	10 (48)	1 (8)

Source Same as Table 9.1

Tomoko Hamaoka, a researcher of Fuji Keizai, attributes the products' success to a blend of functionality and fashion, which together met the needs of young women ("Mono" 2009). Fuji Keizai noted that the market gradually grew as more and more companies started making products to meet the emerging demand ("Mono" 2009).[2] Indeed, transparent insoles were fashionable while touting a walking support function through shock absorption and/or anti-slide benefits. They were fashion-oriented in three ways: they were designed to be used in trendy shoes, such as high-heeled mules, sandals, or pumps; they were transparent and therefore inconspicuous when shoes were taken off; and the products were exquisite.

The fashionable qualities of the product itself, such as the brand name, shape, and color, were evident when compared with those of the early walking support insoles that increased in popularity in the 1990s. The names of fashion-oriented transparent insoles emphasized cuteness and beauty. For instance, there was Scholl Japan's "Party Feet" series ("Tsumasaki" 2004); Kowa's "Cute Step Gel Pad" series ("Jūshin idō" 2010); and Serendip's "Insole de Bikyaku" (Insole for beautiful legs) ("Lame" 2011). In contrast, the walking support insoles from the 1990s that were discussed in Chap. 9 had names that emphasized health functions. For instance, Kobayashi Pharmaceutical's "Odor-Eaters Hizatsu Taisakuū Taisaku" (Odor-Eater knee pain prevention) ("Nakajiki" 1996); Scholl Japan's "Back Ease" ("Nakajiki tsukai" 1994); Columbus's "Shoe Fitter Insole" ("Ashi ni au" 1995); "Shoe Fitter Sandal Yō" (Shoe Fitter Insole for Sandals) ("Sandal to ashi" 1997); and Morito's "Comfort Zone" ("Kutsu no nakajiki" 1999). As for the shape and color, the fashion-oriented transparent insoles were only a few millimeters thick and delicate and were either transparent or pastel in color, sometimes with gritter (e.g., "Arakawa Sangyo, 'Jewelry Soles'" 2001; "MD guide" 2003), whereas the early walking support insoles had molded surfaces to support the soles of the feet and achieve comfortable walking and were beige in color to imitate the standard leather shoe insert ("Mono" 2009).

However, how did walking support insoles with enhanced fashionable qualities and functionality come to fruition in the first place? The following sections analyze the process, focusing on the dynamics among insole suppliers, distributors, and consumers.

10.2 Morito's "Non-slide": the First Transparent Insole

The transformation of the walking support insole market was triggered by the release of Morito's "Non-Slide" insole in 2000 when high-heeled mules were popular. Mules, or backless sandals, do not cover the heel. In the second half of the 1990s, the women's shoe segment saw high-heeled mules that began to grow in popularity among young women ("Kakato" 1997; Katase et al. 2001). It was already difficult for people to find pumps that fit well as they have no instep support. It was even harder to find well-fitting mules and sandals as they have no instep and heel support. Without support,

[2] Asahara Takako, a journalist, has noted the same points (Asahara 2004).

mules and sandals caused wearers' feet to slip forward when walking, which often led to painful shoe sores and blisters on the forefoot (Katase and Hirabayashi 2002) and often caused wearers' feet to slip right off the edge, leading to falls and ankle sprains (Katase et al. 2001). Nevertheless, young women preferred to wear trendy high-heeled mules. In a survey conducted in July 2000, among 333 female university students at Kinjo Gakuin University, 90% owned at least one pair of mules (Katase et al. 2001). One student said that she wore mules because "Just wearing them makes you look elegant. You can't fight the fads" (Katase et al. 2001, p. 33).[3]

Morito addressed this issue. Morito was the top insole manufacturer in Japan and had developed walking support insoles as part of its product line, including "Foot Assist" for blisters, calluses, and shoe sores, "Foot Support" of shock-absorbing pads, and "Foot Helper" for bunions and metatarsal bones (Sugawara 1999). According to Hitoshi Yamazoe, a development engineer at Morito, the company believed that a partial insole at the forefoot could help wearers avoid the pitfalls of mules and developed a new insole that would meet the following conditions.[4] It would be made from a material that would prevent the feet from slipping, made thin to avoid narrowing the shoe, and be transparent so that it would be inconspicuous when the shoes were removed. The material that satisfied all those requirements was silicone. However, there is one problem—adhesive cannot adhere to silicone. Without adhesive, the insole would slip off the shoe. Morito overcame this technical difficulty and commercialized the "Non-Slide," a transparent, 0.7 mm thick silicone insole with adhesive ("Morito" 2002).[5]

Non-Slide became a popular product. The company test-marketed the product in 2000 at the Hankyu Department Store in Osaka and the Tokyu Hands (a variety store) in Nagoya. The test products at Tokyu Hands Nagoya garnered significant media attention, making appearances on talks, news, and variety shows that profiled the insoles' ability to safeguard against slippage in high-heeled mules and sandals.[6] With anticipation building nationwide, Morito ramped up production of the Non-Slide and launched the insoles at ¥600 (US$ 4.9) full-scale in the summer of 2001 ("Morito" 2002).[7] The effort was an unexpected success. The sales of the Non-Slide topped 300,000 in the first year because of media coverage and its ability to address the issues with wearing high-heeled mules ("Morito" 2002).[8]

---

[3] Translated from Japanese by the author.

[4] Hitoshi Yamazoe, MD Section, Retail Products Sales Division, Morito Japan Co., Ltd. (interview, May 17, 2021).

[5] Hitoshi Yamazoe, MD Section, Retail Products Sales Division, Morito Japan Co., Ltd. (interview, May 17, 2021). Tōichirō Maeda stated that the Non-Slide might not be silicone because it had an adhesive finish (President of Arakawa Sangyo Co., Ltd., interview, May 10, 2021). This indicates that silicone with adhesive was a conundrum.

[6] Hitoshi Yamazoe, MD Section, Retail Products Sales Division, Morito Japan Co., Ltd. (interview, May 17, 2021).

[7] Hitoshi Yamazoe, MD Section, Retail Products Sales Division, Morito Japan Co., Ltd. (interview, May 17, 2021). The price is calculated based on the dollar-yen rate in 2001.

[8] Hitoshi Yamazoe, MD Section, Retail Products Sales Division, Morito Japan Co., Ltd. (interview, May 17, 2021).

10.3 Arakawa Sangyo's "Jewelry Soles": Intention to Be Fashionable

The first firm to seize the opportunities created by Morito's success was Arakawa Sangyo, a dealer in shoe-related goods. Creating an insole and turning it into a marketable product entails the time-intensive process of developing metal production molds. It took at least six months to launch new insoles.[9] Arakawa Sangyo had an edge over other companies. As a member of the footwear industry, the company got word almost instantly from its clients that the Non-Slide was performing well and that inventory was running low.[10] Moving quickly, Arakawa Sangyo set out to develop transparent silicone insoles that could fill the Non-Slide shortage. By polishing the silicone to a mirror finish, Arakawa Sangyo overcame the difficulty of adhesive failure on silicone, drawing on its years of experience in dealing with rubber for shoe repair.[11] If silicone is polished to a mirror finish, it is less slippery and sticks in place better, similar to plastic wrap.

Arakawa Sangyo named the insoles "Jewelry Soles" and differentiated them from the Non-Slide by incorporating a fashion element. From their glittery accents and pastel color lineup (purple, pink, green, gray, and clear) to their attractive, eye-catching packaging with a view of their interior, the insoles leaned into the "Jewelry" name. Their approachable, "accessory" quality caused Jewelry Soles to resonate with young women, which was in line with Arakawa Sangyo's intention to target that segment ("Arakawa Sangyo, 'Jewelry Soles,'" 2001; "MD guide" 2003). Jewelry Soles debuted in February 2001 for ¥500 (US$ 4.1) and circulated in department stores.[12] They sold over 300,000 pairs in their first year of sale ("Arakawa Sangyo, sandal" 2003).

Before launching Jewelry Soles, Arakawa Sangyo had been importing health-oriented walking support insoles, Tacco Insoles, from Germany since 1997 ("Arakawa Sangyo, 'Jewelry Soles,'" 2001). It offered health-function-first insoles for people with flat feet, bowlegs, or knock knees, and was priced at ¥600–1,500 (US$ 4.9–12.3). Arakawa Sangyo made a clear distinction between Tacco Insoles and Jewelry Soles. It defined the German imports as health "functional" products and Jewelry Soles as "enjoying a sense" of fashion products ("Arakawa Sangyo, 'Jewelry Soles,'" 2001, p. 21).[13] Tacco Insoles needed a salesperson's explanation due to their full-fledged health orientation, but the Jewelry Soles were designed to sell without explanation because of their pretty appearance as fashionable goods.[14]

---

[9] Tōichirō Maeda, President of Arakawa Sangyo Co., Ltd. (interview, May 10, 2021).

[10] Tōichirō Maeda, President of Arakawa Sangyo Co., Ltd. (interview, May 10, 2021).

[11] Tōichirō Maeda, President of Arakawa Sangyo Co., Ltd. (interview, May 10, 2021).

[12] Arakawa Sangyo later changed its insole name to "Jewelry in Soles" (Tōichirō Maeda, President of Arakawa Sangyo Co., Ltd., interview, May 10, 2021). The price is calculated based on the dollar-yen rate in 2001.

[13] Words in quotation marks are translations from Japanese by the author.

[14] Tōichirō Maeda, President of Arakawa Sangyo Co., Ltd. (interview, May 10, 2021).

10.4 Beauty, Health, and Hygiene Goods Suppliers' Insoles: Becoming Fashion Items

Following up on the successes of the transparent insoles from Morito and Arakawa Sangyo and the related media coverage, an influx of new market entrants in subsequent years intensified competition ("Arakawa Sangyo, sandal" 2003).[15] According to Yamazoe, 14 companies, which comprised beauty, health, and hygiene goods suppliers as well as shoe-related manufacturers, entered the market between 2001 and 2002.[16]

The entry of beauty, health, and hygiene goods companies further promoted the development of fashionable qualities in transparent insoles. As other beauty, health, and hygiene goods of those companies had been sold through drugstores and variety stores, the transparent insoles were also distributed in these stores.[17] Since these channels were self-service, there was no support from sales staff, which made it necessary to compete through packaging, product design, and brand name (Fuji Keizai 2003). Drugstores had a wide range of customers; however, the main customers of variety stores at that time were young women in their 20s and 30s (Asahara 2002). Therefore, beauty, health, and hygiene goods suppliers developed their product designs, packaging, and product names to target young women (Asahara 2004; Fuji Keizai 2010; "Item-betsu" 2010). For example, some were rose-shaped, some were glittery, and some were pastel-colored and transparent and sold in cute packages (Asahara 2004; "Arakawa Sangyo, 'Jewelry Soles'" 2001; "Mono" 2009). The product names also appealed to the cuteness of the product, as shown in Sect. 10.1. Beauty, health, and hygiene goods companies were skilled at such methods.

10.5 Scholl Japan's "Party Feet": a Big Success

The biggest latecomer success story in the fashion-oriented transparent insole market was Scholl Japan, a global foot care goods company. As shown in Fig. 10.2, Scholl Japan increased its insole sales. Scholl Japan had previously focused on foot care products, such as bunion pads and health-oriented walking support insoles, under Dr. Scholl's brand name. Examples include "Tsuchi Fumazu Support" (foot arch support) insoles and "Walk Soft Arch Support" insoles, which were launched in 1989. Scholl Japan had already launched a transparent insole, "Clear Gel Cushion Gel Insoles for Pumps," in March 2001 ("Ashi ni fit" 2001), but the company began rolling out transparent insoles that foregrounded fashion orientation in 2004. It launched

---

[15] Hitoshi Yamazoe, MD Section, Retail Products Sales Division, Morito Japan Co., Ltd. (interview, May 17, 2021).

[16] Hitoshi Yamazoe, MD Section, Retail Products Sales Division, Morito Japan Co., Ltd. (interview, May 17, 2021).

[17] Hitoshi Yamazoe, MD Section, Retail Products Sales Division, Morito Japan Co., Ltd. (interview, May 17, 2021).

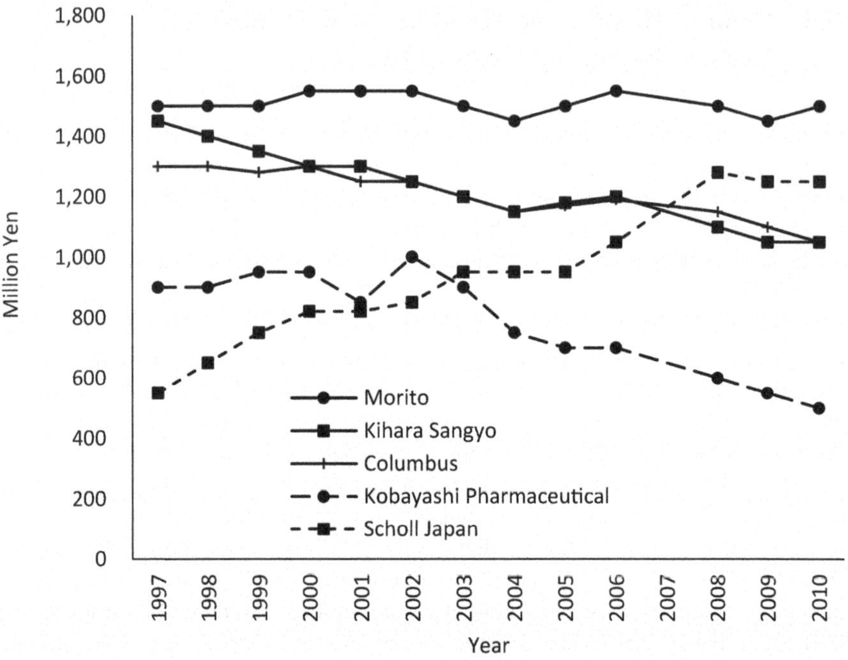

Fig. 10.2 Trends in insole sales by supplier. *Source* Miura (2021, Fig. 3.1, p. 53), modified by the author. *Note* Data for 2007 is unknown

transparent insoles for high-heeled shoes like mules and pumps under the "Party Feet" brand ("Mono" 2009). Akihiko Ōmura, the marketing manager of SSL Healthcare Japan (the successor company of Scholl Japan) stated that the product concept was different from the previous insoles; "Rather than a solution product for the problems we had in the past, this is a line to help people enjoy fashion in a positive way, and it is a series we want to focus on" (Asahara 2005, p. 86).[18] The "Party Feet" brand name invoked a festive, glamorous feel, and the packaging featured delicate and sweet images of high-heeled shoes and mules against a lavender background ("Tsumasaki" 2004). The "Party Feet Tsumasakisenyō Gel Half Insole" (Party Feet gel half-insole for forefoot) was priced at ¥700 (US$ 6.5).[19] Scholl Japan increased its "Party Feet" product lineup from 2005 onward and established itself in the fashion-oriented transparent insole market through TV commercials and women's fashion magazine advertisements (Fuji Keizai 2006, 2007, 2010).

As a foot care goods company, Scholl Japan shipped Party Feet primarily to drugstores ("MD guide" 2003). The sales grew in parallel with the drugstore channel ("Drugstore" 2010), but not all manufacturers saw a successful performance in the

[18] Translated from Japanese by the author.

[19] The price is calculated based on the dollar-yen rate in 2004. The product had sold 10 million units worldwide within a year and a half of its launch (Asahara 2005).

drugstore market. Kobayashi Pharmaceutical, which had been using drugstores as its main channel, saw its insole sales drop after 2002 (Fig. 10.2). Having established a position as the purveyor of Odor-Eaters, a major brand in the hygienic insole segment and early beige walking support insole segment, Kobayashi Pharmaceutical did not introduce any transparent insoles in the 2000s.[20] The fact that the drugstore-focused insoles of Kobayashi Pharmaceutical lost steam in the 2000s suggests that Party Feet's success stemmed from more than the growth of the drugstore channel alone; the nature of the products and the advertisement also played an important role.[21]

Figure 10.2 shows underperforming sales of Kihara Sangyo's and Columbus's insoles, which were long-standing suppliers of shoe-related goods and had strong relationships with traditional footwear channels—shoe specialty stores, department stores, general merchandise stores (GMS), and supermarkets (SM).[22] The relationship between the rise and fall of each channel and insole sales is examined in the next section.

10.6 Drugstores and Variety Stores Expanding Sales of Fashion-Oriented Transparent Insoles

In response to the entry of beauty, health, and hygiene goods suppliers into the transparent insole market, including Scholl Japan, and the increase in fashion-oriented transparent insole products, the distribution channel side also actively stocked these insoles (Fuji Keizaii 2007). The channel that had connections with beauty, health, and hygiene goods suppliers were drugstores and variety stores, and these stores increased the variety of insoles they handled, including fashion-oriented transparent insoles, developing and expanding footcare product corners (Asahara 2001, 2002; Fuji Keizai 2003, 2004). Specifically, large variety store chains, such as Tokyu Hands, Loft, and Sony Plaza, actively expanded their sales floors.

These stores actively selected fashion-oriented transparent insoles because they perceived demand from young women for insoles that were fashionable and comfortable when wearing high-heeled mules and pumps (Asahara 2004; "MD-guide"

[20] Hitoshi Yamazoe, MD Section, Retail Products Sales Division, Morito Japan Co., Ltd. (interview, May 17, 2021).

[21] The price range for Odor-Eaters and Party Feet remains the same. Medical Odor-Eaters Yōtsū Taisaku (Odor-Eaters countermeasure for lower back pain) was ¥1100 (US$ 9.5), Medical Odor-Eaters Gaihanboshi Taisaku (Odor-Eaters countermeasure for bunions) was ¥1100, Miss Odor-Eaters Ashishū Taisaku (Odor-Eaters countermeasure for foot odor) was ¥700 (US$ 6.0), and Miss Odor-Eaters Ashi-mure Taisaku (Miss Odor-Eaters countermeasure for foot-crowding) was ¥480 (US$ 4.1). Party Foot Gel Insole was ¥1300 (US$ 11.2), Gel Half Insole was ¥700, Gel Heel Cushion was ¥900 (US$ 7.7) (Fuji Keizai 2006, p. 116). Prices in U.S. dollars are calculated based on the dollar-yen rate in 2006.

[22] Kihara Sangyo traded materials for shoe inserts and Columbus traded shoe polishes. In addition, Morito, which maintains the number one position in insole sales, originally traded snaps and hook-and-loop fasteners for shoes.

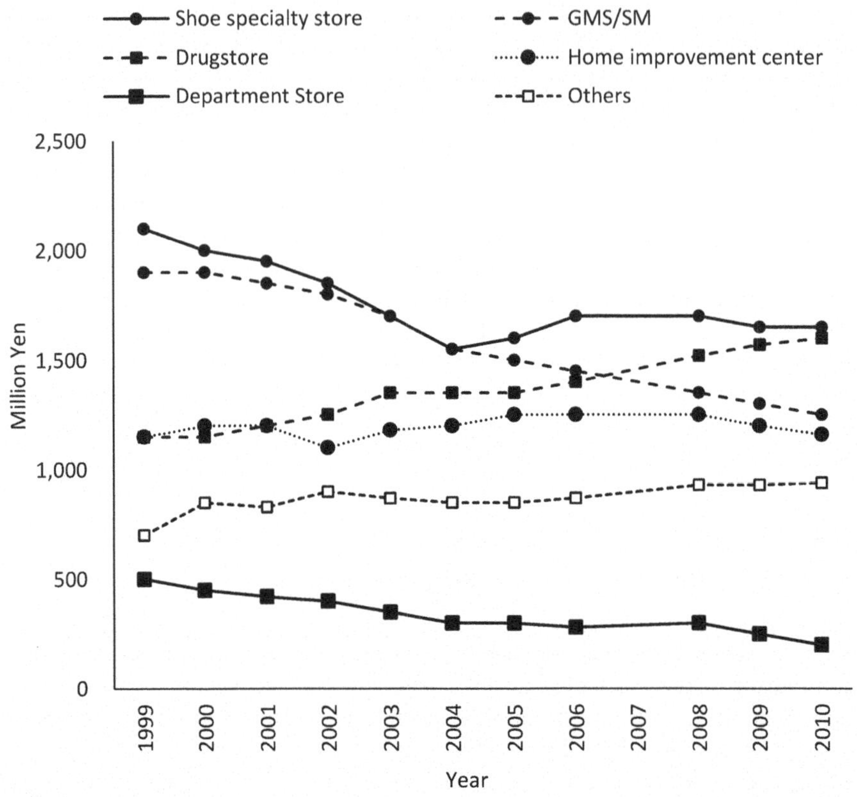

Fig. 10.3 Trends in insole sales by channel. *Sources* Prepared by the author based on Fuji Keizai (2001, p. 137, 2002, p. 155, 2003, p. 141, 2004, p. 140, 2005, p. 129, 2006, p. 111, 2007, p. 112, 2010, p. 124, 2011, p. 116)

2003; "Mono" 2009). Drugstore customers had a wide age range, but variety store customers were mainly women in their 20s and 30s (Asahara 2002) and these insoles fulfilled young women's demands and sold well. Yumi Ōtsuka of Sony Plaza Ginza Shinjuku Lumine said, "it has become commonplace to seek comfort through the adjustment of insoles and other products" (Asahara 2004, p. 61).[23] As these were self-service stores, the competition for fashion quality in the products themselves and in their packaging and names grew, as confirmed in Sect. 10.4.

Active handling of insoles in drugstores and variety stores was a successful outcome. As shown in Fig. 10.3, sales of insoles at drugstores increased throughout the 2000s. There are no sales data for insoles at variety stores, but the sales increases in other channel categories came from variety stores, such as Tokyu Hands, Loft, and Sony Plaza (Fuji Keizai 2001, 2003, 2004, 2005, 2006, 2007, 2011).

[23] Translated from Japanese by the author.

It is important to note that the channel fluctuations affected the transition of insole sales for each channel. Distinguishing them from the impact of expanded handling of the insoles is difficult because of limited data. Drugstores continued to grow in number and sales throughout the 1990s ("Drugstore" 2010). Tokyu Hands was struggling in the 2000s but Loft was growing its sales figures. As for other channels, the number of stores and sales of home improvement centers increased until the first half of the 2000s, after which the sales leveled off while the number of stores continued to increase. This was approximately consistent with the shifts in insole sales (Japan DIY and HC Association, n.d.). Traditional footwear channels, such as shoe specialty stores, department stores, GMS, and SM did not perform well and their insole sales declined accordingly (Fuji Keizai 2011). Particularly with GMS/SM, in addition to the slump in business conditions, their insole sales decreased because SMs had narrowed their offerings to food products, decreasing product handling (Fuji Keizai 2005).

Although it is difficult to distinguish the effects of fashion-oriented transparent insoles on insole sales for each channel from the influence of the rise and fall of the channels, insoles became more popular in drugstores and variety stores that were unrelated to shoes, and insole sales in these stores increased (Fig. 10.3). Conversely, sales at shoe sales floors, such as shoe speciality stores, department stores, GMS, and SM, declined. As of 2010, insole sales at drugstores had increased to the similar level as those at shoe speciality stores, and the sales at variety stores also increased. Thus, owing to young women's desire to wear shoes in a fashionable and comfortable manner, the enhancement of fashion-oriented transparent insoles by beauty, health, and hygiene goods suppliers, active handling of these insoles at drugstores and variety stores, and the strong performance of the channels worked together to achieve the increase in insole sales at drugstores and variety stores.

10.7 Function of Fashion-Oriented Transparent Insoles

Fashion-oriented transparent insoles were questionable in terms of eliminating foot problems when wearing high-heeled mules and pumps. From Yamazoe's perspective, the majority of insoles from later firms were completely different from Morito's, except being transparent.[24] By managing to overcome the problem of adhesive on silicone, Morito's Non-Slide was 0.7 mm thin with minimal effect on shoe size and prevented it from coming off. Arakawa Sangyo, which introduced silicone transparent insoles following Morito, overcame this problem by polishing the silicone to a mirror finish. However, later suppliers used elastomers (clear gel) to make transparent insoles. Although elastomer insoles were considerably thicker (at least 3 mm thick) by nature, their slight stickiness allowed them to somewhat (but not fully) stick

[24] Hitoshi Yamazoe, MD Section, Retail Products Sales Division, Morito Japan Co., Ltd. (interview, May 17, 2021).

to the shoe's insides and they were cheaper than silicone.[25] The thickness of elastomer insoles was out of the question for Morito, as a shoe-related goods company, since thick insoles reduced the space for the foot. However, beauty, health, and hygiene goods suppliers did not seem to be concerned about the issue.[26] Elastomer's low cost and stickiness were more attractive for beauty, health, and hygiene goods suppliers; therefore, the elastomer was their material of choice.

Furthermore, the beauty, health, and hygiene goods companies reframed the thickness of elastomer insoles as "extra cushioning" ("Mono" 2009), thereby, spinning a negative into a perceived positive. If the problem with high-heeled mules, pumps, or sandals is that the foot slips forward, causing shoe sores and blisters, then the foot needs to stop slipping. Cushioning is irrelevant to preventing the feet from slipping forward. Moreover, elastomer insoles, while soft to the touch, are not good shock-absorbents; hence, for shock-absorbing functionality, other materials are more suitable.[27]

Even Yamazoe recognized that the Non-Slide had been a "half success, half failure."[28] The Non-Slide was a highly functional product but it opened the door for later beauty, health, and hygiene goods companies to stake out large market shares with fashionable transparent insoles in drugstores and variety stores. In shoe stores and department stores, the sales staff might convey the functional advantage of Morito's Non-Slide. However, there was virtually no way for Morito to reach customers with detailed explanations of the functional advantages in the self-service settings of variety stores and drugstores.[29] The newcomers excelled at presenting their products with attractive designs, packaging, and naming while maintaining a semblance of functionality in the form of a comfortable foot "feel" through "extra cushioning." They understood how to thrive in self-service stores.

Previous paragraphs have discussed statements based on Morito's products and views, but it should be noted that both SF and SA retailers and medical doctors have expressed concerns about the easy use of insoles that do not consider the individual foot and the shoe. Kazuyuki Takayama, the shop master of Ginza Washington Ginza, a traditional shoe retail chain and an SF retailer, stated that "Shoe fitting is a world of 1-mm margins. Carelessness can immediately result in foot problems, so I listen to customers' concerns and always take them seriously when recommending footcare and insole products" (Asahara 2002, p. 88).[30] Hiroshi Yoshino, the store manager of the SA retailer, Ortho Fits Kichijoji, also stated, "At our store, our priority is to

---

[25] Hitoshi Yamazoe, MD Section, Retail Products Sales Division, Morito Japan Co., Ltd. (interview, May 17, 2021).

[26] Hitoshi Yamazoe, MD Section, Retail Products Sales Division, Morito Japan Co., Ltd. (interview, May 17, 2021).

[27] Hitoshi Yamazoe, MD Section, Retail Products Sales Division, Morito Japan Co., Ltd. (interview, May 17, 2021).

[28] Hitoshi Yamazoe, MD Section, Retail Products Sales Division, Morito Japan Co., Ltd. (interview, May 17, 2021).

[29] Hitoshi Yamazoe, MD Section, Retail Products Sales Division, Morito Japan Co., Ltd. (interview, May 17, 2021).

[30] Translated from Japanese by the author.

select shoes that fit the feet. Then [we select] an insole" (Asahara 2004, p. 61).[31] Dr. Kōichi Kondō, Director of Ryōgoku Ashi no Clinic, a foot clinic in Ryōgoku, Tokyo, explained the potential dangers, "When it comes to wearing insoles, doing things your own way can restrict the space inside your shoes and lead to foot problems." "People should understand that insoles provide temporary relief to certain symptoms. What people should really focus on is choosing the right shoes," he said ("Mono" 2009, p. 16).[32]

10.8 Summary

10.8.1 Rise of the Fashion-Oriented Transparent Insole Market

This chapter has clarified how walking support insoles became fashion-oriented in the 2000s. In the late 1990s, the walking support insoles market emerged, as discussed in Chap. 9. Following this trend, Morito and Arakawa Sangyo introduced transparent insoles with health functionality that stopped the feet from slipping forward and prevented shoe sores and blisters when wearing high-heeled mules. However, this popular product resulted in the entry of beauty, health, and hygiene goods companies, which were unrelated to shoes, and transparent insoles became more fashionable. Differentiating themselves from other companies in drugstores and variety stores, which were the main channels for beauty, health, and hygiene goods companies, the design of products, packages, and names were refined to become fashion variety goods. Drugstores and variety stores also actively marketed fashion-oriented transparent insoles. These insoles, which were fashionable and seemed to reduce the pain of wearing high-heeled shoes, could be easily purchased at variety stores and drugstores for a few hundred yen. This marketing mix was appealing to young women, which resulted in high sales volumes for fashion-oriented transparent insoles.

Both insole suppliers and retailers stated that they launched their products in response to the growing awareness of foot health—young women did not want to endure pain and wanted to walk comfortably in high-heeled shoes. JIF's initiatives aroused awareness among Japanese consumers that wearing shoes should not be painful and young women began to desire to wear high-heeled shoes comfortably and without pain. Given this consumer awareness, the chain reactions of activities of insole manufacturers, beauty, health, and hygiene goods suppliers, drugstores, and variety stores resulted in walking support insoles becoming fashionable and the emergence and expansion of the fashion-oriented transparent insole market as a separate category in the insole market.

[31] Translated from Japanese by the author. The square brackets were added by the author.

[32] Translated from Japanese by the author.

10.8.2 The Market Unintended by JIF and Inconsistent with Foot Health

The increased awareness of foot health triggered by JIF's activities led to these behavioral changes of non-target companies and consumers, which were not what JIF had intended. JIF's target was shoe retailers, not insole manufacturers, beauty, health, and hygiene goods suppliers, drugstores, or variety stores. However, beauty, health, and hygiene goods suppliers began to produce fashionable insoles, and drugstores and variety stores aggressively developed their sales floors for these insoles. Young women came to want the fashion-oriented transparent insoles marketed in these stores to enjoy comfortable high-heeled shoes.

The resultant emergence of the fashion-oriented transparent insole market was also not what JIF had intended, and the market was inconsistent with JIF's superordinate goal of protecting the health of Japanese people's feet. It was questionable whether fashion-oriented transparent insoles would truly solve the problem of high-heeled shoes. As high-heeled shoes resemble a slippery slope, it is easy to lose balance when walking in high-heeled shoes and unbalanced walking causes shoe sores and blisters (Tanaka 2010). Therefore, the non-slip function of insoles is effective in keeping a balanced gait. However, this was not prioritized in the fashion-oriented transparent insoles by beauty, health, and hygiene goods companies.

Considering foot health, the sale of insoles like fashion items in the self-service stores was also problematic. The emphasis on their fashionable nature was due to the competition in drugstores and variety stores. These sales floors, which were self-service and had nothing to do with shoes, became the main battleground. SF and SA retailers and medical doctors have pointed out the risks of easy use of insoles (Asahara 2002, 2004; "Mono" 2009). To enable balanced walking, insoles require delicate adjustments to fit the foot and shoe and, before that, the shoe must fit the foot well. Therefore, it was problematic that fashion-oriented transparent insoles were selected for their name, design, and packaging without any assistance from sales staff who could look at the feet, shoes, and insoles at the same time. Self-service insole selection might not have been a problem if consumers had sufficient knowledge; however, many consumers did not know which insole to choose to alleviate their foot problems (Aasahara 2001). Under these circumstances, insoles being bought like fashion items was problematic from the standpoint of foot health.

Even if fashion-oriented transparent insoles were truly functional and used in conjunction with the foot and shoe, the transparent insole market was still problematic as it developed as a complementary goods market and encouraged the wearing of high-heeled mules and pumps. Fashion-oriented transparent insoles were a hit because of the demand of young women who wanted to wear trendy mules and high-heeled shoes without pain. It is of course desirable that the use of such insoles can help prevent foot slippage and alleviate pain by providing some cushioning when wearing high-heeled shoes. However, the supply of high-heeled shoes and consumer demand were problematic. JIF had been addressing the neglect of foot health in favor of fashionable shoes. Even if high heels were considered beautiful and mules were considered trendy, the uncritical use of these high-heeled shoes with no instep and/or heel support and instability was problematic (JIF 1988b, 1992b). Nevertheless, the growing awareness of foot health mobilized consumers who wanted to wear high-heeled shoes without pain.

In sum, the health function of these insoles for high-heeled shoes was questionable. They were chosen like fashion items, rather than to match the foot and shoe. The insoles were complementary products that encouraged the uncritical wearing of high-heeled shoes. The fashion-oriented transparent insole market was the result of a chain of actions by companies and consumers influenced by JIF's initiatives. However, the market was not consistent with JIF's superordinate goal of protecting foot health.

10.9 Discussion of Part III

Existing research on social movements targeting companies has indicated that social movements are variables that influence the creation of new markets and has focused on the emergence of markets in line with the superordinate goals of the SMOs (Dubuisson-Quellier 2013; Sine and Lee 2009; Weber et al. 2008). Existing research assumed three points: (1) the intended target companies of the SMOs will change their behavior according to the group's demands; (2) only target companies respond to the activities of the SMOs; and (3) consumers change their awareness and behavior as the SMO intends. Therefore, existing studies suggest that new market categories, consistent with the superordinate goals of the SMOs, emerge.

This study suggests that target companies, non-target companies, and consumers who are directly and indirectly affected by the activities of the SMOs can learn; therefore, they do not necessarily change their behavior as requested by the SMO. Thus, this study assumes that (1) targeted companies do not necessarily implement behavioral changes as demanded by the SMOs, but rather react in diverse ways (Balsiger 2015; de Bakker et al. 2017; den Hond et al. 2010; Hiatt et al. 2009; McDonnell and King 2013; Yue et al. 2013; Zald et al. 2005; Zietsma and Winn 2008); (2) both the companies that are intentionally targeted by SMOs and non-targeted companies react to the efforts of the SMOs (den Hond et al. 2010; Gupta and Briscoe 2020; Hiatt et al. 2009; Yue et al. 2013); and (3) consumers do not necessarily change their behavior in line with the SMOs' superordinate goals, rather, they exhibit diverse responses. These diverse reactions of companies and consumers make room for the emergence of diverse markets, unintended by the SMOs, some of which may not be consistent with the superordinate goals of the SMOs.

The case study of JIF demonstrates that targeted firms, non-targeted firms, and consumers reacted to JIF's initiative and its success based on their respective interests, resulting in the emergence of three markets—the comfort shoe market, the European comfort shoe market, and the fashion-oriented transparent insole market. The comfort shoe market emerged as an intended indirect effect of JIF. The other two markets emerged from the unintended reactions of the companies and consumers to the success of JIF's initiatives. While the European comfort shoe market was unintended, yet in line with JIF's superordinate goal, the fashion-oriented transparent insole market was unintended and inconsistent with JIF's superordinate goal. These markets emerged because target companies, non-target companies, and consumers possessed the ability to learn and act according to their respective interests and needs.

Based on this finding, two issues are indicated for further research on social movements targeting companies and the emergence of markets. The first issue is the attention paid to diverse consumer reactions. Although existing research on the direct effects of activism on companies has pointed out that targeted companies do not always react the way SMOs require (Balsiger 2015; Zietsma and Winn 2008; Zald et al. 2005), it has overlooked the diverse responses of the consumers. Thus, existing research has implicitly assumed that consumer reactions are uniform. However, this study confirmed that consumers exhibit diverse reactions, giving rise to business opportunities. Therefore, it is possible that some markets that both do meet and do not meet the SMO's superordinate goals may arise.

Assuming that consumers, as entities with intentions and learning abilities, exhibit changes in awareness and behavior in response to the SMOs' initiatives, how diverse are these changes? A pattern that is suggested by this study is that consumers respond differently to the issues presented by the SMOs depending on whether their concerns or experiences strongly resonate with those issues or not.

JIF, which emphasizes health functions rather than the fashionable qualities of shoes, argued that shoe selection is important because foot pain should not be endured, but should be resolved through shoe selection, which resulted in a general increase in awareness of foot health. Those with serious foot problems strongly resonated with this message and, not content with JIF's intended comfort shoe market, supported the emergence of the European comfort shoe market. Consumers who had severe foot problems chose shoes that solved their problems; even if European comfort shoes were unfashionable and expensive, the functionality of those shoes were explained and felt because of SA retailers' knowledge and skills, they were preferred. Therefore, the European comfort shoe market emerged as an unintended consequence of the JIF that was consistent with its superordinate goal. By contrast, consumers who did not have serious foot problems and wanted to wear fashionable high-heeled shoes without pain lightly resonated with JIF's claim and supported the emergence of the fashion-oriented transparent insole market. It was an unintended consequence of JIF that was inconsistent with its superordinate goal. The main customers of the European comfort shoe market were middle-aged and older women, whereas, the main customers of the fashion-oriented transparent insole market were young women. As people age, their muscle strength decreases and they are more likely to have foot problems. Therefore, the difference in the customer base between the two markets could be interpreted not by age, but rather by foot problem severity.[33]

[33] As purchasing power increases with age, in general, it is possible to view age differences as a proxy variable for purchasing power. However, purchasing power alone is unlikely to explain the differences between the customers of the two markets. This is because customers with purchasing

Thus, the depth of foot problems or the strength of resonance with SMO's claims and initiatives produced different reactions among consumers. However, this was just one pattern. It is expected that research on social movements targeting companies and market emergence will develop by accumulating studies on how and why consumers respond differently to various initiatives of SMOs.

The second potential issue for further research is attention to the chain of entrepreneurs' actions. Existing research has indicated that non-target companies of SMOs are indirectly affected and undergo behavioral changes (den Hond et al. 2010; Hiatt et al. 2009; Yue et al. 2013). However, it has focused on the short-term reactions of companies with relatively close relationships with targeted companies. Specific examples include Target's store opening adjustments in response to the campaign to block Walmart's store opening (Yue et. al. 2013) and Reebok's improvements in the working conditions in its factories in response to the anti-sweatshop campaign against Nike (den Hond et al. 2010). Both of them are the target companies' competitors.

The insole market saw a chain of actions by diverse companies. JIF's non-targeted company, Morito, which developed walking support insoles in response to a growing interest in foot health, first introduced transparent insoles. Arakawa Sangyo adopted fashion trends, which led to a rapid increase in fashion-oriented transparent insoles by beauty, health, and hygiene goods suppliers. Distributors different from the shoe retailers targeted by JIF, such as drugstores and variety stores, were also mobilized. This led to fashion-oriented transparent insoles being sold at non-shoe sales floors. It was through this long process that walking support insoles changed from health-oriented to fashion-oriented products. This chain of actions created a market that was far removed from the SMO's superordinate goals.

This suggests that a chain of actions by companies can be one of the mechanisms by which markets that do not conform to the superordinate goals of SMOs emerge. Therefore, research on social movements targeting companies and market emergence needs to focus on such long chains of actions.

---

power without foot problems are unlikely to purchase non-fashionable comfort shoes. Meanwhile, if they have foot problems but weak purchasing power, they may not buy expensive European comfort shoes and are unlikely to purchase fashion-oriented transparent insoles. They would either purchase less expensive, domestic comfort shoes or beige walking support insoles, which were developed before transparent insoles. Therefore, while the difference in purchasing power is a variable that partially explains the difference between the two customer groups, the extent of foot concerns, or the strength of resonance with JIF's claims and initiatives, is a more important variable.

Part IV
Unintended Consequences of Successful Activism

Part IV summarizes the discussions presented in this volume. It reviews the discussions aimed at resolving the issues associated with research on social movements targeting companies developed in Part I through Part III and clarifies the contributions made. It then discusses three implications of the book: unintended market emergence resulting from successful social movements, difficulties in mobilizing consumers, and expanding the scope of research on social movements targeting companies.

Chapter 11
Conclusion

Against the backdrop of increasing corporate power, SMOs try to bring changes to the society by influencing corporate behavior as well as changing governments and laws. Thus, social movement studies have begun to focus on social movements targeting companies as well as governments (Bartley and Child 2011; Fremeth et al. 2022; Jaffee 2012; King and Pearce 2010; Rao 2009; Soule 2009; Walker et al. 2008).

Research on social movements targeting companies has been developed on the direct effects of activism and the indirect effects of activism. The direct effect of activism is the change in corporate behavior brought about by SMOs, and the indirect effect of activism is the change in the society because of this spillover effect from the direct effect of activism (Briscoe and Gupta 2016). One of the indirect changes of activism that occurs in society is the emergence of new market categories (Briscoe and Gupta 2016).

This study presents two key issues related to existing research on social movement targeting companies and examines these two issues through the case study of the post-war footwear industry in Japan. (1) How can SMOs on the periphery of an industry change corporate behavior? This relates to the direct effect of activism. (2) Are the markets that emerge owing to the activities of SMOs always intended by the SMOs, and when the market emergence is unintended by SMOs, specifically one that is inconsistent with the superordinate goals of SMOs, how does this emergence occur? This relates to the indirect effects of activism.

This chapter summarizes the arguments developed regarding the two issues and discusses the implications for research on social movements that target corporations derived from the analysis of JIF's case.

S. Miura, *Successful Social Activism and Unintended Market Emergence*,
https://doi.org/10.1007/978-981-99-9291-1_11

11.1 Two Issues

11.1.1 Direct Effect of Activism: How SMOs Change Corporate Behavior

The SMOs seek to influence companies to change their behavior to create their desired society. They do this by attempting to either delegitimize existing corporate behavior that they want to stop or legitimize new corporate behavior that they want to promote (den Hond and de Bakker 2007; Sine and Lee 2009). Existing research has shown that it is crucial for SMOs to mobilize companies directly and also to mobilize primary corporate stakeholders, such as the media, consumers, and shareholders (Balsiger 2010; Dubuisson-Quellier 2013; King and Soule 2007; Weber et al. 2008). As SMOs are secondary stakeholders of companies, it is difficult to get companies to accept their claims (Stevens et al. 2005; Vasi and King 2012). Thus, in addition to appealing directly to companies, SMOs should also appeal to primary stakeholders, effectively mobilizing them to disapprove companies that continue their existing corporate behaviors or to support companies that adopt new behaviors (Frooman 1999; King and Soule 2007).

The first issue discussed in this book is how SMOs, being on the periphery, develop effective strategies to change corporate behavior, even when they know that mobilizing primary stakeholders is an effective measure. The SMOs are secondary stakeholders of the companies that they are attempting to change their behavior, and therefore, they are situated at the periphery of an industry. Thus, they cannot be expected to be familiar with it. It is difficult for SMOs to identify which companies to target, which influential stakeholders to mobilize, and which framing to adopt. However, existing research has overlooked this point.

To consider this issue, it is helpful to classify SMOs' strategies into disruptive and persuasive strategies (Briscoe and Gupta 2016). This problem is more critical in the case of persuasive strategies, which aim to make target companies adopt a new behavior, than disruptive strategies, which aim to force target companies to stop their conventional behavior, for the following reasons. In the case of a persuasive strategy, the behavior required of a company is new, and therefore, ambiguous, while in the case of disruptive strategies, the behavior that SMOs claim for companies to cease is apparent. The companies that are likely to adopt the new behavior are also uncertain, while the companies that are behaving in a way that SMOs aim to stop are apparent. The frames that are likely appropriate to mobilize the target companies and their primary stakeholders are also uncertain. It could be framed based on the economic benefits of the new action, the social benefits, or the costs of not changing the action, and a combination of these factors is also possible. The threat employed in a disruptive strategy that a company's sales and reputation will be damaged if the company continues its behavior is simpler.

How can an SMO on the periphery with limited knowledge about the industry create an effective persuasive strategy? Analysis of JIF's case shows that the key to solving this problem is the introduction of the dynamic strategy change model.

Even if an SMO's strategy is initially built with limited resources, strategies can be revised through learning by doing, with effective strategies emerging *ex-post facto*. The change in JIF's strategy and the resulting proliferation of shoe fitters among shoe retailers demonstrates this.

Though JIF's superordinate goal was consistently protecting the foot health of Japanese people, JIF's initial strategy was unrelated to shoe fitters. The original target of JIF was shoe manufacturers, and its frame to cater to the foot health issue was that shoe manufacturers had the responsibility to make shoes that fitted Japanese feet well, as shoes support foot health rather than just appear fashionable. This strategy did not work. Most shoe manufacturers were indifferent to what the JIF claimed. However, JIF learned through their actions that many Japanese feet were damaged due to ill-fitting shoes, and there is a role called shoe fitter in Europe. Thus, the JIF changed its strategy to promote shoe fitters. From the initial SF training workshop and the book publication (JIF 1984h), JIF learned about the demands of shoe retailers and consumers and further modified its strategy. In the revised strategy, shoe retailers became JIF's target and it asked them to attain certifications on shoe fitting and select shoes that fit customers well. The frame that JIF adopted highlighted the huge demand of consumers for proper shoe selection, which shoe fitters could help with, and how having shoe fitters made stores unique. The revised strategy worked, and JIF succeeded in popularizing shoe fitters in the footwear industry. Thus, JIF built an effective strategy *ex-post facto* through learning by doing.

SMOs are secondary stakeholders of companies in an industry; they are located on the fringes and are not well-informed about the workings within the industry, making it nearly impossible to come up with effective persuasive strategies. However, the case analysis suggests it is possible for SMOs to get to know the workings of an industry gradually through a process of learning by doing and accordingly revising strategy to be effective.

Additionally, JIF's case also shows that, in addition to JIF, the targeted companies also learned through their own experiences. Among the shoe retailers targeted by JIF, small and medium-sized shoe retailers gave their own interpretation of having a shoe fitter. They reasoned that having a shoe fitter in their stores was a strategic way to support their survival in the tough competition from shoe discounters. This interpretation served to boost the proliferation of shoe fitters among small and medium-sized shoe retailers. Small and medium-sized shoe retailers learned and changed their actions by identifying their own interests in the efforts of the SMOs and using them to their advantage.

This shows that targeted companies as well as SMOs learn. If target companies are to learn in the same way as SMOs, research on social movements targeting companies should examine the process by which SMOs and target companies learn from each other and revise their strategies.

11.1.2 Indirect Effect of Activism: Emergence of Markets Unintended by SMOs

Attempts by SMOs to change corporate behavior sometimes lead to the emergence of new market categories (Briscoe and Gupta 2016). The initiatives of SMOs to change corporate behavior are attempts to bring about sociocultural changes in society, and these sociocultural changes help to create opportunities for entrepreneurs to set up new businesses, thus leading to new markets (Briscoe and Gupta 2016).

The second issue discussed in this book is whether the markets that emerge owing to the activities of SMOs are always those intended by the SMO. Moreover, it also discusses how the emergence of markets that are unintended by SMOs and inconsistent with their superordinate goals occurs.

Existing research has examined the emergence of new market categories that are intended by SMOs and that are therefore consistent with the superordinate goals of SMOs. Extent research has assumed the following: (1) The intended target companies of the SMOs will change their behaviors according to the group's demands; (2) only target companies respond to the activities of SMOs; and (3) consumers also change their awareness and behavior as the SMO intends (Dubuisson-Quellier 2013; Sine and Lee 2009; Weber et al. 2008). Therefore, existing studies suggest that new market categories consistent with the superordinate goals of SMOs emerge. However, these assumptions are simplistic.

This study suggests that (1) targeted companies do not necessarily implement behavioral changes as demanded by the SMOs, but rather react in diverse ways (Balsiger 2015; de Bakker et al. 2017; den Hond et al. 2010; Gupta and Briscoe 2020; Hiatt et al. 2009; McDonnell and King 2013; Yue et al. 2013; Zald et al. 2005; Zietsma and Winn 2008); (2) both companies intentionally targeted by SMOs and non-targeted companies react to the efforts of SMOs (den Hond et al. 2010; Hiatt et al. 2009; Yue et al. 2013); and (3) while the diverse responses of consumers have been overlooked in existing research, they also do not necessarily change their behavior in line with SMOs' superordinate goals—instead, they exhibit diverse responses. These diverse reactions of companies and consumers can create various markets that the SMOs did not intend, including markets that are inconsistent with their superordinate goals.

The case of JIF shows that a variety of markets emerged as a result of its initiatives. The comfort shoe market was the market JIF intended and that aligned with its superordinate goal of protecting and promoting foot health. However, markets unintended by JIF also emerged, such as the European comfort shoe market and the fashion-oriented transparent insole market. In the JIF's superordinate goal of protecting the foot health of the Japanese, the European comfort shoe market pursued foot health protection at a higher level than the shoe-fitter-based comfort shoe market. In contrast, the fashion-oriented transparent insole market was questionable in terms of foot health protection and inconsistent with JIF's superordinate goal.

The comfort shoe market was JIF's intended market that emerged as a result of the popularization of shoe fitters. The increasing number of shoe fitters in shoe stores and the improvement of consumer awareness of foot health propelled the comfort shoes market. Shoe manufacturers saw business opportunities in the changes of consumer awareness and started to make comfort shoes. Shoe retailers also saw business opportunities to sell comfort shoes with shoe selection services by shoe fitters as they faced competition from shoe discount chains. Thus, JIF ultimately succeeded in getting shoe manufacturers to make shoes that emphasize health over fashion, which was its original strategic aim. The emergence of the comfort shoe market was the indirect and intended consequence of the success of JIF in changing shoe retailers' behavior.

In contrast, the European comfort shoe market was an unintended market that emerged as a result of companies and consumers responding to the initiatives of JIF. Small and medium-sized shoe retailers who felt that the shoe fitting skills acquired through the SF Training Workshop were insufficient to cater to the needs of consumers, learned collectively how to adjust shoes and insoles from European master orthopedic shoemakers. Some consumers with severe foot problems were not satisfied with the skills of the shoe fitters and wanted more advanced shoe fitting. These were not the behavioral changes that the JIF demanded or anticipated from shoe retailers and consumers; rather, JIF's promotion of shoe fitters elicited these reactions. Combining this with the expectations and actions of companies importing comfort shoes from Europe, the European comfort shoe market emerged.

The fashion-oriented transparent insole market was also an emergent market resulting from non-target companies and consumers reacting to JIF's initiatives in a way that JIF did not intend. Insole manufacturers saw a business opportunity in response to an increased awareness of foot health triggered by JIF's activities and introduced walking support insoles. As high-heeled mules became popular amidst an increasing number of walking support insoles, insole manufacturers introduced transparent insoles to make high-heeled mules comfortable to wear. Seizing the opportunities in these initiatives, beauty, health, and hygiene goods suppliers began to produce highly fashionable transparent insoles, with drugstores and variety stores actively adding them to their sales floors. This product met the needs of consumers who desired trendy high-heeled mules but wanted to avoid sore feet. Interactions among the insole manufactures, beauty, health, and hygiene goods suppliers, distributors, and consumers led to the emergence of the fashion-oriented transparent insole market. JIF did not target any of the insole manufacturers, beauty, health, and hygiene goods suppliers, or drugstores and variety stores. However, the growing awareness of foot health triggered by the activities of JIF brought about a chain reaction. JIF also did not foresee that some consumers would pursue comfort without giving up wearing fashionable shoes. However, such consumers mobilized. The fashion-oriented transparent insole market emerged as a result of the diverse reactions of various players to the increased awareness of foot health generated by the activities of JIF.

The case of the footwear industry suggests that markets that emerge as a result of SMOs initiatives do not always align with SMOs' goals. This point has been overlooked in existing studies. It can be concluded that behind the emergence of these diverse markets lies the diverse reactions of target and non-target companies to the initiatives of SMOs, and the diverse reactions of consumers to the same. The targeted and non-targeted companies learn and do not always make the behavioral changes desired by SMOs. Similarly, consumers learn and do not always make the behavioral changes desired by SMOs. As consumers respond in different ways, and companies find business opportunities, the chain of their actions may create a variety of markets including one inconsistent with SMO's superordinate goals.

If target companies, non-target companies, and consumers affected by the activities of an SMO can learn and change their behaviors, it is not an exception when unintended consequences occur after the activities of SMOs; this situation may occur frequently. From this perspective, it is crucial to elucidate the process and mechanism of the long-term and indirect emergence of diverse markets as a result of the initiatives of SMOs.

11.2 Discussion

11.2.1 Unintended Markets Emerging from Successful Social Movements

A longitudinal case study of the activities of JIF suggests that an SMO successfully achieving its immediate goal may potentially result in the emergence of a market that is not necessarily in line with its superordinate goals as an indirect ripple effect. Hiatt et al. (2009) have suggested this possibility, and the analysis in this research clearly demonstrates it.

The SMO's success in creating behavioral changes in the target companies and the emergence of a market as a result also points toward the successful mobilization of consumers. The greater the SMO's success in mobilizing companies and consumers, the more likely it is to affect an even wider range of companies and consumers (Weber et al. 2008). When the reactions of the affected consumers are not uniform, as seen in this research, various business opportunities may arise and various companies create various new businesses for such consumers. This phenomenon is easy to understand by examining the opposite case. If an SMO fails to mobilize companies or consumers, there is no market change, and thus there would be no room for the emergence of new businesses or markets. The greater the success of the initial initiative, the more extensive the unexpected reactions of companies and consumers, and the more variety in the markets that emerge. The JIF succeeded in improving consumer awareness of foot health and achieved the immediate goal of highlighting the importance of shoe fitters for shoe retailers. The success affected a diverse range of consumers and companies, which led to the emergence of the European comfort shoe market and fashion-oriented transparent insole market. The fashion-oriented transparent insole market was ironically contradictory to the goals of JIF.

Though it may be argued that the emergence of the unintended market is simply the consequence of the shortcomings of the SMO, it is incorrect. In fact, the JIF and shoe fitters were sometimes criticized for the insufficiency of their abilities and activities that could not produce enough improvements in the footwear industry. However, the case study shows that the issue is not that simple. Rather, the fashion-oriented transparent insole market, which was questionable in terms of foot health, emerged because of the success of JIF's initiatives. As JIF's shoe fitter training activities achieved a certain degree of success, the success provoked responses and actions from a wide variety of companies and consumers and various markets emerged in the footwear industry, including the fashion-oriented transparent insole market.

Thus, when SMOs succeed in achieving their immediate goals, they influence a variety of players, including consumers and companies, producing unintended market changes. The emergence of new markets involves the actions of various players. It is difficult for an SMO to control the broad ripple effect of its success. Although providing an argument for resolving this issue is beyond the scope of this research, a key factor in this process is the mobilization of consumers, which is discussed in the next section.

11.2.2 Difficulties in Mobilizing Consumers

Based on the case of JIF and the footwear industry, it can be argued that one of the difficulties that may arise from the success of activism is the mobilization of companies and consumers with diverse interests and intentions beyond SMO's initial target. JIF's activities to emphasize the importance of foot health led to the mobilization of the needs of young women who wanted to comfortably enjoy wearing fashionable, trendy high-heeled shoes. Insole manufacturers and beauty, health, and hygiene goods suppliers saw an opportunity and developed a fashion-oriented transparent insole. As a result of interactions among the consumers and the companies, the fashion-oriented transparent insole market emerged.

Research on social movements targeting companies has primarily focused on SMOs and companies—it began when companies, not just governments, became powerful. However, consumer behavior must also be analyzed to understand contention in the marketplace. Although companies wield power in society, consumers do as well. Thus, we need to include SMOs and their counterparts—consumers as well as companies—and examine their interactions and the outcomes of such interactions.

This research shows that consumers react in various ways to the activities of SMOs, and do not always react as expected. However, the question of what separates the reactions that SMOs desire from those they do not, and which of these reactions will prevail in society, remains unanswered. Companies are organizations, and their actions are rational in their intentions. However, consumer behavior may be more capricious and diverse than organizational behavior. Thus, mobilizing consumers so that they behave in the desired manner may be harder than doing the same for companies. Further research is necessary on the premise that companies and consumers, possess intentions and the ability to learn, and therefore, may react in unintended ways. Based on this premise, further research must examine the ways in which consumers are mobilized in various social movements.

11.2.3 Scope of the Research on the Consequences of Social Movements Targeting Companies

The scope of the research on the indirect effect of social movements targeting companies has been relatively limited. Although the impact of social movements on non-targeted companies has been studied, the research often has focused on the short-term effect on non-targeted companies that are close or similar to targeted companies. For example, Target's response to the protests against Walmart (Yue et al. 2013) and Reebok's response to the protests against Nike have been studied (den Hond et al. 2010). Both are the target companies' close competitors. Consumers have also been treated uniformly, and their diverse reactions have received little attention. However, this research shows that the influence of initially successful social activities impacts various companies, and the actions of such companies can become interconnected. Additionally, various consumers can be impacted, resulting in diverse behavioral changes. The long-term dynamics between these various companies and consumers can create unintended market-related changes. Though this is a complex process, deciphering it is essential to understand the consequences brought about by successful social movements.

It is a difficult task for SMOs to successfully change corporate behavior, and it is also difficult for SMOs to control the results of the success of such endeavors. Although there is no silver bullet for this, research on social movements targeting companies needs to explore the process and consequences of social movements targeting companies from a broad and long-term perspective by deciphering the interactions among the players involved.

Appendix 1
Interview List

No	Name	Affiliation	Type of organization in the left column[a]	Former affiliation (type of organization)[b]	Date	Place	Interview main topic[C]
1	Abe, Kaoru	Ph.D., CPO, Professor, Chair, Niigata University of Health and Welfare	University		3/25/2017	Okayama	A
2	Asahi, Naoko	Kutsu no Asahiya Co., Ltd.	Shoe retailer		11/8/2021	Nagano	C
3	Asahi, Sadayoshi	President, Kutsu no Asahiya Co., Ltd.	Shoe retailer		11/8/2021	Nagano	C
4	Asahi, Yoshiyuki	Second Shoe Making	Shoe manufacturing and repair store		11/8/2021	Nagano	C
5	Endoh, Michio	President, Van San-Sho, Inc.	Shoe wholesaler and retailer		1/11/2018	Tokyo	C
6	Fujiwara, Hiroshi	J.B.Co., Ltd.	Shoe manufacturer	Hotei Gomu (rubber shoe manufacturer)	1/4/2015	Hyogo	B
7	Fukuhara, Ichirō			Otsuka Seika (shoe manufacturer)	5/15/2017	Tokyo	B

(continued)

S. Miura, *Successful Social Activism and Unintended Market Emergence*,
https://doi.org/10.1007/978-981-99-9291-1

(continued)

No	Name	Affiliation	Type of organization in the left column[a]	Former affiliation (type of organization)[b]	Date	Place	Interview main topic[C]
8	Fukui, Toshimi	Fukui Shoelast Mfg. Co. Ltd.	Shoe last manufacturer		4/28/2016	Tokyo	B
9	Fukui, Toshimi	Fukui Shoelast Mfg. Co. Ltd.	Shoe last manufacturer		9/11/2019	Tokyo	B
10	Funakawa, Yōichi			Morito Co., Ltd. (shoe sub-material manufacturer)	5/19/2014	Hyogo	B
11	Harada, Shigeru	Foot, Footwear and Health Association	SMO		3/11/2016	Tokyo	B
12	Hasegawa, Tokiko			Administrative Office, Japan Institute of Footwear (SMO)	2/10/2016	Tokyo	B
13	Herbst, Eduard	President, OSM Herbst Co., Ltd.	Prosthetics and orthotics manufacturer	Alice (shoe retailer)	2/26/2019	Hyogo	C
14	Igari, Takayuki	Catch Ball, Co. Ltd.	Shoe retailer		11/29/2019	Ibaraki	C
15	Inagawa, Minoru	Deputy Director, Leather Industry Museum	Museum	Trotto Seika (shoe manufacturer)	11/11/2014	Tokyo	A
16	In'nami, Jun	Dinus Shoe Corporation	Shoe manufacturer		11/12/2013	Tokyo	B
17	In'nami, Shū	Dinus Shoe Corporation	Shoe manufacturer		11/12/2013	Tokyo	B
18	Kanbe, Shunpei	Managing Director, Foot, Footwear and Health Association	SMO		11/25/2013	Tokyo	B
19	Kanbe, Shunpei	Managing Director, Foot, Footwear and Health Association	SMO		3/11/2016	Tokyo	B

(continued)

(continued)

No	Name	Affiliation	Type of organization in the left column[a]	Former affiliation (type of organization)[b]	Date	Place	Interview main topic[C]
20	Katō, Hideyuki	Morito Japan Co., Ltd.	Shoe sub-material manufacturer		5/17/2021	Online	D
21	Katō, Shōichi	Owner, Bon Pied	Shoe manufacturer	Owner, Studio S. K. (shoe design)	2/10/2014	Chiba	B
22	Katō, Shōichi	Owner, Bon Pied	Shoe manufacturer	Owner, Studio S. K. (shoe design)	3/12/2014	Chiba	B
23	Katō, Shōichi	Owner, Bon Pied	Shoe manufacturer	Owner, Studio S. K. (shoe design)	1/23/2015	Chiba	B
24	Kida, Michiko	President, Alpha Miki	Shoe retailer		10/4/2018	Hokkaido	C
25	Kimura, Katsutoshi	Director of Administrative Office, Foot, Footwear and Health Association	SMO		11/25/2013	Tokyo	B
26	Koga, Toshitake	Asahi Corporation Co., Ltd.			12/1/2016	Fukuoka	A
27	Kubota, Kayo	Schritt	Shoe wholesaler		3/9/2018	Tokyo	C
28	Kubota, Michiko	Owner, Shoes Frontia	Shoe sales consultant	The Seibu Department Stores, Ltd. (department store)	5/15/2017	Tokyo	B
29	Kuribayashi, Kaoru	President, Footmind	Shoe retailer		1/31/2019	Nagoya	C
30	Kuze, Yasuo	President, Schritt Co., Ltd./President, Alka Co., Ltd.	Shoe wholesaler/ Shoe retailer		3/9/2018	Tokyo	C
31	Madono, Hiroyuki	Kawamura Gishi	Prosthetics and orthotics manufacturer		12/12/2018	Osaka	C
32	Madono, Hiroyuki	Kawamura Gishi	Prosthetics and orthotics manufacturer		1/23/2019	Osaka	C

(continued)

(continued)

No	Name	Affiliation	Type of organization in the left column[a]	Former affiliation (type of organization)[b]	Date	Place	Interview main topic[C]
33	Maeda, Tōichirō	President, Arakawa Sangyo Co., Ltd.	Shoe sub-material manufacturer		5/10/2021	Tokyo	D
34	Makiya, Mitsuko	Maki no Kutsu	Shoe retailer		10/1/2017	Okinawa	C
35	Matano, Yoshihiro	Foot, Footwear and Health Association	SMO		3/11/2016	Tokyo	B
36	Matoba, Ken			Ozaki Co., Ltd. (shoe sub-material manufacturer)	5/19/2014	Hyogo	B
37	Miyazaki, Shigeyuki	Kutsu no Miyazaki	Shoe retailer		5/18/2017	Kanagawa	B
38	Morino, Jun'ichi	Ginza Yoshinoya Co., Ltd.	Shoe wholesaler and retailer		8/8/2014	Tokyo	B
39	Morino, Jun'ichi	Ginza Yoshinoya Co., Ltd.	Shoe wholesaler and retailer		11/11/2014	Tokyo	B
40	Moriya, Kanjirō			(Leather cutting company)	1/18/2014	Tokyo	A
41	Murakawa, Minoru	Asahi Corporation Co., Ltd.	Shome manufacturer		12/1/2016	Fukuoka	A
42	Nakajima, Takeshi	Tokyo Metropolitan Leather Technology Center	Public research institute		1/8/2015	Tokyo	A
43	Nakajima, Takeshi	Tokyo Metropolitan Leather Technology Center	Public research institute		2/12/2015	Tokyo	A
44	Nakamura, Kimitaka	President, Nakamura Co., Ltd.	Shoe retailer		10/29/2021	Hiroshima	C

(continued)

(continued)

No	Name	Affiliation	Type of organization in the left column[a]	Former affiliation (type of organization)[b]	Date	Place	Interview main topic[C]
45	Nishiyama, Mutsuko	Director, Kinboshi Shōten Co., Ltd. (Store name is Nishiyama Kutsu Kenkyūjo)	Shoe retailer		8/30/2022	Osaka	C
46	Ozawa, Toshiyuki	Marketing director, Ozawa Ichiba Limited (Store name is Kutsu no Ozawa)	Shoe retailer		5/16/2017	Tokyo	B
47	Sakata, Shigehiro	Owner, Shoe Laboratory Condor	Shoe retailer		7/29/2019	Hyogo	C
48	Sasō, Hideyuki	Managing director, Toukutsu Kyōkai	Shoe retailer's association	Otsuka Seika (shoe manufacturer), Hiewadō Kutsuten (shoe retailer)	8/4/2014	Tokyo	B
49	Satō, Shigemoto	Asics Japan	Shoe manufacturer		7/14/2014	Hyogo	B
50	Shimizu, Shōichi	Director, Ashi to Kutsu no Kagaku Kenkyūjo Co., Ltd.	Shoe wholesaler, Shoe retailer		12/14/2017	Nagoya	C
51	Tanaka, Sumiko	Managing Director, Schöne	Shoe retailer		1/15/2020	Saitama	C
52	Tatesaka, Keiko	Grace Co., Ltd.	Shoe retailer		10/26/2021	Aomori	C
53	Tatesaka, Kunihiko	President, Grace Co., Ltd.	Shoe retailer		10/26/2021	Aomori	C
54	Tatesaka, Wataru	Grace Co., Ltd.	Shoe retailer		10/26/2021	Aomori	C

(continued)

(continued)

No	Name	Affiliation	Type of organization in the left column[a]	Former affiliation (type of organization)[b]	Date	Place	Interview main topic[C]
55	Teramoto, Masateru	President, Monet Teramoto	Shoe retailer		2/1/ 2019	Osaka	C
56	Tobe, Yukio	Owner, Tobe Seika Kōgyō	Shoe manufacturer		10/ 31/ 2013	Tokyo	A
57	Tsukamoto, Yūji	Operating Director, Asahi Corporation Co., Ltd.			12/ 1/ 2016	Fukuoka	A
58	Umemiya, Yoshimasa	Director, Tomizuka Kigata Co., Ltd.	Shoe last manufacturer		10/ 31/ 2013	Tokyo	A
59	Yamamoto, Hiromu			Director of Administrative Office, Japan Institute of Footwear (SMO)	12/ 8/ 2015	Phone	B
60	Yamazoe, Hitoshi	Morito Japan Co., Ltd.	Shoe sub-material manufacturer		5/ 17/ 2021	Online	D
61	Yashiro, Hiroo			Ginza Yoshinoya (shoe wholesaler and retailer)	5/ 17/ 2017	Tokyo	B
62	Yasui, Daisaku	President, Kinboshi Shōten Co., Ltd. (Store name is Nishiyama Kutsu Kenkyūjo)	Shoe retailer		8/ 30/ 2022	Osaka	C
63	Yoshiki, Akiko	Owner, Alkomeister	Shoe retailer		11/ 30/ 2019	Nagoya	C

(continued)

(continued)

No	Name	Affiliation	Type of organization in the left column[a]	Former affiliation (type of organization)[b]	Date	Place	Interview main topic[C]
64	Yoshiki, Hidetoki	Owner, Alkomeister	Shoe retailer		11/30/2019	Nagoya	C

Notes

[a] Affiliation is based on the time of the interview

[b] A former affiliation is listed when relevant to the content of the interview and different from the current affiliation

[c] Regarding the main content of the interviews, *A* represents the footwear industry in general, *B* represents SF retailers, comfort shoes, and the comfort shoe market, *C* represents SA retailers, European comfort shoes, and the European comfort shoe market, and *D* represents insole supplies, insoles, and the insole market. However, this does not suggest that these were the only contents of the interviews

Appendix 2
Fieldwork List

No.	Date	Fieldwork
1	October 9–10, 2013	International Shoe & Leather Goods Fair (Tokyo)
2	September 26, 2014	The 28th Annual Meeting of Japanese Society for Medical Study of Footwear (Fukuoka)
3	October 18, 2014	The 30th Scientific Meeting of the Japanese Society of Prosthetics and Orthotics (Okayama)
4	January 31, 2015	The 11th Academic Conference of International Verband der Orthopädie-Schuhtechniker (IVO, International Association for Orthopaedic Shoe Technicians) Japan (Tokyo)
5	June 4, 2015	Lecture on Feet Education, Part I by Nobuko Hiroshima, owner of Mama to Kodomo no Ashi no Salon Nemunoki (Kanagawa)
6	July 7, 2015	Lecture on Feet Education, Part I I by Nobuko Hiroshima, owner of Mama to Kodomo no Ashi no Salon Nemunoki (Kanagawa)
7	November 20–21, 2015	The 29th Annual Meeting of Japanese Society for Medical Study of Footwear (Aichi)
8	January 20, 2016	FHA SF Training Workshop, Primary Course Day 1 (Tokyo)
9	January 21, 2016	FHA SF Training Workshop, Primary Course Day 2 (Tokyo)
10	February 10, 2016	The FHA 50th Anniversary Celebration
11	February 18, 2016	FHA SF Training Workshop, Primary Course Day 3 (Osaka)
12	September 23–24, 2016	The 30th Annual Meeting of Japanese Society for Medical Study of Footwear (Kyoto)
13	March 24–25, 2017	The 15th Annual Meeting of the Japanese Society for Foot Care (Okayama)
14	May 16, 2017	i/288 (Shoe retail store) (Tokyo)

(continued)

S. Miura, *Successful Social Activism and Unintended Market Emergence*,
https://doi.org/10.1007/978-981-99-9291-1

(continued)

No.	Date	Fieldwork
15	February 18, 2018	The 14th Academic Conference of IVO Japan (Kyoto)
16	February 24, 2019	The 15th Academic Conference of IVO Japan (Hyogo)

Appendix 3
Quota and Tariff Rates for Leather Footwear

Year	Quota quantity (thousand pair)	Primary tariff rate (%)	Secondary tariff rate	
			Shoes for adults	Shoes for children
1986	24,530	30.0, 27.0, or 21.6	60.0% or ¥4,800.0	60.0% or ¥4,800.0
1987	27,000			
1988	31,100			
1989	35,800			
1990	41,200			
1991	48,300			
1992	57,960			
1993	69,550			
1994	83,460			
1995	100,150	29.3, 26,3, or 21.1	56.3% or ¥4,737.5	56.3% or ¥4,500.0
1996	120,190	28.5, 25.7, or 20.5	52.5% or ¥4,675.0	52.5% or ¥4,200.0
1997	120,190	27.8, 25.0, or 20.0	48.8% or ¥4,612.5	48.8% or ¥3,900.0
1998	120,190	27.0, 24.3, or 19.5	45.0% or ¥4,550.0	45.0% or ¥3,900.0
1999	120,190	26.3. 23.6, or 18.9	41.3% or ¥4,487.5	41.3% or ¥3,300.0
2000	120,190	25.5, 23.0, or 18.4	37.5% or ¥4,425.0	37.5% or ¥3,000.0
2001	120,190	24.8, 22.3, or 17.8	33.8% or ¥4,362.5	33.8% or ¥2,700.0
2002	120,190	24.0, 21.6, or 17.3	30.0% or ¥4,300.0	30.0% or ¥2,400.0

Source METI (n.d.b)

S. Miura, *Successful Social Activism and Unintended Market Emergence*,
https://doi.org/10.1007/978-981-99-9291-1

References

Akita, H. (2002). *Mono to ningen bunkashi 104 geta: Kami no hakimono* [A cultural history of things and people 104 geta: Footwear of the Gods]. Hosei University Press.

Aldrich, H. E., & Fiol, C. M. (1994). Fools rush in? The institutional context of industry creation. *Academy of Management Review, 19*(4), 645–670. https://doi.org/10.2307/258740.

Anata no sentaku ketsudan, shoe fitter, ashi no kosei o tsukamu [Shoe fitters make the right choices for your feet's unique features]. (1992, May 29). *Yomiuri Shimbun*, Osaka morning edition, 16.

Aoshima, Y., Takeishi, A., & Cusumano, M. A. (2010). *Made in Japan wa owarunoka* [The End of Made in Japan?]. Toyo Keizai.

Arakawa Sangyo, 'Jewelry Soles' to 'Tacco insoles' de kaisō" [Arakawa Sangyo cruising with strong sales of jewelry soles and tacco insoles]. (2001, August). *Footwear Press*, 21–22.

Arakawa Sangyo, sandal no suberidome sheet 'New Jewelry Soles o 12-shoku de tenkai [Arakawa Sangyo to roll out New Jewelry Soles, its new sandal non-slip sheets, in 12 colors]. (2003, June). *Footwear Press*, 27.

Asahara, T. (2001, March). Item-betsu marketing, footcare & kōkinō insole, ashi no kenkō to biyō e no kanshin no takamari kara, wakai josei no juyō ga nobiru [Item-specific marketing: rising interest in foot health and beauty drives demand for footcare and high-functionality insoles among young women]. *Footwear Press*, 103–108.

Asahara, T. (2002, December). Item-betsu marketing, footcare & kōkinō insole, ashi no tsukare o torinozoku footcare shōhin to insole no juyo ga chakujitsu ni kakudai [Item-specific marketing: growing demands for footcare goods and insoles to remove foot fatigue]. *Footwear Press*, 86–92.

Asahara, T. (2004, March). Item-betsu marketing, footcare yōhin & insole: Sandal to Mule yo¯ de juyo¯ kakudai. Kaitekisei to oshare kan ga shigekisuru [Item-specific marketing, footcare products & insoles: Increased demand for foot care products and insoles for sandals and mules due to their comfort and stylishness]. *Footwear Press*, 60–65.

Asahara, T. (2005, December). MD-guide Insole, footcare yōhin & saishin jōhō: Tōmei na half-insole ga dai hit kakusha 2-keta–100% zō to kōcho [Transparent half insoles were a big hit, with double-digit to 100% growth for each company.]. *Footwear Press*, 83–89.

Ashi ni au kinō jūjitsu: Kutsu kakusha ga aitsugi shinseihin [Enhanced fitting functions: New products by shoe companies] (1995, June 23). *Nikkei Sangyo Shimbun*, 27.

Ashi ni fit shite nuide medatazu, Dr. Scholl's shin seihin [Insole that fits your foot and inconspicuous, Dr. Scholl's new product]. (2001, March 29). *Nikkri Ryutsu Shimbun*, 25.

Association for Technical Aids. (n.d.). *Gishi sōgushi jōhō* [prosthetists and orthotists imformation]. https://www.techno-aids.or.jp/senmon/.

S. Miura, *Successful Social Activism and Unintended Market Emergence*, https://doi.org/10.1007/978-981-99-9291-1

Balsiger, P. (2010). Making political consumers: The tactical action repertoire of a campaign for clean clothes. *Social Movement Studies*, *9*(3), 311–329. https://doi.org/10.1080/14742837.2010.493672.

Balsiger, P. (2015). Managing protest: The political action repertoires of corporations. In D. D. Porta & M. Diani (Eds.), *The Oxford handbook of social movements* (pp. 653–666). Oxford University Press. https://doi.org/10.1093/oxfordhb/9780199678402.001.0001.

Bank of Japan. (n. d. a). *BOJ time-series data serch*. Bank of Japan. https://www.stat-search.boj.or.jp/index_en.html.

Bank of Japan. (n. d. b). *Prices*. Bank of Japan. https://www.boj.or.jp/en/statistics/pi/index.htm.

Baron, D. P. (2003). Private politics. *Journal of Economics & Management Strategy*, *12*(1), 31–66. https://onlinelibrary.wiley.com/doi/abs/10.1111/j.1430-9134.2003.00031.x.

Bartley, T., & Child, C. (2011). Movements, markets and fields: The effects of anti-sweatshop campaigns on US firms, 1993-2000. *Social Forces*, *90*(2), 425–451. https://doi.org/10.1093/sf/sor010.

Baumgartner, R., Möller, M., and Stinus, H. (2016). *Pedorthics: Foot disorders, foot orthoses, footwear*. C. Maurer.

Benford, R. D., & Snow, D. A. (2000). Framing processes and social movements: An overview and assessment. *Annual Review of Sociology*, *26*(1), 611–639. https://doi.org/10.1146/annurev.soc.26.1.611.

Biyō, Kenkō kanren shōhin, shōhinryoku kimete: Shiseido no biyōeki, Kobayashi Seiyaku no kutsu no nakajiki [Product appeal is important for beauty and health products: Shiseido's milky lotion, Kobayashi Pharmaceutical's insoles]. (1994, March 30). *Nikkei Sangyo Shimbun*, 21.

Bosi, L., Giugni, M., & Uba, K. (2016). The consequences of social movements: Taking stock and looking forward. In L. Bosi, M. Giugni, & K. Uba (Eds.), *The consequences of social movements* (pp. 3–37). Cambridge University Press. https://doi.org/10.1017/CBO9781316337790.001.

Briscoe, F., & Gupta, A. (2016). Social activism in and around organizations. *Academy of Management Annals*, 10(1), 671–727. https://doi.org/10.5465/19416520.2016.1153261.

Buyer's guide: Import brand 180 [Buyer's guide: 180 import brands]. (1990, October). *Footwear Press*, 45–60.

Buying box: Comfort special [Comfort shoes buying guide]. (1991, November). *Footwear Press*, 128–131.

Cabinet Office. (n.d.) *National Accounts of Japan*. Cabinet Office. https://www.esri.cao.go.jp/en/sna/menu.html.

Church, R. A. (1968). The effect of the American export invasion on the British boot and shoe industry 1885–1914. *The Journal of Economic History*, *28*(2), 223–254. https://doi.org/10.1017/S002205070006931X.

Church, R. A. (1970). Labour supply and innovation 1800–1860: The boot and shoe industry. *Business History*, 12(1), 25–45. https://doi.org/10.1080/758533830.

Chūō Bussan, bei Combe-sha kara kasseitan-iri kutsu no nakajiki, "Odor-Eaters" o yunyū, hanbai e [Chūō Bussan to import and market "Odor-Eaters," the activated-carbon shoe inserts made by Combe (US)]. (1976, June 6). *Nikkei Ryutsu Shimbun*, 7.

Comfort ni ikiru: Sapporo, Alpha Miki [Comfort shoe specialty store: Alpha Miki in Sapporo-city]. (1991, December). *Footwear Press*, 45–48.

'Comfort' ni ikiru senmonten Motoyoshi, Tokyo Kita-ku [Comfort shoes specialty store Motoyoshi, Kita-ku, Tokyo]. (1991, September). *Footwear Press*, 28–31.

Comfort shijō o semeru: Shutten kigyō ni kiku wagasha no hanbaihōshin to mitōshi [Capturing the comfort shoe market: Exhibitors' sales policy and market forecast]. (1989, July). *Footwear Press*, 44–49.

Comfort yūryoku, chūmoku brand ichiran [Leading and notable brands of comfort shoes]. (1992, December). 42–43.

Dai 8-kai Comfort 21 [The 8th Comfort 21]. (1995, April). *Footwear Press*, 111–120.

Dai 9-kai Comfort 21 [The 9th Comfort 21]. (1995, September). *Footwear Press*, 58–59.

Dai 10-kai Comfort 21 [The 10th Comfort 21]. (1996, April). *Footwear Press*, n. a.

Dai 11-kai Comfort 21 [The 11th Comfort 21]. (1996, October). *Footwear Press*, 90–91.
Dai 12-kai Comfort 21 [The 12th Comfort 21]. (1997, March). *Footwear Press*, pp. 82–86.
Dai 13-kai Comfort 21 [The 13th Comfort 21]. (1997, September). *Footwear Press*, n. a.
Dai 14-kai Comfort 21 [The 14th Comfort 21]. (1998, March). *Footwear Press*, 147–150.
Dai 15-kai Comfort 21 [The 15th Comfort 21]. (1998, September). *Footwear Press*, 119.
Dai 16-kai Comfort 21 [The 16th Comfort 21]. (1999, March). *Footwear Press*, 117.
Dai 17-kai Comfort 21 [The 17th Comfort 21]. (1999, September). *Footwear Press*, n. a.
Dai 18-kai Comfort 21 [The 18th Comfort 21]. (2000, March). *Footwear Press*, n. a.
Dai 19-kai Comfort 21 [The 19th Comfort 21]. (2000, September). *Footwear Press*, 95–96.
Dai 20-kai Comfort 21 [The 20th Comfort 21]. (2001, March). *Footwear Press*, 61–66.
Dai 21-kai Comfort 21 [The 21st Comfort 21]. (2001, September). *Footwear Press*, 61–64.
Dai 22-kai Comfort 21 [The 22nd Comfort 21]. (2002, March). *Footwear Press*, n. a.
Dakara kono brand wa kaiteki nanda: Comfort Shoes-ten '88 yori [Comfortable shoe brands from Comfort Shoes Exhibition 1988]. (1988, September). *Footwear Press*, 55–63.
de Bakker, F. G. A., den Hond, F., & Laamanen, M. (2017). Social movements: Organizations and organizing. In C. Roggeband & B. Klandermans (Eds.), *Handbook of social movements across disciplines* (2nd ed., pp. 203–231). Springer International Publishing. https://doi.org/10.1007/978-3-319-57648-0_8
den Hond, F., & de Bakker, F. G. A., (2007). Ideologically motivated activism: How activist groups influence corporate social change activities. *Academy of Management Review, 32*(3), 901–924. https://doi.org/10.5465/amr.2007.25275682.
den Hond, F., de Bakker, F. G. A., & de Haan, P. (2010). The sequential patterning of tactics: Activism in the global sports apparel industry, 1988-2002. *International Journal of Sociology and Social Policy*, *30*(11/12), 648–665. https://doi.org/10.1108/01443331011085240.
Doitsu seikeigeka gutsu kenkyūkai ga kouriten no yūshi de hossoku [German Orthopaedic Shoe Research was established by retailers]. (1999, October). *Footwear Press*, 38–39.
Drugstore jittai chōsa: sōuriagedaka wa 4% zō no 5 chō 4430 oku en: Tenposū, uriagedaka tomo zōka tsuzuku [Drugstore study: Store count and sales continue to climb, with total sales up 4% to 5.443 trillion yen]. (2010, March 17). *Yakuji Nippō*. https://www.yakuji.co.jp/entry18544.html.
Dubuisson-Quellier, S. (2013). A market mediation strategy: How social movements seek to change firms' practices by promoting new principles of product valuation. *Organization Studies*, *34*(5–6), 683–703. https://doi.org/10.1177/0170840613479227.
Eesley, C., & Lenox, M. J. (2006). Firm responses to secondary stakeholder action. *Strategic Management Journal*, *27*(8), 765–781. https://doi.org/10.1002/smj.536.
Endoh Michio, Van San-sho shachō [Endoh Michio, President, Van San-sho]. (2005, December 5). *Diamond Weekly*, 132–133.
Foot, Footwear and Health Association. (2002, June 24). Kōseirōdōshō to no ginō kentei ni tsuite no shitsugi ōto memo [Memo of questions and answers with the Ministry of Health, Labor and Welfare regarding the National Trade Skill Test]. Foot, Footwear and Health Association.
Foot, Footwear and Health Association. (2023, June 1). *Shoe fitter kensaku* [Shoe fitter search]. http://fha.gr.jp/search.
Foot, Footwear and Health Association. (Ed.). (2015). *Ashi to kutsu to kenkō o kangaeru: Shoe fitterno chiisana kiseki* [Thinking about foot, footwear and health: Shoe fitter's little miracles]. *Senken Shimbun.*
Foot, Footwear and Health Association. (Ed.). (2017). *Shoe fitter ni tanomeba aruku koto ga motto tanoshikunaru* [If you rely on a shoe fitter, walking becomes more enjoyable]. Kikurosu Shuppan.
Freeman, J. (1979). Resource mobilization and strategy: A model for analyzing social movement organization actions. In M. N. Zald, & J. M. McCarthy (Eds.), *The dynamics of social movements* (pp. 167–189). Winthrop Publishers.
Fremeth, A. R., Holburn, G. L., & Piazza, A. (2022). Activist protest spillovers into the regulatory domain: Theory and evidence from the US nuclear power generation industry. *Organization Science, 33*(3), 1163–1187. https://doi.org/10.1287/orsc.2021.1473.

Frooman, J. (1999). Stakeholder influence strategies. *Academy of Management Review, 24*(2), 191–205. https://doi.org/10.5465/amr.1999.1893928.
Fuji Keizai. (1999). *'99 Toiletry goods marketing yōran no. 3* ['99 Toiletries marketing directory no. 3]. Fuji Keizai.
Fuji Keizai. (2000). *Toiletry goods marketing yōran 2000 no. 3* [Toiletries marketing directory 2000 no. 3]. Fuji Keizai.
Fuji Keizai. (2001). *Toiletry goods marketing yōran 2001 no. 3* [Toiletries marketing directory 2001 no. 3]. Fuji Keizai.
Fuji Keizai. (2002). *Toiletry goods marketing yōran 2002 no. 3* [Toiletries marketing directory 2002 no. 3]. Fuji Keizai.
Fuji Keizai. (2003). *Toiletry goods marketing yōran 2003 no. 3* [Toiletries marketing directory 2003 no. 3]. Fuji Keizai.
Fuji Keizai. (2004). *Toiletry goods marketing yōran 2005 no. 3* [Toiletries marketing directory 2004 no. 3]. Fuji Keizai.
Fuji Keizai. (2005). *Toiletry goods marketing yōran 2005 no. 3* [Toiletries marketing directory 2005 no. 3]. Fuji Keizai.
Fuji Keizai. (2006). *Toiletry goods marketing yōran 2006 no. 1* [Toiletries marketing directory 2006 no. 1]. Fuji Keizai.
Fuji Keizai. (2007). *Toiletry goods marketing yōran 2007 no. 1* [Toiletries marketing directory 2007 no. 1]. Fuji Keizai.
Fuji Keizai. (2010). *Toiletry goods marketing yōran 2010 no. 1* [Toiletries marketing directory 2010 no. 1]. Fuji Keizai.
Fuji Keizai. (2011). *Toiletry goods marketing yōran 2011 no. 1* [Toiletries marketing directory 2011 no. 1]. Fuji Keizai.
Fukyō shirazu de kotoshi mo antei seichō: Comfort and walking [Stable growth this year despite recession: Walking shoes and comfort shoes]. (1995, December). *Footwear Press*, 52–53.
Fukyō shirazu no comfort [Recession-proof comfort shoes]. (1992, December). *Footwear Press*, 22–38.
Funabashi, M. (2012). *Waga keiei* [My management]. Chiyoda.
Gaihanboshi no shinkō o yōbō, Kobayasi Seiyaku (Shin seihin). [Preventing bunions from worsening, Kobayashi Pharmaceutical, new product]. (1993, September 25). *Nikkei Ryutsu Shimbun*, 6.
George, A. L., & Bennett, A. (2005). *Case studies and theory development in the social sciences.* MIT Press.
German Orthopaedic Shoe Research (n. d.). G. O. S. R. no Katsudō 1999–2008 [Activities of GOSR 1999–2008]. https://gosr.jp/history/history-1.html.
Ginza Yoshinoya 90-nenshi Hensanshitsu (1997). *Okyakusama to tomoni: Ginza Yoshinoya 90-nenshi* [With our customers: 90-years history of Ginza Yoshinoya]. Ginza Yoshinoya.
Giugni, M. G. (1998). Was it worth the effort? The outcomes and consequences of social movements. *Annual Review of Sociology, 24*(1), 371–393. https://doi.org/10.1146/annurev.soc.24.1.371.
Gomuhouchi Shinbunsha. (1978). *1979-nenban Kutsu Nenka*n [1979 shoe yearbook]. Gomuhouchi Shinbunsha.
Gomuhouchi Shinbunsha. (1979). *1980-nenban Kutsu Nenkan* [1980 shoe yearbook]. Gomuhouchi Shinbunsha.
Gomuhouchi Shinbunsha (1980). *1981-nenban Kutsu Nenkan* [1981 shoe yearbook]. Gomuhouchi Shinbunsha.
Gomuhouchi Shinbunsha (1981). *1982-nenban Kutsu Nenkan* [1982 shoe yearbook]. Gomuhouchi Shinbunsha.
Gomuhouchi Shinbunsha. (1982). *1983-nenban kutsu nenkan* [1983 shoe yearbook]. Gomuhouchi Shinbunsha.
Gomuhouchi Shinbunsha. (1983). *1984-nenban kutsu nenkan* [1984 shoe yearbook]. Gomuhouchi Shinbunsha.

Gomuhouchi Shinbunsha. (1984). *1985-nenban kutsu nenkan* [1985 shoe yearbook]. Gomuhouchi Shinbunsha.

Gupta, A., & Briscoe, F. (2020). Organizational political ideology and corporate openness to social activism. *Administrative Science Quarterly, 65*(2), 524–563. https://doi.org/10.1177/0001839219852954.

Hana no kaori, kasseitan o naizō shiteirutame kutsu no iya na nioi o kyūshū [Insole with flower scent contains activated carbon to absorb shoe odors]. (1987, October 27). *Nikkei Ryutsu Shimbun*, 11.

Hensmans, M., Johnson, G., and Yip G. (2013). *Strategic transformation: Changing while winning*. Palgrave Macmillan London. https://doi.org/10.1057/9781137268464.

Hiatt, S. R., Sine, W. D., & Tolbert, P. S. (2009). From Pabst to Pepsi: The deinstitutionalization of social practices and the creation of entrepreneurial opportunities. *Administrative Science Quarterly, 54*(4), 635–667. https://doi.org/10.2189/asqu.2009.54.4.635.

Hikakusangyō Enkakushi Hensan Iinkai. (1959). *Hikaku sangyō enkakushi, jōkan* [History of the leather industry, part 1]. Tokyo Hikaku Seinenkai.

Hikakusangyō Enkakushi Hensan Iinkai. (1989). *Hikaku sankgyō enkakushi, gekan* [History of the leather industry, part 2]. Tokyo Hikaku Seinenkai.

Hīrugutsu nimo nakajiki, 'insole' de kaiteki hokō: Ashi no katachi ni micchaku, futan keigen [Close-fitting, burden-reducing insoles support comfortable walking in heeled shoes]. (November 22, 2006). *Nihon Keizai Shimbun*, morning edition, 37.

'Hitotsu ue o iku hakigokochi' o teiansuru tenjikai the 7th Comfort 21[The Comfort 21 suggested higher level comfortable shoes]. (1991, September). *Footwear Press*, 72–73.

Ichida, K. (2000). Edo jidai no geta [Geta in the Edo period]. In Edo Jidai Iseki Kenkyūkai (Ed.), *Edo jidai no kōkogaku* [Archaeology of the Edo period] (pp. 26–54). Yoshikawa Kōbunkan.

Imanishi, U. (1962). *Nihon hakimono hensen-shi* [The history of Japanese footwear]. Nihonhakimono Shinbunsha.

Inagawa, M. (2013). *Seiyō gutsu kotohajime: Nihonjin to kutsu no deai* [The beginnings of Western-style shoes: An encounter between Japanese people and shoes]. Gendai Shokan.

Inagawa, M. & Yamamoto Y. (2011). *Kutsuzukuri no bunka-shi: Nihon no kutsu to shokunin* [A history of shoemaking culture: Japanese shoes and shoemakers]. Gendai Shokan.

Insole hanbai dōkō [Insole Sales Trends]. (2006, Septemnber). *Footwear Press*, 81.

Interview Fuss und Schuh Institut, Rijichō Endoh Michio shi: Kaikō 10 shūnen o mukae, senmongijutsu o sonaeta shūryōsei ga 1000-nin o koeru [Interview with Michio Endoh, President of Fuss und Schuh Institut: Celebrating its 10th anniversary, the school has more than 1,000 graduates with specialized skills]. (1999, September). *Footwear Press*, 44–46.

Interview hassō no genten: Schritt shachō Kuze [Interview, origin of ideas: Kuze, President of Schritt]. (2001, September). *Footwear Press*, 36–38.

Interview, sōgyō 15 shūnen o mukaeta Alice: Doitsu no kenkōgutsu o nihon ni shōkai, comfort shoes sijō o kaitaku [Alice Inc. marked its 15th anniversary: Cultivating the comfort shoe market with German health shoes]. (1999, March). *Footwear Press*, 104–105.

Interview tenki ni tatsu: Van San-sho Endoh Michio shachō [Interview, at a turning point: Van San-sho President Michio Endo]. (1996, November). *Footwear Press*, pp. 54–55.

Ishida, M. & Yoshinaga, N. (Ed.). (2009). *Arukeru karada ni naru tame ni: Yomu to arukitakunaru hon* [How to get your body ready to walk: A book that makes you want to walk]. BAB Japan.

Ishikawa, Y. (2019). *#KuToo: Kutsu kara kangaeru honki no feminism* [#KuToo (Coinage of the word "shoes" and "pain,"): Sincere feminism from a shoe perspective]. Gendai Shokan.

Ishizuka, T. (1983) *Kutsu o machigaeru to byōki ni naru* [Wrong shoes make you sick]. Shufunotomo.

Itami, H. (1998). *Nihon Sangyō Mittsu no Nam*i [Three waves of Japanese industry]. NTT Publishing.

Itami, H., & Roehl, T. W. (1991). *Mobilizing invisible assets*. Harvard University Press.

Item-betsu marketing: Comfort, ladies [Item-specific marketing: Comfort shoes for women]. (1988, May). *Footwear Press*, 67–71.

Item-betsu marketing: Comfort shoes [Item-specific marketing: comfort shoes]. (1994, September). *Footwear Press*, 67–70.

Item-betsu marketing: Insole & footcare yōhin [Item-specific marketing: Insoles and footcare products]. (2010, January). *Footwear Press*, 60–64.

Iwamoto, S. (2014). Ifuku sangyō-shi kenkyū no dōkō: Kobetsu-shi kara zentai-shi e [The survey of research on apparel industry history]. *Study of Economic History, 17*, 103–121. https://doi.org/10.24712/keizaishikenkyu.17.0_103.

Jaffee, D. (2012). Weak coffee: Certification and co-optation in the fair trade movement. *Social Problems*, 59(1), 94–116. https://doi.org/10.1525/sp.2012.59.1.94.

Japan Automobile Manufacturers Association. (n. d.). *The automotive manufacturing industry as a key industry*. The Automotive Manufacturing Industry. http://www.jama.or.jp/industry/industry/index.html.

Japan DIY, HC Association. (n.d.). *Nenkan sōuriagedaka to homecenter-sū, suikeichi* [Estimated total annual sales and number of DIY centers]. https://www.diy.or.jp/i-information/association/jigyo/transition.html.

Japan Institute of Footwear. (1970). *JIF size iinkai chūkan hōkokusho* [JIF size committee interim report]. Japan Institute of Footwear.

Japan Institute of Footwear. (1971). *Dai 1-ki ashigata keisoku jicchi yōryō* [First phase foot measurement implementation guidelines]. Japan Institute of Footwear.

Japan Institute of Footwear. (1972). *Shoe report tokushū: Fitting no tame no yasashii kutsu no chisiki* [Shoe report selection: Easy shoe knowledge for fitting]. Japan Institute of Footwear.

Japan Institute of Footwear. (1975, October 22). *Dai 1-ki ashigata keisoku shiryō no itchibu* [Part of the first phase foot shape measurement data]. Japan Institute of Footwear.

Japan Institute of Footwear. (1979, September 31). *Seikaiin meibo* [List of regular members]. Japan Institute of Footwear.

Japan Institute of Footwear. (1981a, May 15). *JIF kaihō 81-2* [JIF News Letter 81-2]. Japan Institute of Footwear.

Japan Institute of Footwear. (1981b, date unknown). *JIF kaihō 81-4* [JIF News Letter 81-4]. Japan Institute of Footwear.

Japan Institute of Footwear. (1982a, September 2). *JIF kaihō 82-3* [JIF News Letter 82-3]. Japan Institute of Footwear.

Japan Institute of Footwear. (1982b, date unknown). *Fitter yōseikouza jisshi yōryō an* [Fitter training workshop plan]. Japan Institute of Footwear.

Japan Institute of Footwear. (1982c, date unknown). *JIF un'eian, '82 9-gatsu–12-gatsu* [JIF Management plan, '82, September–December]. Japan Institute of Footwear.

Japan Institute of Footwear. (1983a, February 2). *JIF rijikai shiryō* [JIF board meeting materials]. Japan Institute of Footwear.

Japan Institute of Footwear. (1983b, May 6). *JIF kaihō 83-3* [JIF Newsletter 83-3]. Japan Institute of Footwear.

Japan Institute of Footwear. (1983c, August 9). *JIF kaihō 83-4* [JIF newsletter 83-4]. Japan Institute of Footwear.

Japan Institute of Footwear. (1983d, October 27). *JIF kaihō 83-5* [JIF Newsletter 83-5]. Japan Institute of Footwear.

Japan Institute of Footwear. (1983e, November 29). *JIF kaihō 83-6* [JIF Newsletter 83-6]. Japan Institute of Footwear.

Japan Institute of Footwear. (1983f, date unknown). *Itaikutsu wa mō hakanai kōkoku boshū* [Advertisements wanted for *Say goodbye to wearing painful shoes*]. Japan Institute of Footwear.

Japan Institute of Footwear. (1983g, date unknown). *Keieisha to chūken shain no tameno dai 1-ki fitter yōseikōza* [The first fitter education program for the top and middle management].

Japan Institute of Footwear. (1983h, date unknown). *Oshirase to onegai* [Notices and requests]. Japan Institute of Footwear.

Japan Institute of Footwear. (1983i, date unknown). *Suisen no goaisatsu* [Recommendation]. Japan Institute of Footwear.

Japan Institute of Footwear. (1984a, March 3). *JIF kaihō 84-1* [JIF newsletter 84-1]. Japan Institute of Footwear.

Japan Institute of Footwear. (1984b, May 10). *JIF kaihō 84-2* [JIF Newsletter 84-2]. Japan Institute of Footwear.

Japan Institute of Footwear. (1984c, April 12). *Kaiin kakui, Kodansha kan Itai kutsu wa mō hakanai haifu ni tsuite* [Dear members, about *Say goodbye to wearing painful shoes* published by Kodansha]. Japan Institute of Footwear.

Japan Institute of Footwear. (1984d, August 1). *Nihon Kutsu Sōgō Kenkyū Kai kanyū no osasoi* [Invitation to join Japan Institute of Footwear]. Japan Institute of Footwear.

Japan Institute of Footwear. (1984e, October 2). *Itai kutsu wa mō hakanai TV de 4-ka kan renzoku hōsō* [Four consecutive day TV programs on *Say goodbye to wearing painful shoes*]. Japan Institute of Footwear.

Japan Institute of Footwear. (1984f, November 21). *JIF kaihō 84-4* [JIF Newsletter 84-4]. Japan Institute of Footwear.

Japan Institute of Footwear. (1984g, date unknown). *Kutsu kouriten sales no tameno shoe fitter yōsei kōza, dai 1-kai* [Shoe Fitter Training Workshop for shoe store sales, first]. Japan Institute of Footwear.

Japan Institute of Footwear. (1985a, March 18). *JIF kaihō 85-1* [JIF Newsletter 85-1]. Japan Institute of Footwear.

Japan Institute of Footwear. (1985b, April 11). *Shoe fitter no minasan e* [Dear shoe fitters]. Japan Institute of Footwear.

Japan Institute of Footwear. (1985c, June 14). *JIF kaihō 85-3* [JIF newsletter 85-3]. Japan Institute of Footwear.

Japan Institute of Footwear. (1985d, July 18). *JIF kaihō 85-4* [JIF newsletter 85-4]. Japan Institute of Footwear.

Japan Institute of Footwear. (1985e, August 5). *JIF kaihō 85-5* [JIF newsletter 85-5]. Japan Institute of Footwear.

Japan Institute of Footwear. (1985f, October 17). *JIF kaihō 85-6* [JIF Newsletter 85-6]. Japan Institute of Footwear.

Japan Institute of Footwear. (1985g, October 17). *JIF kaihō 85-6* [JIF newsletter 85-6]. Japan Institute of Footwear.

Japan Institute of Footwear. (1985h, November 26). *JIF kaihō 85-7* [JIF newsletter 85-7]. Japan Institute of Footwear.

Japan Institute of Footwear. (1985i, date unknown). *Kutsu kouriten sales no tameno shoe fitter yōsei kōza, dai 2-kai* [Shoe Fitter Training Workshop for shoe store sales, second]. Japan Institute of Footwear.

Japan Institute of Footwear. (1985j, date unknown). *Kutsu kouriten sales no tameno shoe fitter yōsei kōza, dai 3-kai* [Shoe Fitter Training Workshop for shoe store sales, third]. Japan Institute of Footwear.

Japan Institute of Footwear. (1988a). *Shoe fitter yōsei tsūshin kōza: Dai 1-kai Jōkyū course goan'nai* [Shoe fitter training corresponding course: The first advanced course]. Japan Institute of Footwear.

Japan Institute of Footwear. (1990, May 10). Nosaka Miyako san NHK shutsuen [Miyako Nosaka appeared on NHK (Nippon Hoso Kyokai, Japan Broadcasting Corporation)]. *Trait d'Union*, 6, 6.

Japan Institute of Footwear. (1992a). *92 Shoe fitter list*. Japan Institute of Footwear.

Japan Institute of Footwear. (1995). *Awanai kutsu wa karada ni warui: Ashigata betsu anata ni pittari no kutsuerabi* [Ill-fitting shoes are bad for your health: Selecting parfect shoes for you based on your foot shape]. Kodansha.

Japan Institute of Footwear. (1997). *Tsūshosangyōshō itaku chōsa: Ashi to kutsu to kenkō ni kansurujinzaiikusei no arikata hōkokusho* [Survey Commissioned by Ministry of International Trade and Industry: Report on human resource development for foot, shoe and health]. Japan Institute of Footwear.

Japan Institute of Footwear. (n.d.a). *Kutsu no hon hakkan, shōhisha taishō, hakkō* [Book about shoe for consumers publication project]. Japan Institute of Footwear.

Japan Institute of Footwear. (n.d.b). *Nihon Kutsu Sōgō Kenkyūkai 'Shoe fitter yōsei kōza' shūryōsha meibo* [List of completers of Japan Institute of Footwear 'Shoe Fitter Training Workshop']. Japan Institute of Footwear.

Japan Institute of Footwear. (n.d.c). *Shōwa 54-nendo jigyō hōkokusho* [1979 convention report]. Japan Institute of Footwear.

Japan Institute of Footwear. (Ed.). (1984h). *Itai kutsu wa mō hakanai, shiranakatta kutsuawase no how to* [Say goodbye to wearing painful shoes: The secrets of finding the right shoes for you]. Kodansha.

Japan Institute of Footwear. (Ed.). (1988b). *Kenkō ni ii kutsu erabi: Pumps kara walking shoes made* [Picking healthy shoes: From pumps to walking shoes]. Chikuma Shuhansha.

Japan Institute of Footwear. (Ed.). (1992b). *Shin kenkō ni ii kutsu erabi: Shoe fittier ga oshieru 101 no point* [Picking healthy shoes, updated: 101 tips suggested by shoe fitters]. Chikuma Shuhansha.

Japan Institute of Women's Footwear. (1967). *Shoe report sensho no.1: Kutsu no tame no ashi* [Shoe report selection no.1: Foot for shoes]. Japan Institute of Women's Footwear.

Japan Institute of Women's Footwear. (1968). *Shoe report sensho no.2: Yoikutsu no jōken nyūmonhen* [Shoe report selection no.2: Requirements for good shoes]. Japan Institute of Women's Footwear.

Japan Institute of Women's Footwear. (1969). *Shoe report sensho no.3: Yoi kutsu no kiso chishiki, sales no jissenteki handbook* [Shoe report selection no.3: Basic knowledge of good shoes, practical handbook for sales]. Japan Institute of Women's Footwear.

Japan Standards Association. (n. d.). *JIS S5037: 1998 kutsu no size* [JIS S 5037:1998 sizing system for shoes]. JSA Group website. https://webdesk.jsa.or.jp/books/W11M0090/index/?bunsyo_id=JIS+S+5037%3A1998.

JIF Fitting Kenshūkai. (1991). *Dai 1-kai, fitthing kenshūkai hōkokusho, 1991* [First fitting workshop, 1991]. JIF Fitting Kenshūkai.

JIF Fitting Kenshūkai. (1992). *Dai 2-kai, fitthing kenshūkai hōkokusho, 1992* [Second fitting workshop, 1992]. JIF Fitting Kenshūkai.

JIF Fitting Kenshūkai. (1994). *Dai 3-kai, fitthing kenshūkai hōkokusho, 1994* [Third fitting workshop, 1994]. JIF Fitting Kenshūkai.

Joyochiiki Kenkyū Center. (2009, July). Taten ga mane dekinai kenkō gutsu no consulting hanbai: Yūgengaisha Catch Ball daihyōtorishimariyaku Igari Takayuki [Consulting sales of health shoes avoiding imitation by other stores: Catch Ball Co., Ltd., President Takayuki Igari]. *Joyo Arc*, 17–18.

Jūshin idō ga smooth ni, Kowa, new product [Smooth shifting of your balance, Kowa's new product]. (2010, October 29). *Nikkei MJ (Nikkei Ryutsu Shimbun)*, 15.

KKO [pseud.]. (1984, August 25). Shoe fitter ni tsuite [About shoe fitters]. *Toukutsu* [Toukutsu Association newsletter].

Kaitekigutsu o teiansuru tenjikai "Confort 21" [Comfortable shoes exhibition, Comfort 21]. (1991, November). *Footwear Press*, 15.

Kajiyama, S. (2018). *Kenkō chōju wa kutsu de kimaru* [Health and longevity are determined by shoes]. Bungeishunju.

Kakato no takai sandal, 'mule,' onnagokoro no ashimoto tsukamu: Kiji, iro hōfu ni [Mules, or high-heeled sandals, sweep women off their feet in a variety of materials and colors]. (1997, April 22). *Nihon Keizai Shimbun*, evening edition, 16.

Katase, M., & Hirabayashi, Y. (2002). Ryūkōgutsu mule chakuyō ni yoru ashi no trouble no jittai [The actual condition of the trouble of the foot which happens by mule]. *Abstracts of Annual Congress of The Japan Society of Home Economics, 54*, 248–248. https://doi.org/10.11428/kasei.54.0.248.0.

Katase, M., Hirabayashi, Y., Sionoya, K., Kuribayashi, K. (2001). Joshidaisei no mule no chakuyō no jittai to ishiki [The investigation into the behavior and attitude of the female students wearing mule sandals]. *Kinjo Gakuin Daigaku Kenkyūjo Kiyō, 5*(1), 25–34. https://cir.nii.ac.jp/crid/1520853834970744960.

Katō, K. (1967). Kutsugata [Shoe last]. *The Japanese Journal of Ergonomics, 3*(2), 147–148. https://doi.org/10.5100/jje.3.136.

Katō, K. (1977). Hakimono to hokō [Gait of man and shoes design research]. *Japanese Journal of Ergonomics, 13*(5), 211–214. https://doi.org/10.5100/jje.13.211.

Katō, K. (1990, November 9). *"Bachelor" oyobi "jōkyu cource" jukōsha no minasama e* [Dear "bachelor" and "advanced course" participants]. Japan Institute of Footwear.

Katō, K. (2002). Shoe fitter no yōsei to genjō [Shoe fitters: Training programs and current conditions]. *Leather Science, 39*(1), 123–132.

Katō, K. (2003). Nihon no shoe fitter sodate no oya [The man who brought up Japan's shoe fitters], *Journal of Artistic Anatomy, 8*(1), 133–135.

Katō, K. & Yamamoto, H. (1986). *Shoe fitter ga kaita kutsu no hon* [Shoe book by a shoe fitter]. Sansuisha.

Katō, K. & Yamamoto, H. (2004). *Jōkyū shoe fitter ga oshieru kutsu erabi de genki ni naru hon* [Advanced shoe fitter teaches how to select shoes to cheer you up]. Kikurosu Shuppan.

Katō, K. & Yamamoto, H. (Eds.). (1976). *Yoi kutsu no kiso chishiki: sales no jissenteki handbook (Revised ed.)* [Basic knowledge of good shoes: Practical handbook for sales (Revised ed.)]. Japan Institute of Footwear.

Katō, K. & Yamamoto, H. (Eds.). (1980). *Yoi kutsu no kiso chishiki: sales no jissenteki handbook (Revised 3rd ed.)* [Basic knowledge of good shoes: Practical handbook for sales (Revised 3rd ed.)]. Japan Institute of Footwesar.

Katō, K. & Yamamoto, H. (Eds.). (1983). *Yoi kutsu no kiso chishiki: sales no jissenteki handbook (Revised 5th ed.)* [Basic knowledge of good shoes: Practical handbook for sales (Revised 5th ed.)]. Japan Institute of Footwear.

Katō, K. & Yamamoto, H. (Eds.). (1987). *Yoi kutsu no kiso chishiki: Sales no jissenteki handbook (Revised 7th ed.)* [Basic knowledge of good shoes: Practical handbook for sales (Revised 7th ed.)]. Japan Institute of Footwear.

Kenkō kutsu ten 'La Moustache' tenchō Tadano Toshio san: Ashino nayami kaiketsu e doitsu no gijutsu shūtoku [Toshio Tadano, owner of health shoes store, La Moustache learned German skills to solve foot problems]. (2015, November 19). *Asahi Shimbun*, morning edition, 26.

Kido, T. (1979). *Shin Katagami Technique* [Technique of the shoe pattern-cutting, updated]. Japan Institute of Footwear.

King, B. (2008). A political mediation model of corporate response to social movement activism. *Administrative Science Quarterly, 53*(3), 395–421. https://doi.org/10.2189/asqu.53.3.395.

King, B. (2016). Reputation, risk, and anticorporate activism. In L. Bosi, M. Giugni, & K. Uba (Eds.), *The consequences of social movements* (pp. 215–236). Cambridge University Press. https://doi.org/10.1017/CBO9781316337790.

King, B., & Pearce, N. A. (2010). The contentiousness of markets: Politics, social movements, and institutional change in markets. *Annual Review of Sociology, 36*, 249–267. https://doi.org/10.1146/annurev.soc.012809.102606.

King, B. G., & Soule, S. A. (2007). Social movements as extra-institutional entrepreneurs: The effect of protests on stock price returns. *Administrative Science Quarterly, 52*(3), 413–442. https://doi.org/10.2189/asqu.52.3.413.

Kishimoto, T. & Ichida, K. (Ed.). (2000). *Kutsu no jiten: Geta o haita?* [Encyclopedia of shoes: Did you wear geta]. Bunensha.

Kobayashi Seiyaku Business Division Kashiwabara Nobuyuki: Nakajiki, gaihanboshi fusegu [Kashiwabara Nobuyuki, Business Division, Kobayashi Pharmaceutical]. (1994, December 19). *Nikkei Sangyo Shimbun*, 16.

Kobayashi, T. (2017). Aruku koto ga motto tanoshikunaru: Senior no kutsuerabi [Make walking more fun: Choosing shoes for seniors]. In Foot, Footwear and Health Association (Ed.), *Shoe fitter ni tanomeba aruku koto ga motto tanoshikunaru* [Shoe fitter help walk more fun] (pp. 87–105). Kikurosu Shuppan.

Koike, C., & Nakao, Y. (1966). Hifuku kōsei no tameno jakunen joshi no keisoku, dai 1-pō [Atlas of women]. *Japanese Journal of Ergonomics*, *2*(4), 15–29. https://doi.org/10.5100/jje.2.4_15.

Kondō, S. (1995). *Ashi to Kutsu no Kagaku* [Science of human and shoes]. *Journal of the Japanese Research Association for Textile End-Uses*, *36*(10), 616–622. https://doi.org/10.11419/sensho shi1960.36.616.

Kondō, S., Terada, K. & Kōhara, Y. (1950). Ashi no keisokuchitōkei no ichishian [On a statistical treatment of measurement of foot]. *The Journal of the Anthropological Society of Nippon*, *61*(4), 167–174. https://doi.org/10.1537/ase1911.61.167.

Koshō, T. (1966). Kin'yū shihon seiritsu-ki ni okeru hikaku sangyō [The leather industry in the establishing period of financial capital]. *Journal of the Faculty of Economics of Komazawa University*, *24*, 222–243. http://repo.komazawa-u.ac.jp/opac/repository/all/21225/.

Kotler, P., & Armstrong, G. (2012). *Principles of Marketing* (14th ed.). Pearson Education.

Kouriten ni interview: Comfort hanbai kō omou [Interview with retailers: Thought on comfort shoe sales]. (1988, July). *Footwear Press*, 51–54.

Kouriten ni kiku: Watashi ni totte 'fitter' towa [Interview with retailers: My thought on a shoe fitter]. (1988, December). *Footwear Press*, 39–41.

Kouriten zadankai: Uriba de ima nani ga okotteiruka [Retailers' discussion: Sales floor today]. (1988, February). *Footwear Press*, 35–41.

Kuremoto, M. (2011). *Jinsei o tanoshiku suru otona no onna no kutsuerabi* [Selecting shoes to make life fun for adult women]. Gentosha.

Kutsu no counseling hanbai hyakkaten de hirogaru: Shoe fitter o zokuzoku haichi [Counseling sales spread in department stores]. (1987, February 19). *Nikkei Ryutsu Shimbun*, 5.

Kutsu no nakajiki: Ashimoto no seiketsu shikō ni match, oshare takinō ga zokuzoku [Insoles: Stylish and multifunctional insoles sell well to people concerned about foot hygiene]. (1990, November 22), *Nikkei Ryutsu Shimbun*, 24.

Kutsu no nakajiki ashiura pitari, Morito new product [Shoe insoles that fit the soles perfectly]. (1999, January 28). *Nikkei Ryutsu Shimbun*, 18.

Kutsu no nakazoko ni mieru nakajiki, Kobayashi Seiyaku (Shinseihin) [Insoles look like the original shoe insert, new product from Kobayashi Pharmaceutical]. (1986, May 1). *Nikkei Ryutsu Shimbun*, 13.

Kuze, Y. (1999). Kutsu de ashi o kenkō ni suru [Shoes and healthy feet]. In E. Machida (Ed.), *Ashi no itami to henkei o naosu hon* [All about curing foot pain and deformities] (pp. 121–166). Makino Shuppan.

Kyakutanka up no kotsu: Report kanrenshōhin o uru [Tips for increasing average sales per customer: Report report on selling related products]. (2009, September). *Footwear Press*, 38–45.

Kyoto University Hospital Kango Jissen Kaihatsu Center (Ed.). (2004). *Tōnyōbyō kanja no footcare: Footcare gairai no system to care no jissai* [Footcare of diabetes patients: Foot care outpatients' system and their care]. Igakushoin.

Lame iri de kutsu no naka oshareni, Serendip's new product [Glittery insole makes shoe inside fashionable, Serendip's new product]. (2011, May 23). *Nikkei MJ (Nikkei Ryutsu Shimbunn)*, 17.

Lounsbury, M., Ventresca, M., & Hirsch, P. M. (2003). Social movements, field frames and industry emergence: A cultural-political perspective on US recycling. *Socio-Economic Review*, *1*(1), 71–104. https://doi.org/10.1093/soceco/1.1.71.

Luders, J. (2006). The economics of movement success: Business responses to civil rights mobilization. *American Journal of Sociology*, *111*(4), 963–998. https://doi.org/10.1086/498632.

MD-guide, footcare and insole: Ashi no kenkō ni taisuru kanshin ga oikazeni. Kinōsei no fukakachi zuke de hanro mo tasai ni [MD guide of footcare goods and insoles: Variety of sales channels for high value-added products with advanced functionality backed by strong awareness of foot health]. (2003, December). *Footwear Press*, 60–66.

Madono, H. (2002). Gishi sōgushi ni taisuru kutsu no kyōiku ni tsuite [Education of orthopaedic footwear for certified prosthetists and orthotists]. *Kutsu no Igaku*, *16*(2), 34–37.

Maeda, Y. (2003, March). Kenzen na comfort shop keiei [Sound comfort shoe store management]. *Footwear Press*, 36–37.

Makiya, M. (1997). *Kutsu de jinsei o kaeru: Yoi kutsu, yoi ashi, handsome walk* [Shoes change your life: Good shoes, good feet, handsome walk]. Hamano.

McDonnell, M. H., & King, B. (2013). Keeping up appearances: Reputational threat and impression management after social movement boycotts. *Administrative Science Quarterly, 58*(3), 387–419. https://doi.org/10.1177/0001839213500032.

Meister technology super comfort Pedx. (1992, December). *Footwear Press*, 32.

Meshida, K. (2017). Fashion-sei ka Jitsuyōsei ka: Kinō de kangaeru shinshigutsu erabi [Selecting men's shoes from a fashion or a function Perspective]. In Foot, Footwear and Health Association (FHA) (Ed.), *Shoe fitter ni tanomeba aruku koto ga motto tanoshikunaru* [If you rely on a shoe fitter, walking becomes more enjoyable] (pp. 49–64). Kikurosu Shuppan.

Ministry of Economy, Trade and Industry. (2022). *Hakimono sangyō o meguru saikin no dōkō* [Recent trends in the footwear industry]. Ministry of Economy, Trade and Industry. https://www.meti.go.jp/policy/mono_info_service/mono/seikatsuseihin/hikaku/downloadfiles/2022hakimonodoukou.pdf.

Ministry of Economy, Trade and Industry. (n.d.a). *Census of Manufactures*. Ministry of Economy, Trade and Industry. https://www.meti.go.jp/statistics/tyo/kougyo/index.html.

Ministry of Economy, Trade and Industry. (n.d.b). *Kako no wariatewaku suii to kanzeiritsu no suii* [Historical trends in quotas and tariff rates]. http(s)://www.meti.go.jp/policy/external_economy/trade_control/03_import/01_kanwari/kanwari_7.html.

Ministry of Finance. (n.d.). *Trade Statistics of Japan*. Ministry of Finance. https://www.customs.go.jp/toukei/info/.

Ministry of Internal Affairs and Communications. (n.d.). *Consumer Price Index*. Ministry of Internal Affairs and Communications. https://www.stat.go.jp/data/cpi/index.html.

Mintzberg, H. (1978). Patterns in strategy formation. *Management Science, 24*(9), 934–948. https://doi.org/10.1287/mnsc.24.9.934.

Mintzberg, H., & Waters, J. A. (1985). Of strategies, deliberate and emergent. *Strategic Management Journal, 6*(3), 257–272. https://doi.org/10.1002/smj.4250060306.

Miranda, J. A. (2004). American machinery and European footwear: Technology transfer and international trade, 1860–1939. *Business History*, 46(2), 195–218. https://doi.org/10.1080/0007679042000215106.

Miura, S. (2014). *Ashi to Kutsu to Kenkō Kyōgikai no katsudōshi (1): Shoe fitter yōseikōza tanjō made* [A History of Foot, Footwear and Health Association, Vol. 1: The Launch of the Shoe Fitter Training Program]. Working Papers of Research Center for Japanese Business Studies, (185), 1–20.

Miura, S. (2017) Senzen no kawagutsu sangyō: Gunju to minju no suikei [Leather shoe production before World War II: An estimation of military and private demand]. *Hitotsubashi Review of Commerce and Management, 12*(1), 54–61.

Miura, S. (2018, August 3–4). *Partnering strategy between NPOs and business organizations: The case of the shoe industry in Japan* [Paper presentation]. Challenges of Sustainable Development and Social Impacts on Cooperatives and Social Enterprises, Bangkok, Thailand.

Miura, S. (2019a). Shakai katsudōdantai no senryaku shūsei to shijō sōzō: kutsusangyō ni okeru shakaikatsudōdantai, kigyō, shōhisha, media no sōgosayō [Adjustments of social activist strategies and new market creation: The interplay of an activity group, companies and their primary stakeholders in the shoe industry]. *Organizational Science, 52*(3), 20–32. https://doi.org/10.11207/soshikikagaku.52.3_20.

Miura, S. (2019b). Shikakunintei jigyō no setsuritsu process: Shoe fitter shikaku o jirei to shite [Establishing private qualification programs: How the shoe fitter qualification program was established]. *Shujitsu Management Studies*, (4), 33–68. https://shujitsu.repo.nii.ac.jp/records/453.

Miura, S. (2020) Naze eranda kutsu de ashi o itamerunoka: Shijō deno kutsu erabi no muzukashisa o saguru [Why do we have trouble with the shoes we wear?: The difficulty of finding shoes that fit in Japan]. *Gakuen*, (958), 16–36. https://swu.repo.nii.ac.jp/records/7011.

Miura, S. (2021). The developmental history of the insole market in Japan: Rising health consciousness and an unintended shift toward fashion (1984–2010). *Japanese Research in Business History*, *38*, 43–61. https://doi.org/10.5029/jrbh.38.43.

Miura, S. (2023). *Retail format innovation and survival of small stores: Evidence from the Japanese shoe trade, 1974–2022*. Institute of Current Business Studies of Show a Women's University Working Paper, (7), 1–34. http://swubizlab.jp/wp/wp-content/uploads/2023/03/2023miura.pdf.

Miyakawa, T. (1994, October). Relax Chokugen: Shizen no nagare [Relax straight talk: Natural course of events]. *Footwear Press*, 20–21.

Miyamoto, S. (1933). *Minkan Fukushokushi Hakimonohen* [Civilian fashion: Footwear]. Yuzankaku.

Mizuho Sōgō Kenkyūjo. (2002, April). Kuze Yasuo, Schritt shachō [Kuze Yasuo, President of Scritt]. *Mizuho Management Report*, 32–37.

Monet Teramoto. (n. d.). *Watashitachi no rekishi* [Our History]. http://www.monet-teramoto.com/info_rekishi.html.

Mono ryūkō: Kutsu no nakajiki, tōmei de medatazu danryokusei mo [Product trends: Transparent, inconspicuous and elastic shoe inserts]. (2009, June 22). *Yomiuri Shimbun*, morning edition, 16.

Morito, mule ya pumps no maesuberi-bōshi pad, 'Non-Slide' [Morito releases the 'Non-Slide,' a pad to prevent slippage in mules and pumps]. (2002, August). *Footwear Press*, 60.

Nakajiki ni keisha hiza no itami keigen, Kobayashi Seiyaku shin seihin [Beveled insoles for knee pain relief]. (1996, December 19). *Nikkei Ryutsu Shimbun*, 16.

Nakajiki tsukai yōtsū o yobō, Scholl Japan shin seihin [insoles to prevent back pain, Scholl Japan's new product]. (1994, February 19). *Nikkei Ryutsu Shimbun*, 7.

Nakajima, T. (2011a). Kutsu no fitting mondai ni tsuite, 1 [Shoe fitting issues, 1]. *Leather & Footwears*, *155*, 6–11.

Nakajima, T. (2011b). Kutsu no fitting mondai ni tsuite, 2 [Shoe fitting issues, 2]. *Leather & Footwears*, *156*, 6–12.

Nakajima, T. (2012). Kutsu no fittingu mondai ni tsuite, 3 [Shoe fitting issues, 3]. *Leather and Footwear*, *159*, 7–12.

Nakao, Y. (1965). Jintai Keisokuchi [Measurements of the Human Body]. *The Japanese Journal of Ergonomics*, *1*(1), 35–39. https://doi.org/10.5100/jje.1.35.

Nikkei Business Publications & Kuze, Y. (Eds.). (1999). *Kawaii! Demo... itakunai: Shippai shinai kutsuerabi* [So cute! And they don't hurt: Failproof shoe selection]. Nikkei Business Publications.

Nippon Seika Shashi Hensan Iinkai. (Ed.). (1990). *Nippon Seika Shashi Steps: Nippon Seika no ayumi 1902–1989* [History of Nippon Seika Steps: The path of Japan-made shoes 1902–1989]. Nippon Seika.

Nishimura, K. (1992). *Koike Chie fashion no michi: Jidai no saki o osietuzukete* [Chie Koike's fashion way: Teachings Ahead of Their Time]. Bunka Publishing Bureau.

Nihsimura, T. (2016). *Sonokutsu itakunai desuka?: Anatani pittarri na kutsu no mitsukekata* [Those shoes hurting you?: How to find the right shoes for you]. Asukashinsha.

Notsu, T. (1968). Kodai fukusō kenkyū (Dai 2hō): Hakimono no kenkyū [A study of ancient costume (Part 2): A study on footwear]. *Bulletin of Shimane Women's Junior College*, *6*, 12–19. https://ushimane.repo.nii.ac.jp/records/955.

Notsu, T. (1969). Kodai Fukusō Kenkyū (Dai 3hō): Hakimono no Kenkyū [A study of ancient costume (Part 3): A study on footwear (2)]. *Bulletin of Shimane Women's Junior College*, *7*, 42–49. https://ushimane.repo.nii.ac.jp/records/956.

Numagami, T. (1995). Kobetsujireikenkyū no datōsei ni tsuite [Validity of single case study]. *Business Review*, *42*(3), 55–70.

Numagami, T. (2000). *Koui no keieigaku: Keieigaku ni okeru ito sezaru kekka no tankyū* [Toward an action system theory of management]. Hakuto-Shobo.

Oohori, A. & Yamazaki, N. (1990). Hokō ni okeru kutsunai suberiryō no keisoku to hyōka [Measurement and evaluation of relative displacement between foot and shoe on walking]. *Japanese Journal of Ergonomics*, *26*, 216–217. https://doi.org/10.5100/jje.26.Supplement_216.
Organisation for Economic Co-operation and Development. (1975). *Kutsu yōgo 6 kakoku taiyakushū* [Footwear industry technical vocabulary] (K. Katō & H. Yamamoto, Trans.). Organisation for Economic Co-operation and Development. (Original work published 1969).
Orthopedic shoes ni kanshin atsumaru: Fashion-sei o kanesonaeta shōhin mo [Orthopedic shoes attracted attention: Some shoes had fashionable look]. (1994, December). *Footwear Press*, 119–121.
Ōtsuka, A. (1991). *Hakigokochi: Kurashi no naka no Kutsu* [Fit and feel: Shoes in everyday living]. Tsukiji Shokan.
Otsuka Seika. (1976). *Otsuka Seika hyakunen-shi* [100-year history of Otsuka Seika]. Otsuka Seika.
Ōtsuka, Y., & Abe, Y. (1990). *Ashi ga abunai! Kutsu de nakanai tame no hon!* [Feet are in danger! Book about how to avoid your shoes making you cry!]. JIOC Publishing.
Ōya, S. (1988, December). Fitting no shūhen, shoe fitter wa ima nani o subekika? [Related to shoe fitting, what should a shoe fitter do now?]. *Footwear Press*, 35–58.
Ōya, S. (1996a, January). Comfort shijō no asu o kangaeru [Thinking about the future of the comfort shoe market]. *Footwear Press*, 100–103.
Ōya, S. (1996b, February). Comfort shijō no asu o kangaeru, 2 [Thinking about the future of the comfort shoe market, 2]. *Footwear Press*, 91–95.
Pacheco, D. F., & Dean, T. J. (2015). Firm responses to social movement pressures: A competitive dynamics perspective. *Strategic Management Journal,* 36(7), 1093–1104. https://doi.org/10.1002/smj.2273.
Paige, R. C., & Littrell, M. A. (2002). Craft retailers' criteria for success and associated business strategies. *Journal of Small Business Management,* 40(4), 314–331. https://doi.org/10.1111/1540-627X.00060.
Pfeffer, J., & Salancik, G. R. (1978). *The external control of organizations: A resource dependence perspective.* Harper & Row.
Porter, M. E. (1980). *Competitive strategy: Thechniques for analyzing industries and competitors.* The Free Press.
Posty Corporation. (1985). *1986-nenban shoes book* [1986 shoe yearbook]. Posty Corporation.
Posty Corporation. (1986). *1987-nenban shoes book* [1987 shoe yearbook]. Posty Corporation.
Posty Corporation. (1987). *1988-nenban shoes book* [1988 shoe yearbook]. Posty Corporation.
Posty Corporation. (1988). *1989-nenban shoes book* [1989 shoe yearbook]. Posty Corporation.
Posty Corporation. (1989). *1990-nenban shoes book* [1990 shoe yearbook]. Posty Corporation.
Posty Corporation. (1990). *1991-nenban shoes book* [1991 shoe yearbook]. Posty Corporation.
Posty Corporation. (1991). *1992-nenban shoes book* [1992 shoe yearbook]. Posty Corporation.
Posty Corporation. (1992). *1993-nenban shoes book* [1993 shoe yearbook]. Posty Corporation.
Posty Corporation. (1993). *1994-nenban shoes book* [1994 shoe yearbook]. Posty Corporation.
Posty Corporation. (1994). *1995-nenban shoes book* [1995 shoe yearbook]. Posty Corporation.
Posty Corporation. (1995). *1996-nenban shoes book* [1996 shoe yearbook]. Posty Corporation.
Posty Corporation. (1996). *1997-nenban shoes book* [1997 shoe yearbook]. Posty Corporation.
Posty Corporation. (2005). *2006-nenban shoes book* [2006 shoe yearbook]. Posty Corporation.
Posty Corporation. (2012). *2013-nenban shoes book* [2013 shoe yearbook]. Posty Corporation.
Posty Corporation. (2013). *2014-nenban shoes book* [2014 shoe yearbook]. Posty Corporation.
Posty Corporation. (2014). *2015-nenban shoes book* [2015 shoe yearbook]. Posty Corporation.
Posty Corporation. (2015). *2016-nenban shoes book* [2016 shoe yearbook]. Posty Corporation.
Posty Corporation. (2016). *2017-nenban shoes book* [2017 shoe yearbook]. Posty Corporation.
Posty Corporation. (2017). *2018-nenban shoes book* [2018 shoe yearbook]. Posty Corporation.
Posty Corporation. (2018). *2019-nenban shoes book* [2018 shoe yearbook]. Posty Corporation.
Posty Corporation. (2020). *2021-nenban shoes book* [2021 shoe yearbook]. Posty Corporation.
Posty Corporation. (2021). *2022-nenban shoes book* [2022 shoe yearbook]. Posty Corporation.

Professional shoe fitting o yomu kai [*Professional shoe fitting* reading group]. (1988, December). *Footwear Press*, 43.

PR Special comfort & high-tech shoes guide. (1988, November). *Footwear Press*, 67–83.

Rao, H. (2009). *Market rebels: How activists make or break radical innovations*. Princeton University Press.

Reinecke, J., & Ansari, S. (2021). Microfoundations of framing: The interactional production of collective action frames in the occupy movement. *Academy of Management Journal*, 64(2), 378–408. https://doi.org/10.5465/amj.2018.1063.

Ryōhanten mo comfort ni chakushu, 1-man en o kitte misesu ni hit [Mass merchandisers also launched comfort shoes, hitting the middle-aged woman market at less than ¥10,000]. (1989, February). *Footwear Press*, 41–42.

Sakai, K. (2018). Thriving in the shadow of giants: The success of the Japanese surgical needle producer MANI, 1956–2016. *Business History*, *61*(3), 1–27. https://doi.org/10.1080/00076791.2018.1424833.

Sandal to ashi no zure fusegu pad, Columbus shin seihin [Pads to prevent feet from slipping in sandals, Columbus's new product]. (1997, March 25). *Nikkei Ryutsu Shimbun*, 23.

Sasō, K. (1982). *Sasō Keigo no kutsu sekkyaku know-how* [Shoe salesperson's know-how by Keigo Sasō]. Japan Institute of Footwear.

Satō, E. (Ed.). (1971). *Kutsu sangyō hyakunen-shi* [A 100-year history of the shoe industry]. Nihon Kutsu Renmei.

Schritt, chokuei no technical shop o open [Schritt opens a technical shop]. (1992, August). *Footwear Press*, 101–102.

Schurman, R. (2004). Fighting "Frankenfoods": Industry opportunity structures and the efficacy of the anti-biotech movement in Western Europe. *Social Problems*, *51*(2), 243–268. https://doi.org/10.1525/sp.2004.51.2.243.

Seikyōdatta "comfort 21": Kakusha seiyakujōkyō ha jōjō [Successful Comfort 21: many contracts signed]. (1993, November). *Footwear Press*, 86–88.

Seki, M. (1975). Kawagutsu sangyō no fukugō kyōsō kōzō to sabetsuka kōdō [Competition in the shoe industry and industrial economics]. *Seijo University Economic Papers*, *51*, 241–271. https://seijo.repo.nii.ac.jp/records/1296.

Shibata, H. (2007). *Hadashi ga ichiban kimochi ii* [Barefoot feels best]. Diamond.

Shiire guide: Comfort brand tokushū 'koko ga chigau.' [Purchasing guide: Features of comfort shoes by brand]. (1988, February). *Footwear Press*, 51–58.

Shimamoto, M. (2020). *National project management: The Sunshine project and the rise of the Japanese solar industry*. Springer. https://doi.org/10.1007/978-981-15-3180-4.

Shimizu, S. (1995). *Arukukoto, ashi soshite kutsu* [Walking, feet and shoes]. Futoh-sha.

Shimizu, S. (1999). *Zoku arukukoto, ashi soshite kutsu* [Part II, walking, feet and shoes]. Futoh-sha.

Shionoya, K. (2012). *Ashi no trouble wa kutsu de naosō: Yōkoso ashi to kutsu no gairai e! (Dai 2han)* [Fix foot trouble with shoes: Welcome to the foot and shoe outpatient clinic! (2nd ed.)]. Chuohoki Publishing.

Shoe fitter Kubota Michiko san [Shoe fitter Michiko Kubota]. (1986, July 28). *Asahi Shimbun*, morning edition, Tokyo area, 21.

Shoe fitter wa ima nanio subekika. (1988, February). *Footwear Press*, 35–38.

Shōgeki Kyūshū, yōtsūtaisaku ni kutu yō nakajiki: Kobayashi Seiyaku, new face [Shock absorption to prevent lower back pain: Kobayashi Pharmaceutical's new product]. (1992, April 22). *Nihon Keizai Shimbun*, morning edition, 17.

Sine, W. D., & Lee, B. H. (2009). Tilting at windmills? The environmental movement and the emergence of the US wind energy sector. *Administrative Science Quarterly*, *54*(1), 123–155. https://doi.org/10.2189/asqu.2009.54.1.123.

Snow, D. A., & Soule, S. A. (2010). *A primer on social movements*. W. W. Norton.

Soule, S. A. (2009). *Contention and corporate social responsibility*. Cambridge University Press. https://doi.org/10.1017/CBO9780511804359.

Stevens, J. M., Kevin Steensma, H., Harrison, D. A., & Cochran, P. L. (2005). Symbolic or substantive document? The influence of ethics codes on financial executives' decisions. *Strategic Management Journal*, *26*(2), 181–195. https://doi.org/10.1002/smj.440.

Suchman, M. C. (1995). Managing Legitimacy: Strategic and Institutional Approaches. *Academy of Management Review*, 20(3), 571–610. http://www.jstor.org/stable/258788.

Sugano, E. (1975). *Kutsu: Ashimoto e no advice* [Shoes: Advice to your foot]. Zukan no Hokurikukan.

Sugawara, S. (1991, June). *Sereis henbōsuru shōken 4 Sendai.* [Changing trade area 4, Sendai city]. *Footwear Press*, 122–129.

Sugawara, S. (1992, October). Kutsu kōgai shijō no trend wa 'ōgataka to grade up' da [Trend in the suburban shoe market is larger and upgraded]. *Footwear Press*, 42–50.

Sugawara, S. (1999, March). Item-betsu marketing, footcare & insole, kenkō shikō no naka de nobiru juyō, senmonten wa fittingu taiō e [Item-specific marketing: Specialty shops to provide fitting services with demand for footcare and insoles growing amid rising health consciousness]. *Footwear Press*, 140–145.

Suzuki-Jhohnson, E. & Nakagawa, S. (2021). *Zukan sekai no kutsu hakimono* [Illustrated book of shoes and footwear of the world]. Gijutsu-Hyohron.

Takayama, K. (2014). *Makizume, Kannyūsō, Gaihanboshi no tokk*ō self care [Extremely effective self care for pince toenails, ingrown toenails, and bunions]. Makino Shuppan.

Takegawa, K. (2007). *Shinshi gutsu o erabu* [Selecting men's shoes]. Kobunsha.

Takeichi K. (1969). Seitaikeisoku ni kansuru kenkyū. [Anthropometric survey of human figure]. *Bulletin of Industrial Arts Institute*, *58*, 35–63.

Takesawa, R. (2005). *Kikuchitakeo no kutsumonogatari* [Takeo Kikuchi's shoe story]. Banseisha.

Tamura, M. (2008). *Gyōtai no seisui: Gendai ryūtsū no gekiryū* [Rise and fall of retail types and formats: Raging stream of modern distribution]. Chikura Publishing.

Tanaka, N. (2010). *Yōtsū, kashitsū no tame no kutsuerabi guid: Karada ni atta tadashii kutsu o haiteimasu ka? Dai 2han* [Guide to selecting shoes for lower back and leg pain: Are you wearing the right shoes for your body? 2nd edition]. Japan Medical Journal.

Tilly, C. (1999). From interactions to outcomes in social movements. In M. Giugni, D. McAdam, & C. Tilly (Ed.), *How social movements matter* (Vol. 10, pp. 253–270). University Minnesota Press.

Tokushū comfort de aruku [Special feature, walking with comfort shoes]. (1988, February). *Footwear Press*, 35–58.

Tokushū 'Comfort' o uru: Case study sekkyaku hanbai kokomade yatterru [Selling 'comfort shoes': Cases of thorough customer service sales]. (1988, July). *Footwear Press*, 35–50.

Tokushū fukyō shirazu no comfort [Comfort shoes sales unafected by the resession]. (1992, December). *Footwear Press*, 22–38.

Tokushū sonogo no comfort shoes hanbai [Special feature, Comfort shoes sales afterwards]. (1991, September). *Footwear Press*, 22–41.

Tokyo Fashion Senmongakko, Fujingutsu design no jisshū seminar [Tokyo Fashion Institute, women's footwear design workshop]. (1987, August 13). *Nikkei Sangyo Shimbun*, 1.

Tokyo Shoe Fair: Care-for shoes from West Germany. (1987, February). *Shoes Kai*, 40–43.

Toukutsu Kyōkai. (1986, August 25). *Toukutsu shoe fitter kōza iyoiyo jisshi* [Toukutsu shoe fitter training workshop begins]. *Toukutsu* [Toukutsu Association newsletter].

Toukutsu Kyōkai. (2021). *Toukutsu Kyokai setsuritus 70-shūnen kinen-shi* [The 70th anniversary of the association of Tokyo shoe retailers]. Toukutsu Kyōkai.

Tsukihoshi Gomu. (1967). *Tukihoshi Gomu 90nenshi* [90 years of Tsukihoshi Gomu]. Tshkihoshi Gomu.

Tsumasaki dake no nakajiki, Dr. Scholl's, new product [Forefoot insoles, Dr. Scholl's new product]. (2004, July 15). *Nikkei MJ (Nikkei Ryutsu Shimbun)*, 11.

Uchida, T. (2003). *Ashi no oyayubi no magari "gaihan boshi" wa jibun de naoseru* [You can heal big toe curvature or "bunions" yourself]. Makino Shuppan.

Uchimura, Y. (1972). Seitaikeisoku ni kansuru kenkyū sokubu no keisoku [Anthropometric survey of human figure: Measurement of leg and foot]. *Bulletin of the Industrial Products Research Institute, 69*, 57–62.

Van San-sho. (n. d.). FSI ortho tech shoe meister no iru omise [Shoe stores with FSI ortho tech shoe master]. https://www.fuss-und-schuh.co.jp/seminar/link.html.

Vasi, I. B., & King, B. (2012). Social movements, risk perceptions, and economic outcomes: The effect of primary and secondary stakeholder activism on firms' perceived environmental risk and financial performance. *American Sociological Review, 77*(4), 573–596. https://doi.org/10.1177/0003122412448.

Wadai no mise Schritt: Orthpaedic seminar de comfort o hirogeru [Popular store: Orthopedic seminar to broaden the comfort shoe market]. (1994, August). *Footwear Press*, 28.

Walker, E. T., Martin, A. W., & McCarthy, J. D. (2008). Confronting the state, the corporation, and the academy: The influence of institutional targets on social movement repertoires. *American Journal of Sociology,* 114(1), 35–76. https://doi.org/10.1086/588737.

Weber, K., Heinze, K. L., & DeSoucey, M. (2008). Forage for thought: Mobilizing codes in the movement for grass-fed meat and dairy products. *Administrative Science Quarterly, 53*(3), 529–567. https://doi.org/10.2189/asqu.53.3.529.

Yahagi, T. (2004). Chain stores: Keieikakushin no renzokuteki tenkai [Chain stores: Continuous development of business innovation]. In T. Ishihara & T. Yahagi (Eds.), *Nihon no Ryūtsū 100nen: Marketing channels, retailing and public policy issues* [Japanese 100-year distribution: Marketing channels, retailing and public policy issues] (pp. 217–261). Yuhikaku Publishing.

Yamazaki, N. (1983). Ashi to kutsu no tekigōsei [Foot and shoe fitness]. *Journal of the Society of Biomechanisms, 7*(2), 14–18. https://doi.org/10.3951/sobim.7.14_1.

Yamazaki, N. (1987). Hakigokochi no kaizen senryaku [Strategies to improve shoe comfort]. *Sen'i Gakkaishi, 43*(6), 228–232. https://doi.org/10.2115/fiber.43.6_P228.

Yamazaki, N. (1992). Kutsu no appakukan to yurusakan [Feelings of pressure and looseness of shoes]. *Journal of the Society of Biomechanisms, 16*(4), 269–273. https://doi.org/10.3951/sobim.16.269.

Yano Research Institute. (1981). *Kutsu, Hakimono Sangyō Nenkan 1981nenban* [Shoes and footwear industry yearbook, 1981]. Yano Research Institute.

Yano Research Institute. (1983). *Kutsu hakimono sangyō nenkan 1983 nenban* [Shoes and footwear industry yearbook, 1983]. Yano Research Institute.

Yano Research Institute. (1985). *Kutsu hakimono sangyō nenkan 1985 nenban* [Shoes and footwear industry yearbook, 1985]. Yano Research Institute.

Yano Research Institute. (1989a). *Kutsu hakimono sangyō nenkan 1989 nenban* [Shoes and footwear industry yearbook, 1989]. Yano Research Institute.

Yano Research Institute. (1989b). *Kutsu hakimono sangyō nenkan 1990 nenban* [Shoes and footwear industry yearbook, 1990]. Yano Research Institute.

Yano Research Institute. (1990). *Kutsu, Hakimono Sangyō Nenkan 1990 nenban* [Shoe and Footwear Industry Almanac, 1990]. Yano Research Institute.

Yano Research Institute. (1998). *Kutsu, Hakimono Sangyō Nenkan '98 nenban* [Shoe and Footwear Industry Almanac, 1998]. Yano Research Institute.

Yano Research Institute. (2003). *Kutsu, Hakimono Sangyō Nenkan 2003* [Shoe and Footwear Industry Almanac, 2003]. Yano Research Institute.

Yano Research Institute. (2009). *Kutsu, Hakimono Sangyō Nenkan 2009* [Shoe and Footwear Industry Almanac, 2009]. Yano Research Institute.

Yano Research Institute. (2014). *Kutsu, Hakimono Sangyō Nenkan 2014 nenban* [Shoe and Footwear Industry Almanac, 2014]. Yano Research Institute.

Yano Research Institute. (2016). *Kutsu, Hakimono Sangyō Nenkan 2016 nenban* [Shoe and Footwear Industry Almanac, 2016]. Yano Research Institute.

Yashiro Y. (1997). *Walk more, be healthy: Ginza Yoshinoya to watashi* [Walk more, be healthy: Ginza Yoshinoya and me]. Ginza Yoshinoya.

Yaziji, M., & Doh, J. P. (2013). The role of ideological radicalism and resource homogeneity in social movement organization campaigns against corporations. *Organization Studies*, 34(5–6), 755–780. https://doi.org/10.1177/0170840613479.

Yin, R. K. (2014). *Case study research: Design and methods* (5th ed.). Sage Publications.

Yoshimura Hisashi san Yoshimura Shōten shachō, watashi no tenki [Hisashi Yoshimura, President, Yoshimura Shōten, my turning point]. (1988, October 5), *Asahi Shimbun*, morning edition, Gunma page.

Yoshinoya Kutsuten no fitter kōza: Jitsugi de 20-nin no ashi hakaru [Yoshinoya Kutsuten fitter training workshop: 20 foot shape measurements]. (1987, February 9). *Nikkei Ryutsu Shimbun*, 21.

Yoshinoya Kutsuten tenchō class taishō ni fitter yōsei kōza [Yoshinoya Kutsuten offers a fitter training workshop]. (1986, July 21). *Nikkei Ryutsu Shimbun*, 21.

Yue, L. Q., Rao, H., & Ingram, P. (2013). Information spillovers from protests against corporations: A tale of Walmart and Target. *Administrative Science Quarterly, 58*(4), 669–701. https://doi.org/10.1177/00018392135112.

Zadankai comfort hanbai no genjō to kongo [Current situation of comfort shoe sales]. (2003, March). *Footwear Press*, 22–27.

Zald, M. N., Morrill, C., & Rao, H. (2005). The impact of social movements on organizations. In G. F. Davis, D. MacAdam, W. R. Schtt, and M. N. Zald (Eds), *Social movements and organization theory* (pp. 253-279). Cambridge University Press. https://doi.org/10.1017/CBO9780511791000.014.

Zennihon Hakimono Dantai Kyōgikai. (1978). *Kutsugata kijun sakusei no tameno chōsa kenkyū hōkokusho: Jisshi Yōryō Sakusei no Tame no Kiso Chōsa* [Research survey report on creating shoe last standards: Basic research for creating guidelines]. Zennihon Hakimono Dantai Kyōgikai.

Zietsma, C., & Winn, M. I. (2008). Building chains and directing flows: Strategies and tactics of mutual influence in stakeholder conflicts. *Business & Society*, *47*(1), 68–101. https://doi.org/10.1177/000765030730664.

Zone betsu MD guide: Comfort [MD guide by product category: Comfort shoes]. (1992, December). *Footwear Press*, 39–43.

People and Organizations Index

S. Miura, *Successful Social Activism and Unintended Market Emergence*,
https://doi.org/10.1007/978-981-99-9291-1

F

G

H

I

J

K

Subject Index

S. Miura, *Successful Social Activism and Unintended Market Emergence*,
https://doi.org/10.1007/978-981-99-9291-1

SPRINGER NATURE

GPSR Compliance

The European Union's (EU) General Product Safety Regulation (GPSR) is a set of rules that requires consumer products to be safe and our obligations to ensure this.

If you have any concerns about our products, you can contact us on ProductSafety@springernature.com

In case Publisher is established outside the EU, the EU authorized representative is:

Springer Nature Customer Service Center GmbH
Europaplatz 3
69115 Heidelberg, Germany

The manufacturer's authorised representative in the EU is Springer Nature Customer Service Centre GmbH, Europaplatz 3, 69115 Heidelberg, Germany. If you have any concerns regarding our products, please contact ProductSafety@springernature.com

Printed and bound by CPI Group (UK) Ltd, Croydon, CR0 4YY
01/10/2026
02225899-0002